IFIP Advances in Information and Communication Technology 575

Editor-in-Chief

Kai Rannenberg, Goethe University Frankfurt, Germany

Editorial Board Members

IFIP – The International Federation for Information Processing

IFIP was founded in 1960 under the auspices of UNESCO, following the first World Computer Congress held in Paris the previous year. A federation for societies working in information processing, IFIP's aim is two-fold: to support information processing in the countries of its members and to encourage technology transfer to developing nations. As its mission statement clearly states:

IFIP is the global non-profit federation of societies of ICT professionals that aims at achieving a worldwide professional and socially responsible development and application of information and communication technologies.

IFIP is a non-profit-making organization, run almost solely by 2500 volunteers. It operates through a number of technical committees and working groups, which organize events and publications. IFIP's events range from large international open conferences to working conferences and local seminars.

The flagship event is the IFIP World Computer Congress, at which both invited and contributed papers are presented. Contributed papers are rigorously refereed and the rejection rate is high.

As with the Congress, participation in the open conferences is open to all and papers may be invited or submitted. Again, submitted papers are stringently refereed.

The working conferences are structured differently. They are usually run by a working group and attendance is generally smaller and occasionally by invitation only. Their purpose is to create an atmosphere conducive to innovation and development. Refereeing is also rigorous and papers are subjected to extensive group discussion.

Publications arising from IFIP events vary. The papers presented at the IFIP World Computer Congress and at open conferences are published as conference proceedings, while the results of the working conferences are often published as collections of selected and edited papers.

IFIP distinguishes three types of institutional membership: Country Representative Members, Members at Large, and Associate Members. The type of organization that can apply for membership is a wide variety and includes national or international societies of individual computer scientists/ICT professionals, associations or federations of such societies, government institutions/government related organizations, national or international research institutes or consortia, universities, academies of sciences, companies, national or international associations or federations of companies.

More information about this series at http://www.springer.com/series/6102

Yuko Murayama · Dimiter Velev ·
Plamena Zlateva (Eds.)

Information Technology in Disaster Risk Reduction

4th IFIP TC 5 DCITDRR International Conference, ITDRR 2019
Kyiv, Ukraine, October 9–10, 2019
Revised Selected Papers

 Springer

Editors
Yuko Murayama
Tsuda University
Tokyo, Japan

Plamena Zlateva
Institute of Robotics
Bulgarian Academy of Sciences
Sofia, Bulgaria

Dimiter Velev
Science Research Centre
for Disaster Risk Reduction
University of National
and World Economy
Sofia, Bulgaria

ISSN 1868-4238   ISSN 1868-422X (electronic)
IFIP Advances in Information and Communication Technology
ISBN 978-3-030-48941-0   ISBN 978-3-030-48939-7 (eBook)
https://doi.org/10.1007/978-3-030-48939-7

This Springer imprint is published by the registered company Springer Nature Switzerland AG
The registered company address is: Gewerbestrasse 11, 6330 Cham, Switzerland

Preface

The effects of disasters are very serious and it may take a very long time to recover from the destruction caused. Related damage can be severe and offering relief may lead to expenses in the billions of euros. There has been an increase in natural disasters that has occurred in the past years and it is expected that their frequency will continue in the coming years.

Due to the multidisciplinary nature of work in the field of disaster risk reduction, people from various backgrounds will be included in this field of research and activity. Their backgrounds are likely to include industry, diverse geographical and global settings, not-for-profit organizations, agriculture, marine life, welfare, risk management, safety engineering, and social networking services.

At present, at global and national levels, a wide range of scientific and applied research activity is conducted in the area of disaster risk reduction concerning individual types of disasters. Modern information and communication technologies (ICT) can facilitate significantly the decision-making processes from the point of view of disaster risk reduction.

Following the increasing number of disasters worldwide and the growing potential of both ICT and ICT expertise, at its General Assembly held during October 8–9, 2015, at the Daejeon Convention Center, South Korea, IFIP established the Domain Committee on Information Technology in Disaster Risk Reduction in order to:

- Promote disaster risk reduction within the ICT community
- Provide an additional opportunity for IFIP members to work with other specialized bodies such as the UN, UNISDR, ICSU, ITU, and ISCRAM
- Coordinate the efforts of member societies as well as different Technical Committees and Working Groups of IFIP in the disaster-related field

The disaster support offered by the Domain Committee is based on the following major pillars:

- Information acquisition and provision
- Shelter information management for local governments
- Disaster Information Systems
- State-of-the-art ICT (such as the Internet of Things, Mobile Computing, Big Data, and Cloud Computing)

IFIP's Domain Committee on Information Technology in Disaster Risk Reduction organized the 4th IFIP Conference on Information Technology in Disaster Risk Reduction (ITDRR 2019), held during October 9–10, 2019, at the Kyiv National University of Culture and Arts, Ukraine.

ITDRR 2019 provided an international forum for researchers and practitioners to present their latest R&D findings and innovations. The conference was focused on various ICT aspects and the challenges of disaster risk reduction. The main topics included areas such as Natural Disasters, Big Data, Cloud Computing, Internet of Things, Mobile Computing, Emergency Management, Disaster Information Processing, and Disaster Risk Assessment and Management.

ITDRR 2019 invited experts, researchers, academics, and all others who were interested to disseminate their work and attend the conference. The conference established an academic environment that fostered the dialogue and exchange of ideas among different levels of academic, research, business, and public communities.

The Program Committee received 53 paper submissions, out of which 19 research papers were successfully accepted. We are grateful to the members of the Program Committee and to paper reviewers for their dedication in helping produce this volume.

April 2020

Yuko Murayama
Dimiter Velev
Plamena Zlateva

Organization

Honorable Chair

Yuko Murayama   Japan
  (IFIP Vice President)

General Chairs

Igor Grebennik   Kharkiv National University of Radio Electronics, Ukraine

Olena Chaikovska   Kyiv National University of Culture and Arts, Ukraine

Program Committee Co-chairs

Dimiter Velev   University of National and World Economy, Bulgaria

Plamena Zlateva   Institute of Robotics, Bulgarian Academy of Sciences, Bulgaria

Finance Chair

Eduard Dundler   Austria
  (IFIP Secretary)

Publicity Chair

Jun Sasaki   Iwate Prefectural University, Japan

Steering Committee

Diane Whitehouse   UK
  (IFIP TC9: ICT
  and Society Chair)

Erich Neuhold (IFIP TC5:   Austria
  Information Technology
  Application Chair)

Jose G. Gonzalez   University of Agder, Norway

A Min Tjoa   Austria
  (IFIP Honoray Secretary)

Program Committee

Andreas Karcher	Universität der Bundeswehr, Germany
Anna Förster	Bremen University, Germany
Benny Benyamin Nasution	Politeknik Negeri Medan, Indonesia
Boris Delibasic	University of Belgrade, Serbia
Chrisantha Silva	Computer Society of Sri Lanka, Sri Lanka
Denis Trcek	University of Ljubljana, Slovenia
Gabriela Marín-Raventós (IFIP Councillor)	Costa Rica
Gansen Zhao	South China Normal University, China
Hans J. Scholl	University of Washington, USA
Henrik Eriksson	Linköping University, Sweden
Hsin-Hung Wu	National Changhua University of Education, Taiwan
Ihor Bondar	Kyiv National University of Culture and Arts, Ukraine
Jaziar Radianti	University of Agder, Norway
Jian Cao	Shanghai Jiaotong University, China
Josune Hernantes	University of Navarra, Spain
Julie Dugdale	University of Grenoble, France
Kai Ranenberg (IFIP Vice President)	Germany
Kaninda Musumbu	Université Bordeaux, France
Kim Hee Dong	Hankuk University of Foreign Studies, South Korea
Kyungsoo Pyo	National Disaster Management Research Institute, South Korea
Leire Labaka	University of Navarra, Spain
Marcos R. S. Borges	Universidade Federal do Rio de Janeiro, Brazil
Mariki Eloff	University of South Africa, South Africa
Mariyana Nikolova	NIGGG, Bulgarian Academy of Sciences, Bulgaria
Michinori Hatayama	Disaster Prevention Research Institute, Kyoto University, Japan
Mihoko Sakurai	University of Agder, Norway
Mike Diver	Australian Computer Society, Australia
Monika Buscher	Lancaster University, UK
Murray Turoff	New Jersey Institute of Technology, USA
Myhailo Poplavskyi	Kyiv National University of Culture and Arts, Ukraine
Norberto Patrignani	Politecnico di Torino, Italy
Naoto Matsumoto	Sakura Internet Research Center, Japan
Nariyoshi Yamai	Tokyo University of Agriculture and Technology, Japan
Nikolai Roenko (Vice-President of UFI)	Miratex, Ukraine

Nirit Bernstein	Institute of Soil, Water and Environmental Science, Israel
Orhan Altan	Istanbul Technical University, Turkey
Patrick Letouze	Universidad Federal do Tocantins, Brazil
Rajan Raj Pant	Information Technology Security Emergency Response Team, Nepal
Remy Dupas	Université Bordeaux, France
Saji Baby	GEO International Environmental Consultation Co., Kuwait
Sergei Kavun	Kharkiv University of Technology, STEP, Ukraine
Sergei Ohrimenco	Laboratory of Information Security, AESM, Moldova
Shi Yizhe	Shenyang University of Chemical Technology, China
Shunsuke Fujieda	University of Tokyo, Japan
Starr Roxanne Hiltz	New Jersey Institute of Technology, USA
Stewart James Kowalski	Norwegian University of Science and Technology, Norway
Tadeusz Czachorski	Institute of Theoretical and Applied Informatics, Polish Academy of Sciences, Poland
Tao Bo	Earthquake Administration of Beijing Municipality, China
Tatsuya Yamazaki	Niigata University, Japan
Tetsuo Noda	Shimane University, Japan
Tullio Tanzi	Institut Mines-Télécom, Télécom ParisTech, France
Valeri Semenets	Kharkiv National University of Radio Electronics, Ukraine
Victor Amadeo Bañuls Silvera	Universidad Pablo de Olavide, Spain
Victor de Pous	Legal Counsel for Digital Technology and Legal Analyst, The Netherlands
Wang Guoxin	Earthquake Engineering Research Institute, Dalian University of Technology, China
Wei-Sen Li	National Science and Technology Center for Disaster Reduction, Taiwan
Wolfgang Reinhardt	Universität der Bundeswehr, Germany
Youwei Sun	Earthquake Administration of Beijing Municipality, China
Yoshitaka Shibata	Iwate Prefectural University, Japan
Yutaka Kikuchi	Kochi University of Technology, Japan
Zong Xuejun	Shenyang University of Chemical Technology, China

Contents

Issues in the Use of the Recovery Watcher for Situation Awareness in Disaster and Inclusive Communications

Yuko Murayama[1(✉)] and Kayoko Yamamoto[2]

[1] Tsuda University, Tsuda-Machi, Kodaira, Tokyo, Japan
murayama@tsuda.ac.jp
[2] The University of Electro-Communications, Chofugaoka, Chofu, Tokyo, Japan
k-yamamoto@is.uec.ac.jp

Abstract. Since the Great East Japan Earthquake and Tsunami in 2011, we have been working on how possibly IT could be used for disaster response and recovery in Japan. From this perspective, we implemented a system, Recovery Watcher, which was designed for sharing information on the recovery process with people inside as well as outside the disaster area. We also applied the system for barrier-free support in a university environment. This paper discusses the further possibilities to use the system for the first responders at disaster as well as inclusive support. We look into the original definition of situation awareness as well as trust issues. Finally, we present our plan to use the system in an island for elderly care as well as tourism in future.

Keywords: Situation awareness · Information sharing · Disaster communications · Inclusive communications

1 Introduction and Motivation

The Great East Japan Earthquake and Tsunami on 11 March 2011, caused severe damage to the northern coast of the main island in Japan, and 15894 people died, 2546 are missing and 6156 are injured [1]. While we have had many natural disasters in Japan, only a few researchers in information processing have been working on the issue such as the use of IT for disaster management. The issue has been researched for long [2, 3]. At the disaster, while the inefficiency of the entire communication network was treated as the major problem for information exchange and situation awareness, we found another important problem that there was no information system available in Japan for immediate use in emergency response.

From this perspective, we try and implement systems to be used in disaster response and recovery so that we could see what could be usable at disaster. One of them is Recovery Watcher, an information sharing system to keep people being aware of how recovery goes in the disaster area by reporting images from the disaster area [5]. We reported its use for barrier-free information provision [6].

In this paper, we look into the related research on situation awareness to look at Recovery Watcher from this viewpoint. We report our recent development of Recovery

© IFIP International Federation for Information Processing 2020
Published by Springer Nature Switzerland AG 2020
Y. Murayama et al. (Eds.): ITDRR 2019, IFIP AICT 575, pp. 1–8, 2020.
https://doi.org/10.1007/978-3-030-48939-7_1

Watcher in terms of inclusive communications as well as its issues. We present both trust issues as well as our plan to use the system as a case study in the recovering area in northern Japan in Miyagi Prefecture. The paper is organized as follows. The next section introduces related work on situation awareness. Section 3 describes our work on Recovery Watcher and Sect. 4 presents its use for inclusive communications. Section 5 describes our future work on the use of our system in Miyagi. Section 6 gives some conclusions.

2 Situation Awareness

The term, situation awareness, was originally from aviation, in particular from aerial warfare, at which a pilot needs to know the current situation correctly to make a decision to achieve the goals [7, 8]. The term is defined by Endsley as follows [7]:

> "Situational awareness or situation awareness (SA) is the perception of environmental elements within a volume of time and space, the comprehension of their meaning, and the projection of their status in the near future."

Endsley introduced the three hierarchical phases of the above definition:

- Level 1. Perception of the Elements in the Environment
- Level 2. Comprehension of the Situation
- Level 3. Projection of Future Status

At Level 1, as the first step, one needs to perceive the status, attributes and dynamics of the relevant elements. At Level 2, based on the Level1, one has to understand the significance of those elements and events to form a holistic view of the environment. Based on the knowledge from Levels 1 and 2, one can project future actions in the near future.

Harrald et al. [9] summarized the above as situational awareness has an information component, a perception component and a meaning component. They described more about information component as follows:

> "To provide the information component required for situational awareness, the sys-tem must be capable of collecting, filtering, analyzing, structuring, and transmitting data. Situational awareness is not only the correct perception of reality, it the correct perception of the relevant elements of the current reality necessary for correct, protective, tactical, and strategic response."

Situation awareness has been applied to the other dynamic and complex environment in which human control is required, such as air traffic control, large system operations such as nuclear power plant, and tactical and strategic systems such as firefighters, police and military as well as medical decision making [8].

Harrald et al. [9] describes that the knowledge acquired from the raw data should allow the decision maker to know the future implications of the current state, necessary interventions, the implied decisions to be made, and actions to be taken. The production of knowledge, along with the imputing of meaning, require trained, experienced receivers. They suggest that the following three steps required for shared situation awareness [9]:

1. technology can provide decision makers in a geographically distributed environment with the same information
2. common methods are available to integrate, structure, and understand the information
3. critical decision nodes share institutional, cultural, and experiential bases for imputing meaning to this knowledge

The first two steps are necessary for the common operating picture. They describe that shared situation awareness is required for military, firefighters and first responders.

3 Recovery Watcher for Situation Awareness

As we introduced in the previous section, IT could provide decision makers in a geographically distributed environment with the same information as the first step of the situation awareness [9]. Recovery Watcher was developed exactly for this purpose [6]. The original idea was to keep people being aware of what is happening at the recovery stage after disaster. It takes long to recover and reconstruct the towns and cities at disaster area, but the interests into such recovery and reconstructions would be faded out outside the disaster area as time goes by. On the other hand, we envisage the system to be used by the first responders at the early stage of disaster management cycle such as emergency response and even at the rescue phase [5].

In this section, we describe the original idea of Recovery Watcher in 3.1 and the use for the first responders in 3.2.

3.1   Original Idea of Recovery Watcher

Figure 1 shows the original model of the system. Cameras are located at multiple places in the disaster area. Images are to be uploaded to the server which provides the image sharing space.

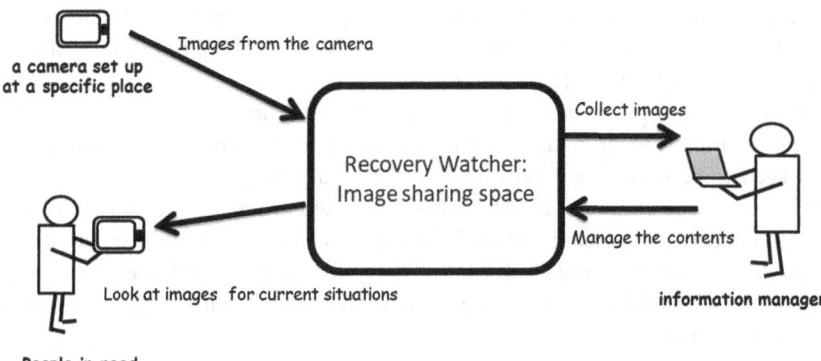

Fig. 1. The original model of Recovery Watcher

The first version of Recovery Watcher for Yamada town in Iwate Prefecture, Japan was set up as live-streaming making use of Ustream [10] for information sharing [6]. However, such video data took much bandwidth over the network, so that we changed into an image-based service with which some photo images would be sent periodically to the server system which acts as information sharing space. The frequency for uploading an image would be tuned accordingly.

Information sharing space could be presented on a map such as Open Street Map (OSM) [11] so that one can look them up thought the map. The information manager may control the uploaded sites so that if we add a new camera site, the new calendar will be prepared by the manager so that we control the camera sites. The users in need for such information on recovery situation in a disaster area would look up for the images, current ones as well as archives through the calendar.

3.2   Recovery Watcher for the First Responders

The recovery watcher system was originally implemented for disaster recovery. However, we could make use of the system for rescue and response at the early stage of disaster management. We interviewed officers, doctors and volunteers who worked for the earthquake and tsunami emergency response in Iwate Prefecture at the Great East Japan Earthquake in 2011 and found that information for situation awareness is needed desperately for the first responders in the beginning of disaster including rescue and response operations [4, 12].

For the use of emergency response, the images need to be uploaded more frequently. We also need to take a picture on demand. Pictures sent from the local users would be of great help as well, so that we would need a function for those users to upload the images if they were in the disaster area. The information manager would need to manage the uploaded images. This part could be done by use of SNS. Hiltz and Plotnick interviewed risk managers on the use of social media and found that trustworthiness is required for them to use social media [13, 14].

The trustworthiness of information from SNS at disaster in Japan could be resolved by DISANA [15] which makes use of tweets from Twitter to present all the related information including bogus information; it is left for the user to decide what to believe. Indeed, Tanaka suggested the needs for critical thinking to decide whether to trust or not the received information [16].

In disaster management, "Levels 2: Comprehension of the Situation" and "Level 3.: Projection of Future Status" suggested by Endsley [7] are important and the decision makers need to be trained and experience for this purpose [9].

There are various kinds of disaster whose cases are different one another. It would be hard to expect that decision makers in disaster management are always trained and experienced in a specific type of disaster. Therefore, we may well need technologies such as Artificial Intelligence and deep learning to produce some suggestions to support the first responders.

4   Recovery Watcher for Inclusive Communications

We introduce the term, inclusive communications, to indicate communications between stakeholders of inclusive support, such as people with disabilities and their supporters. In this section, we report the use of Recovery Watcher for inclusive communications in the next subsection and related work on IT use for inclusive communications in 4.2.

4.1   Use of Recovery Watcher for Inclusive Communications

In Japan, according to Act for Eliminating Discrimination against Persons with Disabilities [17], a university is expected to provide the students with barrier free environment on a best effort basis. It needs a lot of effort in terms of human factors as well as budget to provide physical barrier-free environment such as a lift in old school buildings [18]. It may well be easier to implement software tools to provide people in need with information on barrier-free situations. From this viewpoint, we tried and used Recovery Watcher for inclusive support.

Indeed, situation awareness is required for such inclusive support. We reported the use of our system for barrier free support for the people with disabilities as well as their supporters to find out the situation of the university campus [5]. We firstly created an accessibility map based on OSM with a geotagged photograph sharing tool, Mapillary [19] and Wheelmap [20] including the information on slopes and toilets [21, 22]. Wheelmap, a wheelchair map system using OSM, shall be introduced later in the next subsection on related work. Our map is intended to share the information on accessibility with those who need barrier-free environment, those supporters at the university inclusive education support office and those who would report the current situation of a place such as how crowded the canteen is. Figure 2 shows the model of this system.

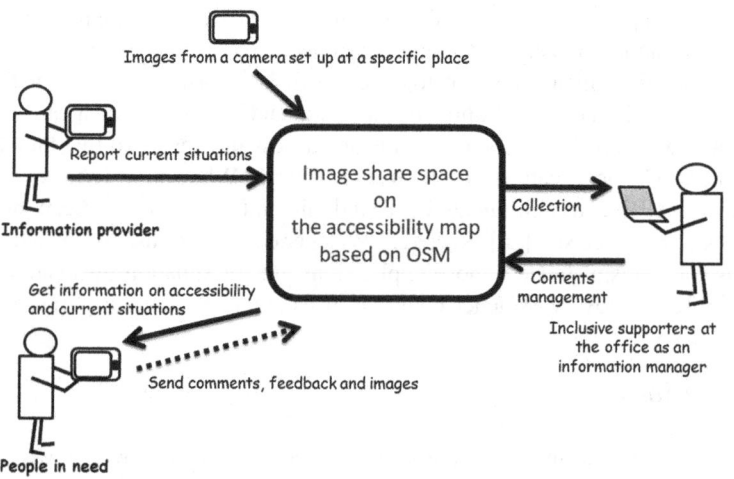

Fig. 2. The model of OSM-based accessibility map for inclusive communications

The difference from the original Recovery Watcher is "Information provider" who would upload images, which they take, as well as any comments. Indeed, "people in need" who look up for the information, may give some feedback comments and upload the images as indicated with the dotted arrow line in Fig. 2, so that the information provided by the information provider could be confirmed by the user; it makes the information more trustworthy and reliable.

4.2   Use of Recovery Watcher for Inclusive Communications

The use of IT for inclusive support has been tried such as Wheelmap [22], which was developed, by a nonprofit organization in Germany, Sozialhelden e.V. and shows wheelchair accessible places on a map using OSM. Users can provide information on accessibility with three levels according to the number of steps and their heights. Photographs can be added as a part of information.

WheeLog created in Japan is a social barrier-free map to be shared by people with and without disabilities [23]. The system was designed from the viewpoint of people with disabilities. With a smartphone, one can trace the wheelchair route and indicate it on a map. The idea is if the route was traced, that route is presumed usable. Ministry of Land, Infrastructure, Transport and Tourism, Japan provides open data on barrier free situations for application developments as a part of the Barrier-free Navi Project [24]. We could provide more useful information to use such open together with Recovery Watcher in future.

5   Future Work

We are planning to make use of Recovery Watcher in Tashirojima Island, one of the small islands in Ishinomaki, Miyagi Prefecture, Japan. The island was hit seriously by the Great East Japan Earthquake and Tsunami in 2011. It is so small as eleven km perimeter with approximately sixty three residents [25]. Although most of those residents are elder fishermen, they got together to make substantial recovery from the disaster [26]. The island is well-known as a "cat island". Cats are taken care of by the residents and worshiped as a god of promising success in fishing, so that they have so many visitors who love cats from all over the world. While they used to have few guidebooks available to introduce the island, the information has been published through SNS and a web site [26]. Recovery Watcher could be of use for the elderly care as well as for tourism. Indeed, those applications are for situation awareness for different purposes. Recovery Watcher could be of use to such different purposes.

6   Conclusions

In this paper, we discuss the use of our system, Recovery Watcher, which was designed originally to observe the recovery process after the Great East Japan Earth-quake and Tsunami on March 11th, 2011.

We introduced the original definition of situation awareness and looked at Recovery Watcher from this view point. As introduced in Sect. 2, for situation awareness has three-level processes according to Endsley [7]. Recovery Watcher can only present the first level which is "Perception of the Elements in the Environment." It requires the other levels 2 and 3, "Level 2. Comprehension of the Situation" and "Level 3. Projection of Future Status" based on the decision maker's experience and knowledge. Those factors are required particularly for the use by the first responders. The experience and knowledge may well be required for the use for inclusive communications as well. For inclusive communications, we need the further research on whether those providers should be identified or not; alternatively, one can geotag the information at submission.

We also need the further research on privacy issue for Recovery Watcher so that we could provide suggestion on how to set up cameras. Currently we avoid to get the image of people. For elderly care, we need to look more into this privacy issue in future.

References

1. National Police Agency of Japan: damage situation and police countermeasures associated with 2011 Tohoku district - off the Pacific Ocean Earthquake. https://www.npa.go.jp/news/other/earthquake2011/pdf/higaijokyo.pdf. Accessed 31 Jan 2018
2. Turoff, M.: Past and future emergency response information systems. Comm. ACM **45**(4), 29–32 (2002)
3. Van de Walle, B., Turoff, M., Hiltz, S.R. (eds.): Information Systems for Emergency Management. Roultedge, Abington (2009)
4. Murayama, Y., Yamamoto, K.: Research on disaster communications. In: Murayama, Y., Velev, D., Zlateva, P. (eds.) ITDRR 2017. IAICT, vol. 516, pp. 1–11. Springer, Cham (2019). https://doi.org/10.1007/978-3-030-18293-9_1
5. Murayama, Y., Yamamoto, K., Sasaki, J.: Recovery watcher: a disaster communication system for situation awareness and its use for barrier-free information provision. In: Murayama, Y., Velev, D., Zlateva, P. (eds.) ITDRR 2018. IAICT, vol. 550, pp. 1–11. Springer, Cham (2019). https://doi.org/10.1007/978-3-030-32169-7_1
6. Saito, Y., Fujihara, Y., Murayama, Y.: A study of reconstruction watcher in disaster area. In: Proceedings of CHI2012 Extended Abstracts, pp. 811–814. ACM, Austin (2012)
7. Endsley, M.R.: Design and evaluation for situation awareness enhancement. In: Proceedings of the Human Factors and Ergonomics Society 32nd Annual Meeting, pp. 97–101 (1988)
8. Endsley, M.R.: Toward a theory of situation awareness in dynamic systems. Hum. Factors J. **37**(1), 32–64 (1995)
9. Harrald, J., Jefferson, T.: Shared situational awareness in emergency management mitigation and response. In: Proceedings of the HICSS-40, pp. 23–23. IEEE, Waikoloa (2007)
10. Ustream (in Japanese). https://ja.wikipedia.org/wiki/Ustream. Accessed 30 Jan 2020
11. The OpenStreetMap Project: https://www.openstreetmap.org/about. Accessed 30 Jan 2020
12. Murayama, Y., Sasaki, J., Nishioka, D.: Experiences in emergency response at the Great East Japan Earthquake and Tsunami. In: Proceedings of the HICSS-49, pp. 146–151. IEEE, Koloa (2016)
13. White, C., Plotnick, L., Kushma, J., Hiltz, S.R., Turoff, M.: An online social network for emergency management. Int. J. Emerg. Manag. **6**(3–4), 369–382 (2009)

14. Hiltz, S.R., Kushma, J., Plotnick, L.: Use of social media by U.S. public sector emergency managers: barriers and wish lists. In: Proceedings of the 11th International Conference on Information Systems for Crisis Response and Management (ISCRAM2014), ID11, ISCRAM, University Park, Pennsylvania, USA (2014)

15. Mizuno, J., et al.: WISDOM X, DISAANA and D-SUMM: large-scale NLP systems for analyzing textual big data. In: Proceedings of the 26th International Conference on Computational Linguistics (COLING 2016) (Demo Track), pp. 263–267. ICCL, Osaka (2016). https://www.aclweb.org/anthology/C16-2055.pdf. Accessed 30 Jan 2020

16. Tanaka, Y., Sakamoto, Y., Honda, H.: The impact of posting URLs in disaster-related tweets on rumor spreading behavior. In: Proceedings of the HICCS-47, pp. 520–529. IEEE, Waikoloa (2014)

17. Cabinet Office. Government of Japan: Annual Report on Government Measures for Persons with Disabilities (Summary) (2015). https://www8.cao.go.jp/shougai/english/annualreport/2015/index-pdf.html. Accessed 30 Jan 2020

18. Shiraishi, J.: A case study for the "barrier-free" environment in a school setting: reconsider how to overcome obstacles to improve school facilities. Hum. Welfare Stud. **7**, 93–102 (2004). (in Japanese). https://hokusho.repo.nii.ac.jp/?action=repostory_uri&item_id=422&file_id=22&file_no=1. Accessed 30 Jan 2020

19. Mapillary: Mapillary, https://www.mapillary.com. Accessed 20 Mar 2020

20. Tsuchida, H.: Development of a bulletin board system for accessibility information using OpenStreeMap, Graduation Thesis, Department of Computer Science, Tsuda University (2019)

21. Noguchi, M., Tsuchida, H., et al.: Use of OpenStreetMap for a bulletin board and a toilet map for accessibility. In: Proceedings of the IPSJ Interaction 2019, pp. 962–966 (2019, in Japanese). http://www.interaction-ipsj.org/proceedings/2019/data/pdf/3P-74.pdf. Accessed 30 Jan 2020

22. Wheelmap. https://wheelmap.org/. Accessed 30 Jan 2020

23. WheeLog. https://www.wheelog.com/hp/. Accessed 30 Jan 2020

24. Ministry of Land, Infrastructure, Transport and Tourism, Japan: Barrier-free Navi Project. (in Japanese). https://www.mlit.go.jp/sogoseisaku/soukou/sogoseisaku_soukou_mn_000002.html. Accessed 30 Jan 2020

25. Ishinomaki City: Introduction to Tashirojima. (in Japanese). https://www.city.ishinomaki.lg.jp/cont/10053500/0050/3639/3639.html. Accessed 30 Jan 2020

26. Naitou, K., Watanabe, A., Yamamoto, K.: Development of web portal to support for remote island. In: Proceedings of the 15th International Congress of Asian Planning Schools Association (APSA 2019 Seoul), Liable Cities and Innovation, 13 p. (2019)

Information Technology Reengineering of the Electricity Generation System in Post-disaster Recovery

Igor Grebennik$^{(\boxtimes)}$, Ata Ovezgeldyyev, Yevhen Hubarenko,
and Maryna Hubarenko

Kharkiv National University of Radio Electronics, Kharkiv, Ukraine
{igor.grebennik, evgen.gubarenko,
maryna.solona}@nure.ua, metanova@yahoo.com

Abstract. The paper considers situations of the impact of various natural disasters on the electricity generating system as part of the energy system of a city or region. The impact of natural disasters in large part change the electricity consumption patterns, which makes it necessary not only to restore the power supply system, but also to conduct a complete review of its operation (reengineering). The paper discusses information technologies that provide a procedure for the reengineering of the electric power system when it is restored after an aggressive external influence, for example, a natural disaster.

Keywords: Information technologies · Natural disasters · Reengineering · Assessing risks · Electricity generation system

1 The Role of Electric Power System

Despite the fact that the humanity has developed various technologies and ability to influence significantly the natural processes, it remains rather vulnerable to aggressive impact of the environment. Natural disaster has become the synonym of inevitable destruction connected with threats to human life, damages to infrastructure and capital goods. Currently, apart from natural, man-made disasters pose a significant threat too, they may affect large regions as well as our planet as a whole, causing the destruction of the biosphere.

A worldwide movement 'Earth Hour' may be used as an example of the population's total dependence on power supply. In 2019 more than 2 billion people in 188 countries of the world took part in this movement [1]. During this hour, the economic activity stops and the social activity drops considerably. Here we talk about an arranged and planned action lasting just one hour once a year. When something like this happens unexpectedly as a result of a natural disaster or accident, the sole fact of electric power lack may become a disaster.

The electric power supply is one of the first life support systems to be repaired. Power supply assures the functioning of various devices, household appliances, technological processes and production. There are various natural disaster consequences for

© IFIP International Federation for Information Processing 2020
Published by Springer Nature Switzerland AG 2020
Y. Murayama et al. (Eds.): ITDRR 2019, IFIP AICT 575, pp. 9–20, 2020.
https://doi.org/10.1007/978-3-030-48939-7_2

the electric power systems, including power line breaks and considerable damage to power generating elements.

2 Specifics of Natural Disaster Consequences

Let us define an electric power system as a network of power generating stations of varied capacity, electric substations (transformers of varying types, capacity and voltage), transmission lines of varying voltage and customers with varying consumption levels. Figure 1 presents a layout of an electric power system with power generating stations depicted as circles with a lightning inside, their size corresponds to the amount of electric power that can be produced. A black circle represents a substation (step-down substation), which lowers the transmission line voltage of hundreds of thousands volt to tens of thousands volt and distributes it to potential consumers. A white circle represents a substation (step-down substation), which lowers the voltage of tens of thousands volt to a level suitable for consumption and distributes it to specific consumers. Grey zones represent consumers: production and residential areas, etc. Black lines are transmission lines (Fig. 2).

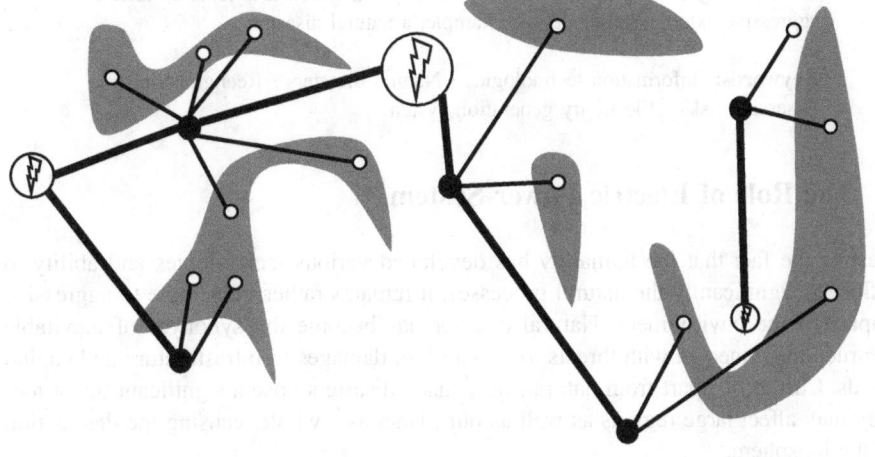

Fig. 1. Layout of an electric power system of a region

Figure 3 shows the objects that are out of order or destroyed, they are marked with a cross. Dashed lines represent power line breaks. Moreover, Fig. 3 shows the consumption areas, which were completely destroyed in comparison to the system's initial state (Fig. 1), they are also marked with dashed lines (Fig. 4).

An important characteristic is also changes to the topology of electric power consumption in the aftermath of a natural disaster. Some changes emerge directly, some after a certain period of time. This may be due to a number of factors such as:

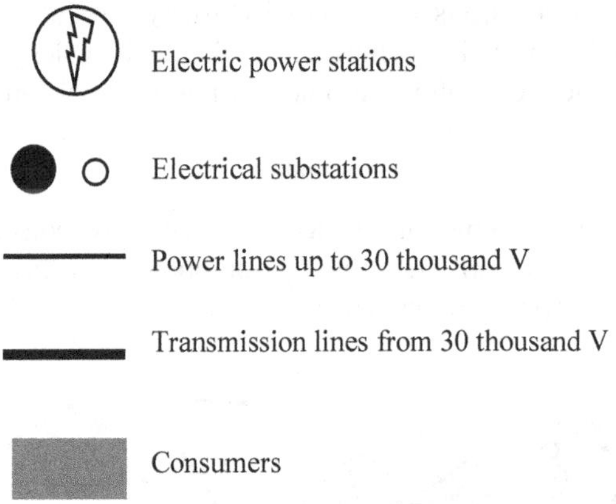

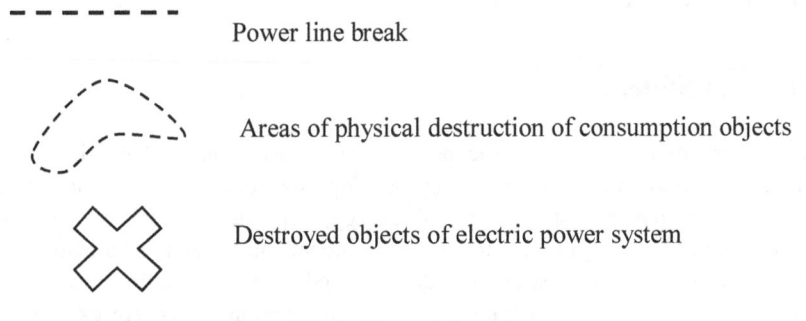

Electric power stations

Electrical substations

Power lines up to 30 thousand V

Transmission lines from 30 thousand V

Consumers

Fig. 2. Figure 1 legend

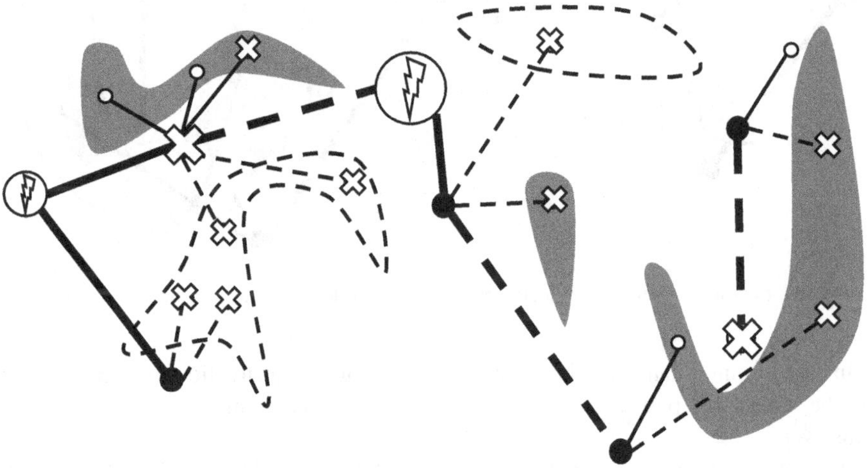

Fig. 3. Example of natural disaster consequences for a region's electric power system

Power line break

Areas of physical destruction of consumption objects

Destroyed objects of electric power system

Fig. 4. Figure 3 legend

- physical destruction of objects consuming electricity (production lines, residential areas), reconstruction of which is time-consuming and challenging;
- changes to infrastructure resulting in hindered raw materials and product delivery logistics;
- short- and long-term relocation of population and production facilities, etc.

Figure 5 shows an example of changes to electricity consumption topology. Marked with the dashed line are the initial consumption areas (Fig. 1), grey areas are the supposed emerging consumption areas.

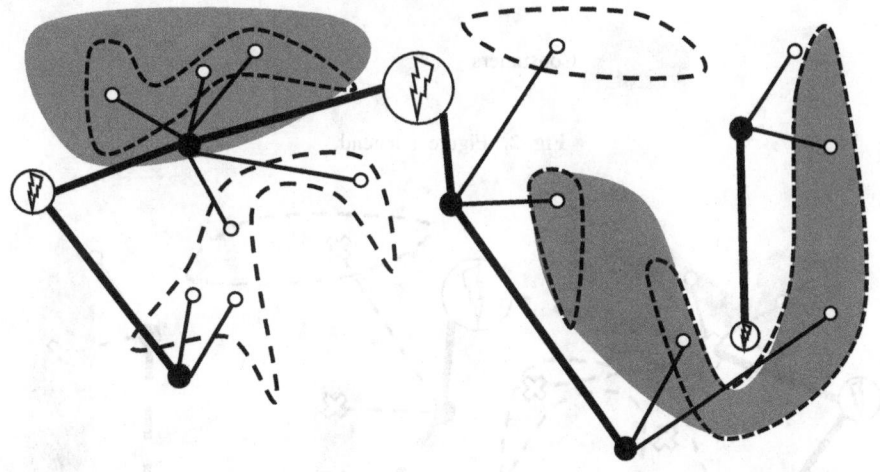

Fig. 5. Layout of changes to electricity consumption topology after a natural disaster

In case of minor damages, the main task is to assure reconstruction measures, which may be taken by public utilities, private maintenance companies or consumers themselves.

In case of complete destructions, the main task is to develop the system from scratch.

Most often, natural disasters cause partial damage to the system, putting some of its elements out of function.

3   Problem Statement

In any country of the world electric power systems wear out and require constant modernisation. Modern societies regularly develop new requirements for the sustainability of electric power systems ("green" energy) [2]. Such systems are, as a rule, large-scale and of high importance for both consumers and the state as a whole. Thus, power system modernisation strategy is to be based on the modelling results of the expected capacity of power generation and its consumption levels. An example of a poorly-planned modernisation process is Australia in 2019, where nearly 200 000 people suffered from rolling blackouts. Australian Minister for Energy Liliana D'Ambrosio stated that the loss of power capacity happened primarily due to the complete close-down of three coal power stations and reduced production on the remaining ones [3]. The power stations were closed within the context of improving sustainability of power production (reduction of CO_2 and sulphur oxide emissions in the process of coal burning). In other words, the abovementioned blackouts in Australia were not caused by an emergency or a man-made disaster, nevertheless, poorly-managed modelling of energy consumption process caused considerable damage.

Under such conditions, the problem of reengineering (redesign of an electric power system considering the damage, emerging technologies and estimations of consumption levels) reads as follows:

Let us suppose, there is an electric power system (Fig. 1). As a result of a natural or a man-made disaster the station was partially damaged (Fig. 3), it has to be restored or modernised.

An electric power system includes:

- sources of electric power production of varying capacity – these may be large and small, fixed and mobile, nuclear, thermal, solar, wind and other power stations;
- electric power transmission system – transmission lines, step-up and step-down substations;
- end consumers;

It is necessary to design a new power station based on the elements of the old power station that will correspond to the estimated changes in the power consumption topology.

- As a rule, the following issues require solutions:
- Which power stations require what kind of modernisation?
- Where should extra power units be located?
- Where should new power stations be located?
- What part of infrastructure should be elaborated and in which area?
- There may also be the task of electric power exchange with other regions (trade, seasonal and daily transmissions).

When it comes to electric power system reengineering, the following aspects should be taken into consideration [4]:

- technologies constantly develop and progress, the issue of their obsolescence emerges almost directly after the completion of construction or modernisation, therefore an important question to answer is whether modernisation is generally appropriate. New technologies have to bring positive effects, corresponding to their costs and outperforming the use of previous technologies. Thus, the decision on replacement or modernisation of obsolete equipment should be taken based on the complex analysis of its costs and effect;
- the scale of electric power systems is so large that even for the strongest economies it is hardly possible to finance the modernisation of the whole system at once;
- electric power systems are large, extensive and operating systems that are of high importance for the economic and social processes of the population. Electric power

outages may lead to accidents and disasters, therefore, the reengineering project has to enable constant electric power delivery;

- equipment amortisation and maintenance measures – any kind of equipment wears out and requires maintenance, therefore after a certain period of time it has to be withdrawn. This has to be taken into account when modernising parts of the electric power systems;
- the need for electric power demand estimations – although the level of power consumption increases, the geography of its demand constantly changes, it may both expand and scale down in a particular region. Therefore, decision on the start of the construction or modernisation has to be taken following the comprehensive modelling based on the estimated changes to demand and development of the region.

Due to the abovementioned difficulties, the reengineering of the electric power systems is as a rule limited to the replacement of the outdated, obsolete or defect equipment. A major incident, such as a natural disaster, may create the space required for a proper electric power system reengineering [5, 6].

As a result, elaborating a project that corresponds to the new operating conditions.

4 Algorithm of the Electric Power System Reengineering

1. Gathering data on the initial state of the power system (Fig. 1). This type of data should be gathered in advance. Apart from the actual information, various action plans in case of a natural disaster have to be elaborated.
2. Gathering data on the operability of the power system elements in the aftermath of a natural disaster (Fig. 3). This type of data is gathered in the immediate aftermath of a natural disaster. It may come from witnesses, unmanned aircrafts, satellites and automatic integrity testers.
3. Forecasting the topology of consumption development (Fig. 5). Estimations may be based on the factual transfer of consumers (production relocation, population resettlement) or on similar situations.
4. Clustering the consumption areas in order to determine approximate installation locations of current and prospective substations (Fig. 6). In order to assure efficient clustering and installation of new power substations, it is necessary to set a variety of parameters, some of them may be determined prior to the natural disaster with the help of modelling.
5. Developing a new electric power station with certain restrictions (Fig. 7).

Specifics of electric power system reengineering [7]:

1. In order decide on the better topology for the power system reengineering, it is required to specify the acceptable solution space.
2. Using the multi-criteria decision-making approach.
3. Optimisation criteria used to develop the system may be defined as the length of power lines, general consumer capacity, general power transmission losses and costs.

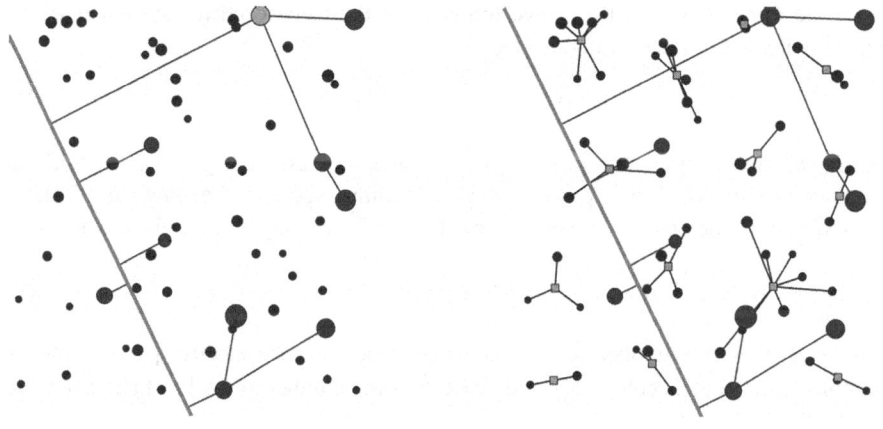

Fig. 6. Example clustering the consumption areas

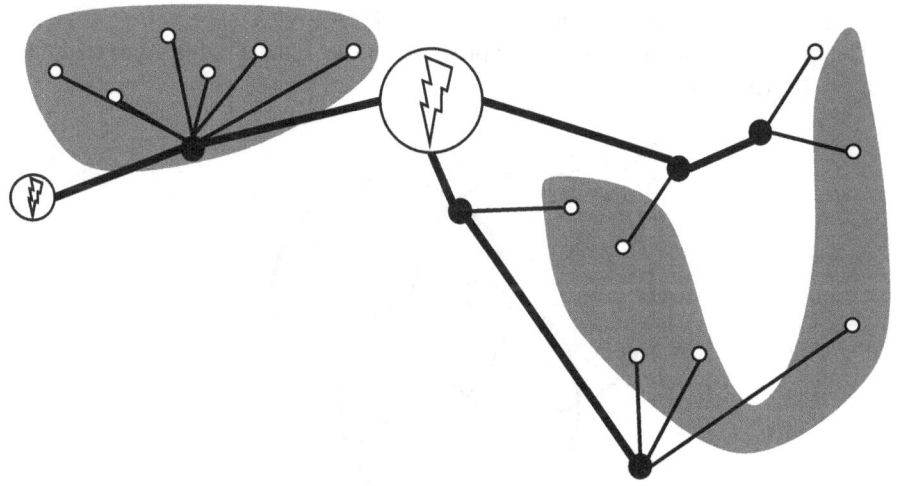

Fig. 7. Example a new electric power station with certain restrictions

4. It will be rational to apply comprehensive criteria compiling all power network efficiency factors.

5 Specifying Feasible Area

Social-economic approach presumes structurisation and detailed description of each of the electric power system element as a set of three constraints. Necessary is to be able to assess the state of the power system in order to compare possible alternative reengineering projects and make a decision on the realisation sequence, which will assure the required values [8]. Thus, the state of the electric power system is determined by the set of characteristics (1).

$$P_C = P_1 \cup P_2 \cup P_3,\tag{1}$$

with P_C as the set of electric power system characteristics; P_1, P_2, P_3 as the tuple of characteristics of the electric power system economic, social and ecological effect.

A variety of the electric power system characteristics may be described as follows:

$$P_i = \langle p_{i,j} \rangle,\tag{2}$$

with $i = \overline{1,3}$ as the number of the limitation block for the electric power systems (economic, social and ecological), and $j = \overline{1,n}$ as the number of the local characteristic of the i-th block.

When applying the limitations to the set of the possible alternatives D, there are three emerging subsets: $S_{P1} \subseteq D$, resulting from the limitations of the economic block P_1; $S_{P2} \subseteq D$, resulting from the limitations of the social block P_2; and $S_{P3} \subseteq D$, resulting from the limitations of the ecological block P_3.

The intersection of the three subsets produces the set of admissible states (feasible area) D^D (3) (Fig. 8).

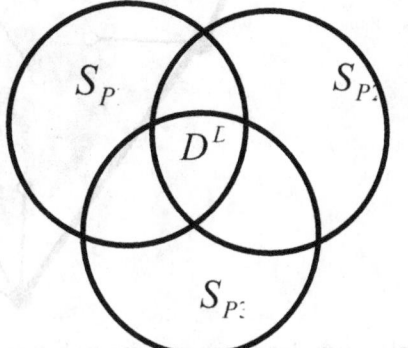

Fig. 8. Schematic representation of determining the admissible value space

$$D^D = S_{P1} \cap S_{P2} \cap S_{P3}.\tag{3}$$

Under the set of possible values (D) we understand any state of the electric power system that can be characterised by the maximum interval of parameter change. This means that these parameters are not limited and define the space of the electric power system's unconditional existence. However, in real-world conditions not all parameter values are admissible due to financial and economic, technical, moral and ethical, social, ecological and other reasons. This results in the necessity to determine the set (space) of admissible parameter values (states) in every single case separately.

The admissible state space (D^D) (3) of any specific electric power system is determined by the limitations of all critical characteristics set in the form of systems of equations or inequations defining certain multivariate space. This means that any admissible state of the socio-economic system may be presented in the form of a point in the space of admissible states.

Defining the admissible space of the socio-economic system states means that all critical characteristics of the electric power system $\langle h_{i,j} \rangle$ (2) have the following limitations

$$p_{i,j}^L \leq p_{i,j} \leq p_{i,j}^U;$$

$$p_{i,j} = p_{i,j}^P, \tag{4}$$

with L, U, P as the corresponding indices of the lowest, highest and admissible values of local characteristics of the electric power system state.

Each of the inequalities or Eqs. (4) defines a local limit, and taken as a set they define a certain area in the n-dimensional space of characteristics. This does not exclude the possibility of uniting several characteristics into functionally related groups. Such interpretation presents the state of every separate electric power system as a multivariate point in the admissible functioning space. Then, the shortest distance from the point showing the state of the system to the limit of the admissible space may be interpreted as a the quantitative index of the system's sustainability. Every local characteristic defines a certain limit of the admissible space, and their functionally related group defines a certain fragment of the limit of the admissible space. Then, the distance from this fragment of the limit to the point of the actual state of the system characterises social, economic, ecological or any other stability of the system.

Given the abovementioned, the formula to determine the characteristic of the electric power system's stability margin based on any local characteristic is in natural indicators and reads as follows

$$\Delta p_{ij} = p_{ij}^R - p_{ij}^B, \tag{5}$$

with B, R as correspondingly border and real values of the characteristic. In relative indicators it reads as follows

$$U_{ij} = \frac{|\Delta p_{ij}|}{p_{ij}^U - p_{ij}^L} \cdot 100\%. \tag{6}$$

Sustainability estimations of a functionally related group of indicators are more difficult to make. In this case, it is suggested to estimate the sustainability according to the following non-dimensional indicator

$$U_i = \sum_{j=1}^{n} a_{ij} p_{ij}^N, \tag{7}$$

with a_i as the non-dimensional indicators of relative importance of i-th characteristic provided that $0 \leq a_{ij} \leq 1$, $\sum_{j=1}^{n} a_{ij} = 1$; and p_{ij}^N as the normalised value of i-th local electric power system characteristic.

The following conditions must be met for normalised local characteristics: dimensionlessness; limitedness, same interval of possible values [0,1]; invariance in regard to the direction of dominance (min, max); non-negativity.

All the abovementioned requirements are met in the following normalisation model [9]

$$p_{ij}^N = \frac{\left| p_{ij}^R - p_{ij}^B \right|}{p_{ij}^U - p_{ij}^L} = \frac{\left| \Delta p_{ij} \right|}{p_{ij}^U - p_{ij}^L}. \tag{8}$$

a_i value is determined by either expert judgement or comparator identification. Sustainability indicator U ranges between [0, 1] and directly characterises stability margin of the socio-economic system based on any group of parameters or as a whole.

The DTW (dynamic time warping) algorithm, enabling analysis and comparison of number sequences, may be used to determine the correlations, analyse the dynamics of electric power consumption and make prognoses [10].

6 Normalization of Criteria Values

If there is no possibility to evaluate one or several variables in cash equivalent, it is then only possible to compare the alternatives and choose the one with the highest efficiency rate. The task of comparing alternative reengineering projects may be reduced to the task of making summarised assessment in the process of multivariate assessment.

The particular circumstances of multivariate assessment are the values lying in the initial informational measuring basis, which have varying semantics and correspondingly varying physical dimensions, interval of possible values, scales of measurement and directions of dominance. This means that all factors included in the model of scalar multivariate assessment have to appear in the normalised form [11]:

$$P(z) = P(\Lambda, K(z)), \tag{11}$$

with $P(z)$ as the summarised scalar assessment; P as the operator defining the structure of the assessment model; $\Lambda = \langle \lambda_t \rangle$, $t = \overline{1, T}$ as the tuple of the normalisation coefficients; $K = \langle k_t \rangle$, $t = \overline{1, T}$ as the tuple of heterogeneous factors.

A more convenient and universal form of the model (11) is the normalised one

$$P(z) \; = \; P(A, \, K^N(z)),$$

with $A \; = \; \langle a_t \rangle$, $t \; = \; \overline{1, T}$ as the tuple of non-dimensional weighting coefficients of the relative importance of local factors; and $K^N \; = \; \langle k_t^N \rangle$, $t \; = \; \overline{1, T}$ as the tuple of normalised local factors.

A tuple requires the following conditions

$$0 \leq a_i \leq 1, \; \sum_{i=1}^{n} a_i \; = \; 1.$$

7 Conclusions

- In the aftermath of natural disasters it is recommended to organise electric power system reengineering instead of reconstruction measures
- Natural disasters may cause shifting of electricity consumption topology
- Electric power system reengineering is a complex multi-step process, its main objective is to redevelop the system so that it corresponds to the new requirements
- We used social-economic approach to specify the acceptable value space as well as mathematical tools of multi-criteria decision-making
- Social-economic approach has proven to assure a sustainable solution

References

1. Earth hour 60+. Earth hour infographic, https://www.earthhour.org. Accessed 09 Dec 2019
2. Midillia, A., Dincerb, I., Ay, M.: Green energy strategies for sustainable development. Energy Policy **34**, 3623–3633 (2006)
3. IA REGNUM. In Australia, tens of thousands of people were left without electricity due to the heat. https://regnum.ru/news/2560864.html. Accessed 09 Dec 2019
4. Hammer, M., Champy, J.: Reengineering the Corporation: A Manifesto for Business Revolution. Harper Business, Manhattan (1993). 223 p.
5. Grebennik, I., Khriapkin, O., Ovezgeldyyev, A., Pisklakova, V., Urniaieva, I.: The concept of a regional information-analytical system for emergency situations. In: Murayama, Y., Velev, D., Zlateva, P. (eds.) ITDRR 2017. IAICT, vol. 516, pp. 55–66. Springer, Cham (2019). https://doi.org/10.1007/978-3-030-18293-9_6
6. Grebennik, I., Reshetnik, V., Ovezgeldyyev, A., Ivanov, V., Urniaieva, I.: Strategy of effective decision-making in planning and elimination of consequences of emergency situations. In: Murayama, Y., Velev, D., Zlateva, P. (eds.) ITDRR 2018. IAICT, vol. 550, pp. 66–75. Springer, Cham (2019). https://doi.org/10.1007/978-3-030-32169-7_6
7. King, T., El-Hawary, M., El-Hawary, F.: Optimal environmental dispatching of electric power systems via an improved Hopfield neural network model. IEEE Trans. Power Syst. **10** (3), 1559–1565 (1995)

8. Jech, T.: Set Theory. Springer, Heidelberg (2006). https://doi.org/10.1007/3-7643-7692-9
9. Dasgupta, A.: Set Theory: With an Introduction to Real Point Sets. Springer, New York (2014). https://doi.org/10.1007/978-1-4614-8854-5
10. Nechiporenko, A., Gubarenko, E., Gubarenko, M.: Authentication of users of mobile devices by their motor reactions. Telecommun. Radio Eng. **78**, 987–1003 (2019)
11. Tzeng, G.-H., Huang, J.J.: Multiple Attribute Decision Making: Methods and Applications. CRC Press Taylor & Francis Group, Boca Raton (2011)

Information Technologies for Assessing the Impact of Climate Change and Natural Disasters in Socio-Economic Systems

Igor Grebennik[(⊠)], Valerii Semenets, and Yevhen Hubarenko

Kharkiv National University of Radio Electronics, Kharkiv, Ukraine
{igor.grebennik,valery.semenets,
evgen.gubarenko}@nure.ua

Abstract. The paper proposes to use the utility theory for the synthesis of multivariate models of assessing the impact of changing climatic conditions and the disaster assessment in the implementation of the socio-economic approach. The work contrasts two situations of environmental impact (external influence) on the society systems. A feature of each of the situations is the duration and intensity of impact, which leads to its unique consequences. Socio-economic approach takes account equally the economic, social and environmental impacts. The paper proposes a universal model to assess the impact of external influences on the system. Considering information technologies that provide a procedure for assessing risks and consequences of natural disasters in socio-economic systems.

Keywords: Information technologies · Natural disasters · Assessing risks · Socio-economic systems

1 Analysis of the Subject Field

Modern society constantly faces various global challenges. Namely, climate challenges, such as global warming and shifting of climate zones or anthropogenic challenges, such as hazardous emissions, fires, tanker or well oil spills and accumulation of waste, etc. In order to ensure successful functioning of a state, its governmental institutions have to consider a wide range of scenarios and if possible counter emerging threats. Taking all potential circumstances and scenario developments into account is rather difficult and unreasonable, particularly in regard to balancing the levels of resource consumption with the achievement of desirable results. Therefore, the two following aspects gain, as a rule, increased attention: firstly, threats to life and health of the country's population, and secondly large-scale destructions or inability to use the country's main production facilities. The abovementioned first aspect assures the fulfilment of a state's main function – protection and realisation of its population potential. The second aspect provides for the public consumption level, and if the state fails to insure the necessary consumption levels, it may result in public tensions, protests, famine or pandemic.

Published by Springer Nature Switzerland AG 2020
Y. Murayama et al. (Eds.): ITDRR 2019, IFIP AICT 575, pp. 21–30, 2020.
https://doi.org/10.1007/978-3-030-48939-7_3

There are hundreds of disasters in the world. The ratio of natural catastrophes to man-made disasters is presented on the Fig. 1 [1].

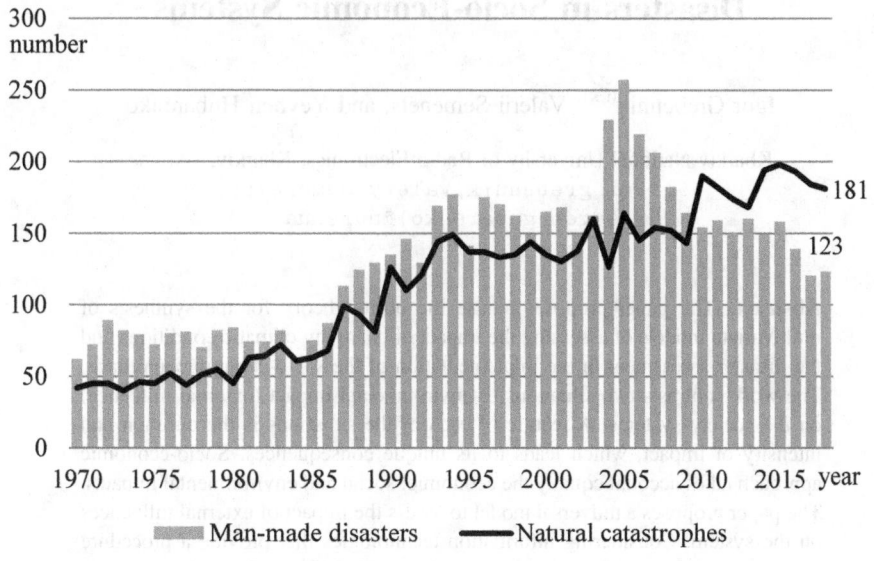

Fig. 1. Number of catastrophic events, 1970–2018.

According to the UN [2], the number of deaths among all types of natural disasters, hydrometeorological disasters come first, geological second and man-made disasters third.

About 3.3 million people (on average 82,500 people per year) worldwide died from earthquakes, hurricanes and other dangerous natural phenomenon from 1970 to 2010. Most lived in poor countries.

These statistics include only the direct victims of natural disasters. Natural disasters often provoke a decrease in consumption, for example, drought can provoke a crop failure and subsequently starvation.

For example, the drought in the USSR – 1921–1923. (about 3 million people), 1932–1933 (from 3 to 10 million people); China – 1939 (200 thousand people), 1942–1943 (about 3 million people); India – 1943 (about 1.5 million people); Kampuchea – 1975–1978 (about 1 million people); Ethiopia – 1983–1988 (about 1 million people); North Korea (about 2 million people).

Since 1980, more than two million people and over $3 trillion have been lost to disasters caused by natural hazards, with total damages increasing by more than 600% from $23 billion a year in the 1980s to $150 billion a year in the last decade [3].

Middle income countries suffer as a rule the greatest damage.

Examples demonstrating that natural and man-made disasters are widespread and often.

As can be seen, natural disasters can occur in any region of our planet. Unquestionably, for a certain type of natural disaster, there are relatively calm regions, but if viewed in a complex, and take into account the changing climate of the planet, all regions of the planet are at risk of natural disasters.

The aggressive impact on the system should include not only natural disasters, but also man-made disasters. Man-made disasters have already equaled many types of natural disasters in their scale and consequences. Yield them only in predictability. Natural disasters are more difficult to predict and to develop an event to compensate the effect.

2 Types of External Influence

During the research, different types of effects of the aggressive environmental impact on the system were identified. Should be allocated:

1. Short-term impact and consequences. For example, a strong gusty wind breaks branches and disrupts outdoor advertising, car fires and more. The point is that an exposure lasts no more than a few days, and it is also possible to completely eliminate the consequences in a few days. For example, fires, torn off roofs, broken tree branches.
2. Long-term impact – short-term consequences. For example, accumulation of garbage, dust, snow. The process is time-consuming, but regular regulatory activities (filter replacement, garbage removal, snow removal) are enough to eliminate the consequences. For example, snowdrifts, abnormal temperatures.
3. Short-term impact – long-term consequences. For example, tsunamis, hurricanes, earthquakes, major industrial accidents involving emissions of toxic substances. All of them last a limited, often small period of time, but the damage is huge and it can be eliminated in a few years. For example, tsunami, flooding, volcanic ash.
4. Long-term impact and consequences. For example, enterprise emissions that gradually poison groundwater and soil, exit points for gas and oil products that mix with groundwater and can accumulate in various cavities in the ground. Poisoning and accumulation of critical mass occurs gradually, purification requires long and costly procedures.

The classification is symptomatic because the time spent on remediation is related to available resources and technologies. Some consequences are not eliminated, leaving nature to overcome the consequences on its own.

Climate change should be placed in the fourth category (long-term impact and consequences).

3 Description of the Problem

3.1 Definition of a System

Undeniably, addressing the issue of countering potential risks should be based on the methods and principles of system analysis [4, 5]. Definition of an abstract system, which is most practical and convenient for modelling, is the set-theoretical one presented in the works by Bourbaki [6].

In this case, a system is defined as a set of homogeneous or heterogeneous elements $M = \{m_i\}$, $i = \overline{1,n}$ with a set of relations $R = \{r_j\}, j = \overline{1,k}$. Then the Cartesian product

$$C = \{M \times R\} \tag{1}$$

defines the universal set of structures of an abstract system. Qualitative and quantitative characteristics of the sets M, R make it possible to determine the exact structure of any system: social, economic, and ecological, etc.

Every particular model of the structure (1) has a certain set of obvious or latent properties $P = \{p_l\}$, $l = \overline{1,g}$. Thus, $P = F(C) = F\{M,R\}$.

Given the abovementioned, the initial definition of an abstract system may be expanded and presented as follows [7]

$$S = \langle \{M \times R\}, P \rangle. \tag{2}$$

3.2 The Process of Decision-Making

Making a decision is an integral part of any purposeful human activity: household, professional, production, environmental, social, and political, etc. Despite the abundance of the application areas, it is possible to list common stages of the decision-making process. They are as follows [8]:

- formulating an objective;
- defining a set of possible X^P and admissible $X \subset X^P$ decisions to achieve the formulated objectives (decisions);
- selecting and conceptualising a metric to determine relative efficiency of possible alternative decisions $x \in X$ i.e. efficiency criterion $K(x)$;
- solving the task of finding an efficient solution

$$x^0 = \arg \underset{x \in X}{extr}\, K(x). \tag{3}$$

According to V.M. Glushkow [9] a solution, which may be considered efficient, meets the following criteria: promptness, integrity (complexity) and optimality. A decision that is prompt is made simultaneously with the occurrence of a hazardous situation, in accordance with the emergence of the reliable initial information neither prior to (in this case it will not reflect the current state of affairs) nor long after it. This means timely, resourceful, logistical and informational coordination of the decision realisation process. A decision that is complex takes as many system affecting factors (variables) and their correlation (interrelations) into consideration as possible. A decision that is optimal reflects the formalisation requirement of the problem in order to enable the use of formal objective methods to define the emergency solution (3) instead of implementing intuitive subjective procedures.

Fulfilment of the abovementioned required efficiency criteria obstructs the decision-making process. Particularly, ensuring the integrity (complexity) criterion requires expansion of the task and increasing the number of variables, including those that are not fully defined, it complicates the models describing their interrelations, and as a result places the issue of decision-making under multi-criteria circumstances as well as partial (interval) uncertainty of the initial data. On the other hand, in the essence of the decision-making process lies the informed choice of one alternative from the set of admissible ones. This means that the process of decision-making is an intellectual, subjective procedure realised individually or collectively by the persons with the delegated decision-making power. Therefore, such persons or experts elaborating the decision are considered the carries of information required for the formalisation of the decision-making process. This raises the issue of getting the necessary information from its carriers. Methodology of the described issue is known as expert assessment.

The issue of getting expert information becomes particularly acute when dealing with multi-criteria optimisation (choice) of decisions. Under multi-criteria circumstances the efficiency criterion $K(x)$ (3) is an n-tuple, rather than a scalar one $K(x) = \langle k_i(x) \rangle$, $i = \overline{1, n}$, with $k_i(x)$ as the criteria, which are heterogeneous in essence and dimension, determined in different scales, with varying direction of dominance and are local (particular), each of the criteria characterises local properties (quality) of decisions, whereas taken as a set these criteria fully describe the system as a whole. In this case, an admissible set of decisions X is a composition of two subsets $X = X^D \cup X^C$, with X^D, X^C as the corresponding subsets of concerted (dominated) and compromise (non-dominated, Pareto-optimal) decisions [7, 10].

According to its definition, optimal decisions belong to the compromise space and the issue of decision-making (3) reads as follows: $x^0 = \arg \underset{x \in X}{extr} \, k_i(x)$, $\forall i = \overline{1, n}$.

According to Hadamard [11] such an objective is incorrect, particularly due to the fact that there is no solution for all different contradictory criteria simultaneously reaching their maximum value.

3.3   Structural and Parametric Identification

The essence of structural identification is limited to the selection based solely on the heuristic considerations of one of the following polynomial models: additive $F_K(x) = \sum\limits_{i=1}^{n} \lambda_i k_i(x)$, multiplicative $F_K(x) = \prod\limits_{i=1}^{n} k_i(x)$, combinational and Cobb-Douglas model $F_K(x) = \prod\limits_{i=1}^{n} k_i^{\beta_i}(x)$, where $\Lambda = \langle \lambda_i \rangle$, $i = \overline{1, N}$ is the tuple of weighting coefficients and $K = \langle k_i \rangle$, $i = \overline{1, N}$ is the tuple of disparate factors. Currently, the most widespread model is the additive one. Each of the listed polynomial is a fragment of the Kolmogorov-Gabor polynomial

$$F(x) = \lambda_0 + \sum_{i=1}^{m} \lambda_i k_i(x) + \sum_{i=1}^{m} \sum_{j=i}^{m} \lambda_{ij} k_i(x) k_j(x) + \sum_{i=1}^{m} \sum_{j=i}^{m} \sum_{k=j}^{m} \lambda_{ijk} k_i(x) k_j(x) k_k(x) + \ldots$$

(4)

The pros of opting for the Kolmogorov-Gabor polynomial list as follows [12]:

- in his work Kolmogorov showed and Gabor subsequently summarised that a polynomial enables precise approximation of any function of disparate variables;
- a polynomial contains both additive and multiplicative linear in their characterising factors $K(x_i)$ components and therefore enables formation of any polynomials on their basis;
- when elaborating values and assessment of such complicated structures as organisational systems, duplication of these values is unavoidable, whereas a polynomial can compensate their influence.

Furthermore, the system utility is a smooth monotonic function, therefore it is recommended to include the terms of maximum second degree. Then it is possible to implement the below mentioned truncated Kolmogorov-Gabor polynomial as a universal model structure (4):

$$F(x) = \sum_{i=1}^{m} \lambda_i k_i(x) + \sum_{i=1}^{m} \lambda_{1i} k_1(x) k_i(x) + \sum_{i=2}^{m} \lambda_{2i} k_2(x) k_i(x) + \ldots + \lambda_{mm} k_m(x) k_m(x).$$

However, it is impossible to make an informed choice of one of the models based on the heuristic method of expert assessment.

In order to objectively identify the polynomial structure, it is recommended to apply the genetic algorithm method [13].

3.4   Problem Statement

A social-economic system of any hierarchal level (large enterprise, district, city, region) is constantly under the threat of an emerging natural or man-made disaster.

Various forecasts and statistical data analyses make it possible to predict with some level of certainty the occurrence of natural disasters. A set of measures $Z = \{z_1, z_2, \ldots, z_n\}$ aimed at the prevention of impact of various natural and man-made disasters may be elaborated based on the statistical data and forecasts.

Every such measure may be aimed not only at the prevention of the impact but also at the reduction of damage following the disaster.

It is important to decide on the subset of measures, which will jointly have the highest efficiency. Efficiency is described as summarised general result of the realisation of a subset of taken measures $z \in Z$. These results may encompass the following:

- reducing the number of casualties among the population due to timely warnings and well-organised evacuation plan;
- reducing material damage – smoke detectors and other elements of fire protection system help to ensure timely fire alarms. Some fire protection systems automatically begin the process of fire outbreak elimination, minimising the reaction time and reducing the damage;
- reducing the environmental impact – emission, leak and breakage, etc. registration systems help to timely alarm the operator about the threat or independently take statutory measures.

4   Features of the Development of Events

It is important to emphasise the following particularities of the given task:

1. Threat-countering scenarios may be mutually exclusive, which may be the case within one threat or scenarios of countering various threats may contradict one another. Namely, one of the scenarios requires a prompt and unhindered escape from the building of great masses of people, whereas another scenario involves setting up extra barriers such as turnstile and metal detectors, etc.
2. Realisation of all threat-countering scenarios is not possible due to the lack of resources.
3. Realisation of a number of scenarios of countering one single threat may be possible, namely, setting up fire suppression systems, smoke detectors, fire-distinguishers, and evacuation plans, organising trainings, etc.
4. Realisation effect of a number of scenarios may differ from the set of expected effects. This has to do with the emergence of the control system as opposed to combined realisation of a number of scenarios.
5. Realisation of a scenario shall have a certain efficiency level of threat-countering, it may either be the complete elimination of consequences or elimination on the $[0, 1]$ scale. On this scale, 0 is a complete lack of threat-countering efficiency (e.g. certain measures are carried out in order to appear to have the situation under control and to calm down the population, thus indirectly countering the threat of panic and riots); and 1 is the successful threat-countering and complete elimination of all consequences (e.g. diversification of critical commodities suppliers, thus in case of a failure to fulfil the contract terms by one or several suppliers, the commodities will be delivered due to an increased participation of other suppliers). Moreover, realisation of a scenario shall have certain social consequences. For example, some measures may be considered by the population as the ones improving their well-being and therefore supported and some as needless waste of taxes and therefore rejected. Apart from economic and social effects, realisation of certain scenarios may have environmental consequences. For example, hazardous emissions may result in changes to regional flora and fauna, making it a barren lifeless area.

Apart from the international standards on the estimation of the impact of natural disasters almost every country has its own procedures and methods to estimate the effects. A greater part of measures to counter natural disaster impacts is limited to economic measures: establishment of contingency funds, insurance, methods and mechanisms to calculate profit and taxation. Unilateral character of these measures reduces the efficiency of solving the problem in general.

5 Synthesis of the Model Formation of a Generalized Assessment

As mentioned above, every scenario, which has to be assessed in order to choose a set of scenarios for realisation, is characterised by the three following aspects: economic, social and ecological. Thus, a summarised assessment of scenario realisation P(z) includes assessments of three indicators:

$$F(z) = F(I_E(z), I_S(z), I_{EC}(z)),$$

with $I_E(z), I_S(z), I_{EC}(z)$ as summarised scalar assessments (indicators) characterising respectively the state of economic, social and environmental elements.

Each of the abovementioned indicators is in its turn a summarised assessment of a certain tuple of indices characterising local properties of each of the abovementioned elements:

$$I_E(z) = I_E(Q_1, Q_2, \dots Q_H), \ I_S(z) = I_S(S_1, S_2, \dots S_K), \ I_{EC}(z) = I_{EC}(O_1, O_2, \dots O_L)$$

with Q, S, O as assessment of a certain tuple of indices; H, K, L as number of indices.

Lower basic level of the analysed hierarchy of the assessment system is composed of directly measured values of the state of the object. These initial assessments form the basis of the corresponding indices, namely: $Q_h = \langle q_r \rangle$, $r = \overline{1, R}$, with q_r as a certain initial property of Q_h index.

Thus, a certain metric (measurement system) of quantitative and qualitative assessments of the stability level of technobiosphere system development is formulated. Main requirements of this system list its informational completeness and description precision of the three interrelated elements (subsystems) forming the technobiosphere system [14].

Numerous organisations and scientific groups constantly research this issue, nevertheless, currently there is no unified generally accepted definition of qualitative and quantitative composition of summarised assessments and methods of their formulation. Furthermore, qualitative and quantitative composition may be adapted to each individual case when elaborating the assessment system, whereas choice of the assessment model is of fundamental importance. Therefore, the main objective of the current subchapter is to synthesise the model of scalar multivariate assessment.

Particular characteristic of multivariate assessment is the fact that its initial information measurement basis is composed of values with differentiated semantics and consequently differentiated physical values, vary in intervals of probable values as well as scales and prevalence direction. This means that all factors of the scalar multivariate assessment model are to be presented in the normalised form: $P(z) = P(\Lambda, K(z))$, with

P(z) as the summarised scalar assessment; P as the operator determining the structure of the assessment model; $\Lambda = \langle \lambda_t \rangle$, $t = \overline{1,T}$ as the tuple of weighting coefficients; $K = \langle k_t \rangle$, $t = \overline{1,T}$ as the tuple of disparate factors.

6 Further Actions

Having made complex scalar assessments P(z) of each separate measure out of the set Z, which incorporate economic, social and ecological aspects of the society life, it is possible to formulate a subset of recommended measures to take.

The list of recommended measures should take the following into account:

1. The number of elements in the subset is limited by the amount of available resources (material, human, financial, informational and organisational). As mentioned above, available resources cannot cover the realisation of all measures, furthermore, some actions require the same resource, i.e. they are mutually exclusive.
2. Some measures require a certain order of execution. One action has to take place only following the completion of the other one. For example, trainings on the evacuation to emergency shelters can take place only after the construction of such shelters.
3. Some measures have to be taken jointly in order to increase their efficiency. For example, having set the fire-extinguishing systems, it is necessary to offer introductory lectures and trainings to inform the employees and residents about the features of the system and enable them to react properly in emergency situations.

In order to decide on the subset of measures out of the set Z, formal or expert methods should be applied. Having formulated varying alternative subsets (lists), it is necessary to make a summarised assessment of every alternative using the multicriteria decision-making approach described above.

The DTW algorithm may be used in order to analyse the dynamics of changes to factors within ecological, economic and social areas [15].

The resulting list of measures will have high efficiency and take different factors and aspects into consideration.

7 Conclusions

This paper defines the issue of countering threats as the process of choosing the set of scenarios to reduce or possibly eliminate the impact of threats consequences. In order to make such a decision it is recommended to thoroughly consider economic, social and ecological aspects. In order to synthesise a summarised assessment including the consumption of material resources, efficiency of threat-countering, social importance and influence on the environment, it is suggested to use the utility theory.

The following aspects should be noted:

- The number of natural and man-made disasters is comparable. The impact of natural disasters is considerably bigger than that of the man-made disasters. This is due to the fact that natural disasters are difficult to predict and therefore to counter efficiently.
- Natural and man-made disasters can occur in any region of our planet.
- Elaborating the measures to prevent damage is a complex and controversial process, requiring nontrivial decisions.
- When choosing the measures to counter the impact of natural disasters, it is important to consider their economic, social and ecological effect.
- In order to elaborate the list of measures to prevent damage, it is possible to apply the mathematical tools of multi-criteria assessment.

References

1. Sigma. Secondary natural catastrophe risks on the front line. https://www.swissre.com/institute/research/sigma-research/sigma-2019-02.html. Accessed 14 Oct 2019
2. The World Bank and The United Nations: Source Natural and Man-Made Disasters: Preventive Measures. Alpina Publisher, Moscow (2011)
3. The World Bank. https://www.worldbank.org/en/topic/disasterriskmanagement/overview. Accessed 14 Oct 2019
4. Dudley, P.: Bogdanov's Tektology. Centre for Systems Studies University of Hull (1996)
5. Bertalanffy, L.: Ludwig General System Theory, New York (1969)
6. Bourbaki, N.: Théorie des ensembles. Diffusion, Paris (1970)
7. Grebennik, I., Khriapkin, O., Ovezgeldyyev, A., Pisklakova, V., Urniaieva, I.: The concept of a regional information-analytical system for emergency situations. In: Murayama, Y., Velev, D., Zlateva, P. (eds.) ITDRR 2017. IAICT, vol. 516, pp. 55–66. Springer, Cham (2019). https://doi.org/10.1007/978-3-030-18293-9_6
8. Grebennik, I., Reshetnik, V., Ovezgeldyyev, A., Ivanov, V., Urniaieva, I.: Strategy of effective decision-making in planning and elimination of consequences of emergency situations. In: Murayama, Y., Velev, D., Zlateva, P. (eds.) ITDRR 2018. IAICT, vol. 550, pp. 66–75. Springer, Cham (2019). https://doi.org/10.1007/978-3-030-32169-7_6
9. Hlushkov, V.: Introduction to ACS, 2nd edn. Tekhnika, Kiev (1974)
10. Tzeng, G.-H., Huang, J.J.: Multiple Attribute Decision Making: Methods and Applications. CRC Press Taylor & Francis Group, Boca Raton (2011)
11. Wang, J.-R., Zhou, Y., Medved, M.: Existence and stability of fractional differential equations with Hadamard derivative. Topol. Methods Nonlinear Anal. 41(1), 113–133 (2013)
12. Jech, T.: Set Theory. Springer, Heidelberg (2006). https://doi.org/10.1007/3-540-44761-X
13. Anastasakis, L., Mort, N.: The development of self-organization techniques in modelling: a review of the group method of data handling (GMDH). Department of Automatic Control & Systems Engineering The University of Sheffield Mappin St., Sheffield, S1 3JD, United Kingdom. Research Report No. 813 (2001)
14. Zgurovsky, M.Z., Kasyanov, P.O., Gorban, N.V., Paliichuk, L.S.: Qualitative and quantitative analysis of weak solutions of energy-balance climate models. Cybern. Syst. Anal. 55, 552–560 (2019). https://doi.org/10.1007/s10559-019-00164-1
15. Nechiporenko, A., Gubarenko, E., Gubarenko, M.: Authentication of users of mobile devices by their motor reactions. Telecommun. Radio Eng. 78, 987–1003 (2019)

Problems of Cultural Heritage Preservation in the Context of the Armed Conflict Growth

Yuliia Trach, Maryna Tolmach[✉], Olena Chaikovska, and Tetiana Gumeniuk

Kyiv National University of Culture and Arts, Kyiv 01601, Ukraine
kn.knukim@gmail.com

Abstract. Attention is paid to the need to preserve cultural heritage in areas of armed conflict and the particular legal protection of its objects. The experience of digitization of cultural heritage in Ukraine through implementation of state and public initiatives is presented.

Keywords: Cultural heritage · Armed conflicts · Digitalization

1 Preservation of Cultural Heritage in the Area of Armed Conflict

1.1 Cultural Heritage as an Integral Part of the Modernization and Development Strategy

Cultural heritage is in fact the main way of existence of the culture. What is not included in cultural heritage ceases to be a culture and ultimately ceases to exist. For his life, man manages to master only a small share of cultural heritage. What remains after him for other generations becomes a common property of all people, all of humanity. However, it can only be so if it is preserved. The social progress of humankind depends on the solution of the problem of preservation of cultural heritage. The main function of cultural heritage at the present stage is the orientation to the socio-cultural result, which allows solving the problems of the development of the socio-cultural sphere in conditions of reforms, to ensure the integrity of the socio-cultural space, to increase the complex effectiveness of cultural activities.

Recently, worldviews on the concept of heritage have undergone significant evolutionary changes.

In particular, globalization processes that have taken place in the world have led to the need to consider heritage in the local-global coordinate system. Being a synergistic resource by nature, heritage is in many ways a "thing in itself", it will not be used, remaining at the level of physical cultural resources, unless it is involved in the life of the local community. Tangible cultural heritage always has a clear localization in one or another locality, always "inscribed" in a specific local community, creating physically tangible landmarks in space and time, a base for local ideology and identity, presenting resources for the implementation of educational programs, tourism development and related sectors of the economy. Thus, based on the use of cultural heritage,

Y. Murayama et al. (Eds.): ITDRR 2019, IFIP AICT 575, pp. 31–44, 2020.
https://doi.org/10.1007/978-3-030-48939-7_4

the local community can build effective social strategies aimed at poverty alleviation and sustainable development. At the same time, undoubtedly, trends in globalization have clearly manifested themselves in the field of cultural heritage.

The potential for the development of cultural heritage holds a special place in the creative economy, which integrates culture, economics, science and education. Firstly, heritage provides cultural continuity in addition to identifying and strengthening individual and collective identity, respect for other cultures and diversity of cultural expressions, as well as affirmation of spiritual, educational, social, economic and other values. Secondly, cultural heritage can be the basis for the development of a creative society and means of promoting local economic development. However, the modern world creates a whole system of threats and challenges to cultural heritage. In a dynamic and increasingly accelerating development, physical cultural resources are at risk of total or partial destruction if they are not included in these processes. Even such a positive trend as tourism development, in the absence of proper control by the authorities, can cause significant damage to heritage sites. Threats to the heritage are also hidden as a result of economic development, industrial development of new territories, new urban development programs, during which entire neighborhoods, environmental pollution, and military conflicts are reconstructed or reconstructed. In many countries of the world, heritage preservation programs suffer from lack of financial, administrative and technical resources due to not enough of attention from government agencies.

1.2   Armed Conflicts as a Special Kind of Social Emergency

The intensification of the interconnection and interdependence of all states and peoples, marked at the turn of the 21st century, quite eloquently indicates that the world society processes of becoming economically and politically wholesome are increasing. In these circumstances, any peripheral or other changes in the system of interstate relations affect the state of international cooperation as a whole. Factors destabilizing this interaction are military conflicts, not only killing millions of lives and undermining the lifeblood of entire nations, but also being a significant complement to those root causes, the action of which greatly exacerbates the entire complex of global problems that already threaten humanity today.

In modern conditions the tendency of quantity of military conflicts and local wars to increase has been marked: in the XVIII century 68 wars occurred, in the XIX the number became 205, in the period of 1900–1990 it was 234 [10, p. 92]. Military clashes between states continue to exist today, posing a serious threat from the point of view of their escalation into a world war, as they occur at a time when the issue of war and peace has not only become an area of global concern, but has also become one of the most serious, affecting the very foundations of the existence of human civilization. Armed conflicts, as very dangerous policy instruments, are bloody and protracted, and human and material casualties in them are incomparable to the results achieved.

All of this is to say that in today's context, the search for effective ways and means of resolving and preventing military conflicts is a pressing need of humanity. Moreover, the right of armed conflicts, applied in the period of armed conflicts, in particular, in non-international ones, lacks modern legal requirements and methods of their humanization and settlement, the necessary control mechanisms, and the nature of the efforts made by international organizations for the implementation of the policy of conflict prevention. In these circumstances, the preservation of cultural heritage is one of the foundations for the preservation of cultural diversity and a powerful tool for cultural dialogue. There is a serious problem requiring international control and responsibility for observing humanitarian law on the protection of cultural property, especially in the event of an armed conflict of international or international conflict.

1.3   Legal Protection of Cultural Heritage in the Event of Armed Conflict

For a long time, objects of cultural heritage, in particular, works of art were the main object of conquest, and it was not until the middle of the 19th century that, thanks to the widespread restitution of cultural values captured by Napoleon in the course of his military campaigns, a customary rule was imposed in Europe, prohibiting it. From that moment, the world community begins to recognize the special legal status behind the objects of cultural heritage, the need to protect them from the adverse effects of the war. However, up to the present day the problem of their protection has not been finally resolved.

In many countries of the world, laws were adopted and special systems for the protection of cultural heritage developed. International charters and agreements provide for provisions that claim that heritage belongs to all people, and therefore require collective responsibility for the protection of cultural heritage, consisting of individuals, their communities, as well as governments at local, regional and international levels. In particular, the role of international organizations (UNESCO, ICOMOS, ICOM, ICCROM, etc.) in the protection of cultural heritage in the armed zones has been limited. In 1945, UNESCO in The Hague published the first protocol on the protection of cultural priority in the event of armed conflict, the second was published in 1999 [14].

It should be noted that The Hague Convention of 1954 and its two additional protocols became the most recognised of legal instruments for the protection of cultural property during armed conflicts. However, compared with the other UNESCO conventions for the protection of cultural heritage and property (especially in relation to the 1970 Illicit Traffic onvention and the 1972 World Heritage Convention), the 1954 Hague convention with its both additional protocols gained less state parties endorsement (Fig. 1).

Since 1970, the UNESCO Convention on the Means of Prohibiting and Preventing the Illicit Import, Export and Transfer of Ownership of Cultural Property has been a major instrument of international protection for cultural heritage. In 1999, the UN Security Council adopted Resolution No. 2347, condemning the unlawful destruction of cultural heritage. At a meeting at the UN headquarters in 2017, the relationship between the destruction of cultural heritage and terrorism and mass violence was announced [13].

The International Committee of the Blue Shield, in conjunction with the Association of its National Committees (in Ukraine this committee exists since 2014), should directly engage in the official protection of cultural heritage in the event of armed conflict on the basis and in accordance with the mandate under the conventions of international humanitarian law. However, despite its mission of strategic dialogue with decision-makers and major international organizations in order to prevent and respond quickly to armed conflicts, the International Committee of the Blue Shield has not achieved the greatest success in this area, as one might to expect, and to save the objects of culture after natural disasters.

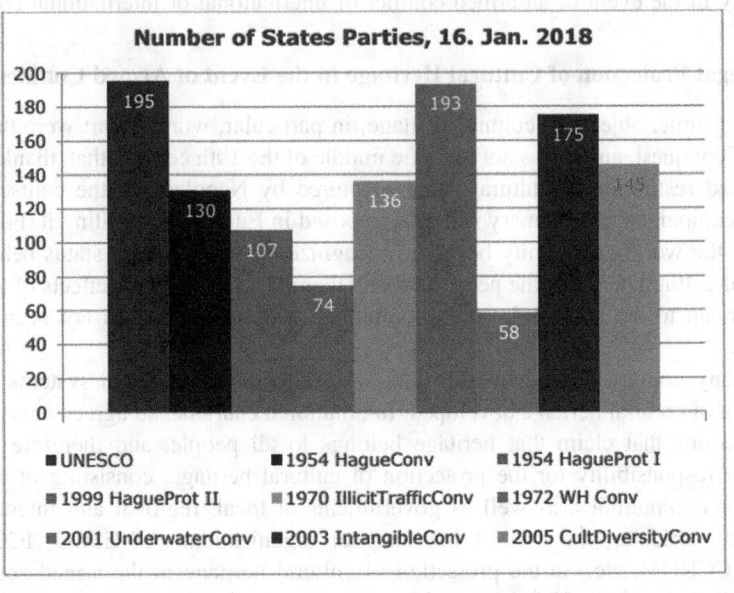

Fig. 1. Number of State Parties to the different UNESCO-Conventions for the protection of cultural heritage

International organizations have tried to protect the world's cultural heritage, but in many cases, their role in protection has been limited due to the lack of adherence to cultural conventions by some countries, the inability to take measures to protect them through legislation, etc. In addition, among the reasons for the inefficient protection of cultural heritage in areas of armed conflict are the lack of effective coordination between international organizations and national institutions working in the field of cultural heritage protection in the area of armed conflict, the limited financial resources, their insufficiency to reach their respective goals and their organizations, repeated attacks on cultural heritage sites and insufficient awareness of the importance of its preservation.

In this context, it is necessary to intensify the development of social partnership mechanisms, new decision-making mechanisms relevant to local communities, between national and regional authorities, public institutions responsible for socio-cultural development, third sector organizations and business entities to integrate cultural heritage into development programs on different levels as well as new decision-making mechanisms significant to local communities. For this purpose, in 2018, the European Commission conducted a wide study and presented a comprehensive review of existing knowledge on the protection of cultural heritage from the effects of natural disasters and threats caused by human activities, in particular military conflicts - "Safeguarding Cultural Heritage from Natural and Man-Made Disasters at the European and international levels. A comparative analysis of risk management in the EU" (Luxembourg, 2018) [5]. This document reflects existing strategies and tools for disaster risk management in 28 Member States, and provides evidence-based recommendations to support European cooperation and better integrate cultural heritage into national platforms for disaster risk reduction.

In the context of the need to prevent the consequences of armed conflict, these recommendations are presented in several blocks: recommendations to the European authorities (in particular, the development of long-term concepts and strategies is necessary); national (in particular, it is necessary to establish or develop civil-military cooperation); regional and local authorities (in particular, information on the need for civil-military cooperation in the field of the protection of cultural property should be initiated at the local level in schools); as well as owners of cultural property (in particular, they must provide adequate records of their property rights and their assets, preferably certified and digitized). Thus, the European Commission pays special attention not only to the study of adaptation strategies, methodologies and other corrective tools in relation to the preservation of cultural heritage, but to the digitization of its objects as one of the inevitable and useful options for preserving the cultural heritage.

2 Digitalization of Cultural Heritage: Ukraine's Experience in the Context of World Trends

2.1 Digitalization as a Fundamentally New Manifestation of Globalization Processes in the Field of Cultural Heritage

Digitalization is a global trend followed by all countries aiming at developing a competitive economy and improving the quality of life of the population. Digitalization is characterized by three leading characteristics: all types of content move from analogue, physical and static to digital, at the same time they become mobile and personal; the transition to simple communication technologies (technology becomes a communication tool), the leading characteristic of the device and technology is controllability; communications become heterogeneous: vertical, hierarchical communication loses relevance, and there is a transition to a network structure of communication [16]. Digitization plays a special role in the field of culture, where multimedia technologies have changed the technological essence of the function of cultural heritage creation and its promotion. In modern conditions, the creation of a collective memory is already real, which will allow us to formulate new models of the global history of culture, to reveal common traditions, to get acquainted with the unique works of large and low-prevalent culture.

In a society where information, technology of acquiring and disseminating knowledge becomes the main value, the legacy with its clearly expressed information essence begins to acquire new traits, as a result of which its value is increased. Among other things, it is the isolation from the legacy of its information component, which begins to live its separate life in international networks - its "virtualization". Another phenomenon is the emergence of new, devoid of one particular type of one-tier non-hierarchical relationships outside the political and administrative frameworks and boundaries, the formation of communities built around certain aspects of heritage activities or policies without unified management or coordination centers operating primarily on the basis of new information technologies.

In the face of such global change, in the face of the threat of cultural unification, the need for efforts to maintain the diversity of cultural heritage as one of the sustainable development resources is increasing. The cultural heritage of different civilizations can and should become the basis for intercultural communication and world progress, a nourishing basis for creativity. For the EU member states, 2018 has become a year of cultural heritage. Much attention was paid to expanding funding and reconstruction of cultural preservation programs. In 2018, the EU approved 10 long-term initiatives in the field of cultural preservation and development, including three programs for the dissemination of cultural knowledge, cultural tourism, combating illicit trafficking in cultural heritage items, as well as improving the skills of creative professionals, involving the society in decision-making on objects cultures and innovative approaches to the preservation and multiplication of cultures of European peoples [1]. Thus, technological and digital innovations have unique potential because they facilitate access to world heritage in a way that has never been achieved in all of human history. At present, digitization of services and the creation of an information space in the cultural environment is one of the most pressing issues in the field of cultural reform. These changes will entail the mass dissemination of cultural values, the convenience of their use, and the involvement of a large audience in the country's historical context.

2.2   The Benefits of Digitalization of Cultural Heritage

Thanks to the modern achievements in the information sphere, the world community is observing a mosaic of unique, unique, unique cultures. The mobile information-landscape matrices of each invariant cultural environment will make constant changes to the general structure of world culture; will be able to ensure the joint movement of cultures of small peoples towards each other. The purpose of such projects is to create a regional segment of cultural heritage networks through the creation and development of collections of information resources. Creating a collection allows you to increase access to information resources; to ensure the development of sufficient and protected resources to maintain the vitality and viability of the region, its sustainable functioning and development; to protect regional cultural values.

Today, the creation of collections is not a technical problem, but a cultural one, since it is necessary to develop a methodology and technology for their creation and development. First, when forming a regional segment in cultural heritage networks, it is advisable to develop a concept, define meaningful boundaries, work out the criteria by which it is created and justify them. Secondly, only on this basis it is possible to develop technological and methodological solutions: determination of the content composition, sources of formation, principles of systematization, ensuring completeness. Thirdly, it is necessary to choose information technologies for creation, support and use of the collection. The leading role is given to the creators who order the technical solution, based on conceptual provisions.

Collections created on this approach will be able to perform many functions in cultural heritage networks. For example informational (the accumulation, systematization and transmission of local history information), epistemological (acquisition of knowledge about the surrounding life, facts from the history of the region), transformative (the transformation of local lore knowledge into spiritual and practical values (conducting local lore, publishing books, discs, creating films, etc.)), function of scientific research (organization and conducting of local lore scientific researches in the field of culture, history, natural science), axiological (rendering assistance to the individual in the realization of significance for oneself, for the society of certain events, phenomena, etc. from the life of the region, participation in the formation of personal relation to these or other regional cultural values; this function is expressed in the choice of thinking behavior), educational (formation of self-consciousness of the person), practical (assistance in solving socio-economic, cultural and other problems in the region), function of security (protection of monuments of history and culture of the region on the basis of conscious action and in accordance with values), integrative (orientation to interdisciplinary regional studies, to the formation of fundamental concepts), regulatory (the establishment of traditional rules and regulations that regulate behavior, passing on local knowledge from generation to generation), cultural (participation in the expansion of horizons, education, self-education, development of culture). Consequently, collections are inherently multifunctional, which means they will be able to solve the global challenges facing culture as a whole.

2.3 Ukraine's Experience in Digitizing Cultural Heritage

In Ukraine, despite the general development of the IT sphere and strong creative ideas, the dialogue between culture and technology is just beginning. The country has adopted the Concept of Development of the Digital Economy and Society of Ukraine for 2018–2020 [12], according to which digitalization is the saturation of the physical world with electronic-digital devices, tools, systems and the establishment of electronic-communication exchange between them, which in fact makes it possible to integrate the interaction of the virtual and the physical, that is, creates cyberphysical space. Also approved is the "List of cultural heritage objects of national importance, which are entered in the State Register of immovable monuments of Ukraine" [8]. However, despite recognizing the decisive role of cultural heritage as the most powerful component of shaping Ukrainian identity along with language, territory, economic life and communion of historical fate, which becomes a factor of national consolidation, awareness of Ukrainians as a single nation, promotion of social issues and promotion of social development. and the preservation of national cultural heritage has been greatly exacerbated. The main reason for the existing shortcomings and problems is the total non-compliance with the current legislation on the protection of cultural heritage as a whole, and individual laws concerning its different types and types.

The situation with the protection of cultural heritage is also exacerbated by the occupation and annexation of the Autonomous Republic of Crimea, parts of Donetsk and Luhansk regions by the Russian Federation in 2014, since those territories have a significant number of cultural heritage sites. According to the published data of the Ministry of Culture of Ukraine, as of 2013, there were 34 museums of different types operating on the territory of the Autonomous Republic of Crimea. In Crimea there were 917.477 objects of the state part of the Museum Fund of Ukraine. There were 5 museum institutions in Sevastopol, 320.163 museum objects of the state part of the Museum Fund of Ukraine were stored. According to the statistics of the Autonomous Republic of Crimea, more than 300 public and departmental museums were also located in the territory of the Autonomy [7, p. 31]. The Russian occupying power poses a direct threat to these prominent cultural heritage sites, for example, on November 16–17, 2015, a tower and a wall fragment of the symbol of the city - the ancient Genoese fortress, which was nominated in two nominations of the Preliminary World Heritage List, collapsed in Sudak. There is documented evidence that Russia is exporting significant cultural values from the occupied Crimea, for example almost all paintings of the famous Aivazovsky Gallery in Feodosia were taken out [7, p. 34].

The use of massive artillery shelling of settlements and industrial sites in the Donetsk and Luhansk regions by Russian military and mercenary groups, as well as by separatist units they support, causes damage and destruction of cultural heritage sites and cultural heritage sites. As of 2013 on the territory of Donetsk oblast, in the sovereign region, 4144 cultural monuments were transferred. Including archeology - 1956, history - 2008, monumental mystery - 32, city architecture and architecture - 148. In the Lugansk region, on the sovereign oblast, 6317 Blvd. Including archeology - 5014, history - 919, monumental mystery - 38, architecture and public garden - 338, garden and park mystery - 8. However, it is difficult to say today how many industrial architectural monuments in these regions have been affected - their identification and accounting have been practically not carried out by local cultural heritage agencies due to either the reluctance of admission of professionals by business owners or due to the regime nature of many industrial sites of objects [7, p. 36]. In addition, it should be noted that until 2014, there were 59 state museums operating in the Donetsk region, of which only 30 (together with branches) and the historical and cultural reserve in the town of Svyatogirsk are in the controlled territory. There are 34 state museums in the Luhansk region, of which only 14 are in the controlled territory. The fate of outstanding cultural assets in uncontrolled territories remains unknown.

Unfortunately, international legal regulation of the protection and return of cultural property has proved to be ineffective for the protection of cultural property in the occupied Crimea and in the area of armed conflict in certain areas of Donetsk and Luhansk regions. Nevertheless, Ukraine and the world community are taking decisive steps not only to preserve and restore illegally exported cultural property, but also to hold those responsible for the deliberate damage to cultural heritage. Under these conditions, it is clearly necessary not only to develop a register of cultural objects to be digitized, but also to make specific projects for the digitization of cultural objects. In addition, the regulatory framework in the field of cultural heritage requires immediate revision, taking into account the use of information technologies not only in accounting for its objects, but also in their digitization [15].

The first steps are already being made. For example, since 2016, the Ministry of Culture of Ukraine has approved standards for the electronic description of museum objects, while emphasizing the importance of complying with them so that they do not then depend on a particular manufacturer or software. This will allow museums that generate information to freely exchange data and submit them to the state register [6]. This possible improvement of cultural property safety would contribute to the renewal of cultural property passports with indication of GPS coordinates and entering cultural property to electronic databases. Creating mirror electronic copies of registers of cultural property of Ukrainian museums, in its turn, would allow to track and find stolen for museums cultural property [19].

This year, on the initiative of the Ministry of Culture of Ukraine, the Ukrainian Center for Cultural Research and other sectoral public organizations, a project was launched - an online platform for digitizing the register of cultural heritage of Ukraine. The project emerged as a response to current cultural realities: paper records are still being kept in paper form. Currently, ministry staff spend about 4 h working to respond to a request for a particular cultural property [11].

In June 2019 the Ministry of Culture launched a pilot project which will be implemented on the basis of the Vinnytsia region with the purpose of practical elaboration of the necessary and important aspects of filling and functioning of the electronic platform with its subsequent implementation at the national level. The implementation of this pilot project is another important step towards not only the preservation and enhancement of cultural heritage, but also the widespread presentation of it at a modern information level [2]. Creating an electronic register of cultural heritage will help to collect, process, analyze and optimize the process of moving 14+ million objects of the museum fund and 130+ thousand objects of tangible and intangible cultural heritage. In doing so, the resource will contribute to the implementation of the Association Agreement with the EU in the context of the preservation and evaluation of cultural and historical heritage. The team also strives to help solve the problem of the return of cultural property from temporarily occupied territories. And the global dream of resource initiators is to promote the self-identification of Ukrainians through the preservation and promotion of cultural heritage.

By design, the project will work on three levels. Yes, art lovers will be able to find information about any cultural heritage monument through the search engine. Specialists will learn analytics and share themed events. Moreover, in the online office of the resource, it will be possible to get 12 administrative services provided by the Ministry of Culture of Ukraine online. The team has already presented a prototype of the register of cultural heritage of Ukraine. The biggest challenge in the implementation of the project was the search for the optimal combination of theoretical problems and their practical IT solutions. The information from the resource will be able to get directly to the European resource Europeana, which will help to present the Ukrainian cultural heritage to the world. The Ministry of Culture plans to take the resource on its balance sheet and develop it as a state-of-the-art portal that provides access to comprehensive information in the fields of culture, the arts, history and is focused primarily on the interest of the end consumer, including for receiving administrative services.

Particularly noteworthy is the large-scale project "Authentic Ukraine", implemented by the Ministry of Culture in collaboration with Google Ukraine, with the involvement of many other organizations interested in preserving and presenting unique Ukrainian authenticity [3]. The Authentic Ukraine Project is a unique virtual space containing a collection of authentic audio and visual examples of Ukrainian authenticity. The virtual platform consists of two parts: "Material Cultural Heritage", represented by virtual tours - wooden churches on the UNESCO World Heritage List, open air museums and opera houses of Ukraine, and "Intangible Cultural Heritage", which consists of 5 sections: oral traditions and forms of expression; performing arts; customs, ceremonies, celebrations; knowledge and practices relating to nature and the universe; traditional crafts. This project opens up new opportunities for exploring and learning about Ukraine's cultural heritage, encourages domestic and foreign tourism, and makes Ukraine more interesting to the world. The platform provides links to all digital heritage resources, is modern, easy to navigate and conveys the atmosphere and emotions of these cultural objects. The Authentic Ukraine electronic resource provides an opportunity to add and expand content. Here you can find copyright texts, audio and video, illustrations, 3D images and virtual tours.

An important part of the project is the educational component. At the end of each section there are interactive tests that can be used by educators during the educational process, which makes the platform a convenient tool for educational activities in schools and public institutions. The information is available in Ukrainian and English.

A significant contribution to filling the void in the theory and practice of digitalization the domestic heritage sector and bringing in the latest knowledge and technologies, world leading practices, and consolidating the efforts of experts in the digital preservation of national historical and cultural heritage are The Digitized Heritage: Preservation, Access, Representation (2013–2017) and The Digitized Heritage: Consolidation, Integration, Creativity (from 2018). The Digitized Heritage is a series of information and training events on the subject of digitizing historical, cultural and scientific heritage. The events have been held in Ukraine, in Kyiv and some other cities since 2013. The initiator was The Specialized Center BALI, LTD, a Ukrainian company dealing with ICT in the culture, education, and science sectors [4]. For over than six years there were 20 informational and training events on digitizing of historical, cultural, and scientific heritage stored in archives, museums, libraries, private collections, and other memory organisations, as well as developing digital libraries, archives and museum collections and enabling open access to them.

The events took place in 6 regions of Ukraine, with the participation of about 600 people from 50 cities and towns of Ukraine, speakers from Ukraine, Italy, United Kingdom, Germany, Belgium, Malta, Poland, Russia. The objective of these events was:

- to acquaint heritage specialists with advanced international practices and train them to use technologies for digitizing, development, and integration of digital collections, access and use methods;
- to promote the construction of a platform in Ukraine for technological development and improvement of digital competences for international professional collaboration and integration of national resources with European digital heritage, with EUROPEANA as a first priority;
- to transfer knowledge on digitizing and technology of digital content and metadata integration to global systems like EUROPEANA according European standards and methods

During 6 years of the Digital Heritage events, it has been possible to form a professional community that tries to keep up with the digital technological development in the heritage sector, bring Memory institutions and their digital resources to a dignified level of digital development awareness and foster the development of cross-sectoral and interdisciplinary collaboration and influence on public administration.

Noteworthy is the experience of the BALI specialized center (http://scbali.com), whose activity is focused on a wide range of scientific and practical works in the field of information and communication technologies in the scientific, educational and cultural sectors, in particular in the field of digitized cultural heritage and digital integration of resources. BALI Center is the developer of the information system «Digitized Content Visualizator» [18] - a new generation tool for the formation of various online digital collections, the creation of a digital museum, with solutions for their integration with the website and other resources, national and world digital heritage systems.

Purpose of the information system "Digitized Content Visualizator":

- creation of databases of metadata, multi-format digital analogues of objects of historical and cultural funds,
- formation of digital collections, funds management;
- multi-format and multifunctional representation and use of digitized objects and digital collections online,
- providing a variety of digital content information services for different categories of users;
- integration into a single digital content system provided in various media formats, its functioning in accordance with standards, practices and trends of development of digital and informational technologies and information services in the web environment.

DS-Visu version 3.0: "Digitized Heritage" is focused on creating digital representations of objects of historical and cultural heritage, forming and managing digital collections formed from funds of memory institutions (libraries, museums, archives), private and other collections, in accordance with existing national, European and world standards in museum, archival, librarian business and leading practices of representations of digitized museum collections in a web-based environment, presenting them in integrated national and global information systems.

DC-Visu operates in a PHP environment optimized for current Javascript enabled browsers. It does not require local installation by the user, provides quick access to digital documents of any size and allows to work with them online.

DC-Visu consists of several modules:

1. administration system (basic functional; access control module; multilingual interface module; statistics);
2. content formation and management system (collection management module; object management module; content generation module);
3. visualization system (web presentation modules for collections; modules for visualization of digitized documents);

4. full-text search system (module of automatic recognition of texts on the basis of system ABBY FineReader Engine; editor-marker of texts; verification and crowd-sourcing module;
5. content conversion system (metadata converter; image converter).

The basic functions are:

– formation of online digital resources: digitized objects and digital collections;
– dynamic creation of lists of digital collections and digitized objects;
– dynamic representation of metadata for digitized objects and digital collections;
– presentation of icons of collections and objects, photos of objects of collections, digitized documents;
– viewing digitized documents page by page and spreadsheets, scaling, rotating page drags;
– navigation by content, composition or kit, pointers, image icons, document page numbers;
– searching for description, content, and index items providing standardized descriptions of the original and the digital copy as an electronic resource,
– forming a bibliographic link/quotation on structural parts of documents, saving images (separate, all) to the file and printing, descriptions and references/quotes and content textual data, integration of electronic analogues of objects in various file formats (text, graphics, multimedia, 3D) and related Internet resources;
– accessing to existing analogues;
– connection of objects with accounting files, related objects from the fund, site, Internet;
– automatic generation of URL addresses of resources and QR-codes of access to these resources through mobile devices;
– exporting metadata to XML source structures.

Within the framework of the Europeana project, one of the European Union's Digital Service Infrastructures for cultural heritage [10], the Bali Center supported the initiative to connect national content to the Europeana collections of digitized cultural heritage in the following thematic areas: Ukrainian science and culture in personalities and facts; World history in documentary funds of Ukraine; Lifetime editions of great authors; Anniversary dates: landmark cities and events. Thanks to the activities of the Bali Center, collections of scientific libraries of the National Dragomanov National Pedagogical University, Taras Shevchenko National University of Kyiv, V. N. Karazin Kharkiv National University, KPI National Technical University, V.O. Sukhomlynskyi State Scientific and Pedagogical Library of Ukraine are presented today in Europeana.

These are only the first steps in the path of digitalization, but now Ukraine has the task of creating a body responsible for interagency cooperation on digitalization. The government should create a mechanism for establishing cooperation between existing institutions, determine the structures (government departments or institutions) that are most suitable for managing large-scale digital transformation projects. In addition, public funding should give impetus to the digitalization of cultural heritage, to begin with in a specific sector or area. A clear vision of the essential elements of digitalization must be ensured by national strategies. Underlying and consistent ICT goals and national broadband infrastructure also remain a prerequisite. Education and awareness raising are critical to implementing digitalization policies. Along with social events and campaigns aimed at disseminating electronic skills and raising the level of digital literacy in society, it is important that the government provide targeted initiatives to meet cultural heritage needs. Countries with an initial digitalization level, including Ukraine, to accelerate the pace of the digitalization process should focus on the development of a constructive policy and regulatory framework, as well as relevant actions by the state, which matured will accelerate digitalization [17].

References

1. A New European Agenda for Culture. Brussels, 22.5.2018 COM(2018) 267 final (2018). https://ec.europa.eu/culture/sites/culture/files/commission_communication_-_a_new_ european_agenda_for_culture_2018.pdf
2. About the implementation of a pilot project for the implementation of electronic accounting of cultural heritage objects. Order of the Cabinet of Ministers of Ukraine from May 22, 2019, No. 374-p, (2019). https://zakon.rada.gov.ua/laws/show/374-2019-%D1%80#n8
3. Authentic Ukraine. https://authenticukraine.com.ua/en. Accessed 21 Aug 2019
4. Barkova, O.: Digitized heritage events – from studying to actions or the Ukrainian digital movement. Uncommon Cult.: Cult. Heritage Real Virtual 7(1/2), (13/14), 186–192 (2018)
5. Bonazza, A., et al.: Safeguarding Cultural Heritage from Natural and Man-Made Disasters - A comparative analysis of risk management in the EU. Corporate Author(s): Directorate-General for Education, Youth, Sport and Culture (European Commission), 207 p. (2018). https://doi.org/10.2766/224310
6. Club Technologies: Six IT Instruments for Culture Development. https://www. culturepartnership.eu/article/six-it-tools-for-developing-culture. Accessed 21 Aug 2019
7. Cot, S.I.: About the state of preservation of cultural heritage of Ukraine. (Information and analysis materials for the parliamentary hearings on "State, Problems and Prospects for the Protection of Cultural Heritage in Ukraine" on April 18, 2018). Kyiv, 42 p. (2018)
8. Decree of the Cabinet of Ministers of Ukraine of September 3, 2009 No. 928 "List of cultural heritage objects of national importance, which are entered in the State Register of Immovable Monuments of Ukraine". https://www.kmu.gov.ua/en/npas
9. Europeana Collections. https://www.europeana.eu/portal/en. Accessed 21 Aug 2019
10. Harris, N.: The Return of Cosmopolitan Capital: Globalization, the State and War, 264 p. I. B.Tauris & Co Ltd. (2003)
11. Ministry as a garage. How state governments create national level startups (2019). https:// nachasi.com/2019/05/17/government-startups/
12. On approval of the Concept of development of the digital economy and society of Ukraine for 2018–2020 and approval of the plan of measures for its implementation. Order of the Cabinet of Ministers of Ukraine; Concept, Plan, Activities from 01/17/2018 # 67-p. (2018). https://zakon.rada.gov.ua/laws/term/40820:65990
13. Our responsibility to protect cultural heritage from terrorism and mass atrocities (2017). http://www.unesco.org/new/en/media-services/single-view/news/our_responsibility_to_ protect_cultural_heritage_from_terrori/
14. Protocol for the Protection of Cultural Property in the Event of Armed Conflict. The Hague, 14 May 1954

15. Resolution of the Verkhovna Rada of Ukraine "On Recommendations of the Parliamentary Hearings on the Status and Problems and Prospects of the Protection of Cultural Heritage in Ukraine". Verkhovna Rada Gazette, vol. 24, p. 91 (2019)
16. Sergeeva, I.L.: The transformation of mass culture in the digital environment (2016). http://publishing-vak.ru/file/archive-culture-2016-6/5-sergeeva.pdf
17. The digitalization scorecard developed by the Broadband Commission provides policy and regulatory guidance for digitalization (2017). https://www.itu.int/en/mediacentre/Pages/2017-PR22.aspx
18. The Information System "Digitized Content Visualizator" (IS DC-Visu): Visualization of Digitized Content and Digital collections management system. http://demo.dcvisu.com/collections/12. Accessed 21 Aug 2019
19. With a shield or a shield?: protection of cultural values in the conditions of armed conflict in eastern Ukraine. In: Bida, O.A., Blaga, A.B., Koval, D.O. (eds.) Ukrainian Helsinki Human Rights Union. Kyiv: KIT, 72 p. (2016). AP Bushchenko

Proposal of Evacuation Support System and Evaluation by Multi-agent Simulation in a Regional Disaster

Makoto Kitsuya[(✉)] and Jun Sasaki

Iwate Prefectural University, Takizawa, Iwate, Japan
g231s008@s.iwate-pu.ac.jp, jsasaki@iwate-pu.ac.jp

Abstract. In Japan, there are many flood and tsunami disasters caused by typhoons, heavy rains and earthquakes. In this case, the residents have an evacuation time to evacuate to shelters after evacuation alerts from a governmental office. However, the limited capacity of shelters and the delay in the rescue of support required people such as elderly and disabled people, the disaster can cause a serious damage. In order to prevent such a damage, we propose an evacuation support system that enables the information sharing of shelters' condition, the support required people and the support team. In this paper, we evaluated the effects of the evacuation support system by multi-agent simulation in a regional disaster. As a result of the simulation for a case study in a regional area with three evacuation shelters on Yahaba town in Iwate Prefecture, Japan, we confirmed that if we had enough evacuation time, the evacuation support system had an effect to increase the number of the evacuees.

Keywords: Evacuation support · Information sharing · Disaster response

1 Introduction

In Japan, natural disasters happen frequently and the total damage amount is 18% in spite of Japanese small land of 0.25% in the world [1]. In the case of flood and tsunami disasters caused by typhoons, heavy rains and earthquakes, the residents have an evacuation time to evacuate to shelters after evacuation alerts from a governmental office. However, the limited capacity of shelters and the delay in the rescue of support required people such as elderly and disabled people, the disaster can cause a serious damage. So, in the case of a regional area disaster, a smooth evacuation is the most important.

The delay in evacuation of suffers has sometimes caused a large human damage. For example, Fig. 1(a) and (b) shows victims' evacuation start time on 2011 Great East Japan Earthquake [2]. The (a) and (b) show the ratio of alive people and that of died people respectively. Though 71% of the alive people evacuated within 120 min, the ratio of evacuated people in the die people was only 22% people. It is difficult for many residents to predict the damage and they tend not to evacuate in the case of a disaster. Therefore, it is an important issue that government offices and supporters give residents a sense of evacuation in the case of a regional disaster. In addition, there are support

© IFIP International Federation for Information Processing 2020
Published by Springer Nature Switzerland AG 2020
Y. Murayama et al. (Eds.): ITDRR 2019, IFIP AICT 575, pp. 45–54, 2020.
https://doi.org/10.1007/978-3-030-48939-7_5

required people who cannot evacuate alone at the time of a disaster such as elderly and disabled people. It is important that the supporters who support the evacuation of such people with sharing the information of the support required people, supporters and shelters' condition, and take evacuation action promptly.

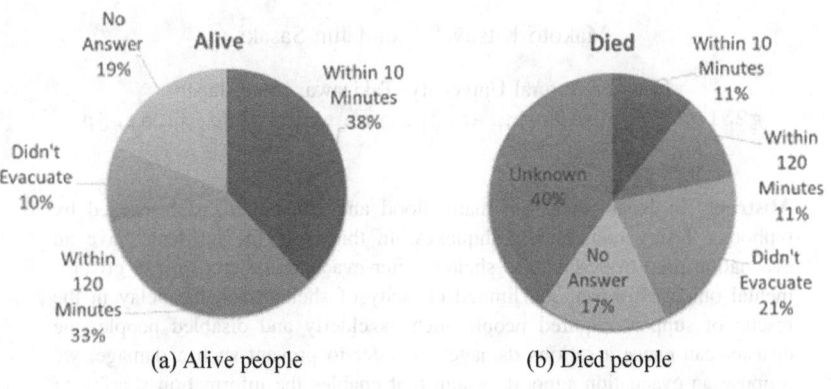

(a) Alive people   (b) Died people

Fig. 1. Victims' evacuation start time on 2011 Great East Japan earthquake

In order to solve above problems, we propose an evacuation support system that enables the information sharing of shelters' condition, the support required people and the support team.

In this paper, we survey the conventional researches on disaster evacuation simulation in chapter 2. Then, in chapter 3, we propose the evacuation support system. Then, in chapter 4, we show the evaluation on the proposed system by multi-agent simulation in a case study of Yahaba town in Iwate Prefecture, Japan. And we conclude the paper in chapter 5.

2   Conventional Researches

Recently, the multi-agent model is widely used for traffic simulation or money flow simulation in the economical field. Muraki, Y. et al. proposed the multi-agent model for wide-area disaster-evacuation simulations with local factors considered [3]. They simulated the situations of Kobe city on the date of the Great Hanshin Awaji earthquake in Japan. The simulation results about the percentage of evacuees who arrived at refuges were in good agreement with the actual data when parameters for evacuation-start timing were adjusted. The earthquake sometimes brings a large damage by tsunami. Liu, Y. et al. also proposed the dynamic route decision model-based multi-agent evacuation simulation and described the case study of Nagata Ward, Kobe in Japan [4]. They were considering group evacuation, landmarks & evacuation signs, and familiarity with the local environment. They also developed a prototype of a multi-agent based evacuation simulation system for the case area of the Oike underground space of Kyoto, Japan and demonstrated the feasibility [5]. Uno, K. et al. developed a simulation system for the disaster evacuation based on multi-agent model using geographical information system (GIS) [6]. They used Dijkstra algorithm to obtain the shortest route to the refuge and showed the evacuation route to understand easily by using virtual reality technique. The system was applied to the evacuation analysis by the flood flow in urban area and was shown to be a useful tool to investigate the damage by natural disasters. Regarding to flood evacuation planning, Lim, H. et al. reviewed many recent studies in the view of behavioral science, risk analysis and transportation modeling [7].

Regarding emergency evacuation in the event of fire and smoke propagation disaster in a large building, Tissera, P. C. et al. proposed a hybrid structure model and simulated people's behavior by using Intelligent Agent model [8]. Gelenbe, E. et al. studied the large scale simulation for human evacuation and rescue in large scale physical infra-structures such as building, campuses, sports and entertainment venues and transportation hubs [9]. There, they surveyed recent research on the use of sensor networks, communications and computer systems to enhance the human outcome of emergency situations. Hawe, G. I. et al. used agent-based simulation to determine the allocation of resources for a two-site incident which minimizes the latest hospital arrival times for critically injured casualties [10].

Minamoto, T, et al. developed a tsunami evacuation simulation system based on Petri Net to find safety areas and to use for emergency evacuation drill [11]. The simulation results were useful to grasp the behavior of inhabitants and to find safety area in the case of tsunami disasters. But, those studies did not consider about the evacuation of vulnerable people who are unable to get away alone, such as elderly and handicapped people.

The Grate East Japan Earthquake, about 60% of the victims of the tsunami was 65 years of age or older. Futagami T. et al. developed a scenario simulator that can be used as a target area where the tsunami is expected to see an animation action of supporters and vulnerable people to evacuate [12]. The system assumes the traffic inhibition and the evacuation behavior of supporters and vulnerable people by using the system.

Kawai Y. et al. also developed a tsunami evacuation simulation system using a game engine and open data [13]. In the simulation system, they prepared multiple types of agent considering the walking speeds and disaster conditions and evacuation behaviors. As results of their simulation in Kamakura city in Japan, the high risk areas became clear.

However, above conventional studies did not mention about the evacuation support system and information sharing method in a disaster conditions. This paper proposes the evacuation support system and information sharing method in the event of a disaster and evaluates the effects using multi-agent simulation.

3   Concept of Evacuation Support System

In Japan, disaster vulnerable people who need evacuation support in the event of a disaster are called "Support Required Person" and they are registered and listed in each local government. The Support Required Person list should be managed and used in the local government, but it is not used even in the emergency case actually because of strong intension of personal information protection. Therefore, we propose to resister more than 3 supporters for each Support Required Person, and to support with 2 of the registered supporters in the event of a disaster. Next, we propose to register multiple disaster ICT volunteers in the area with an official evacuation site (shelter). Finally, we propose to use a behavior information sharing system among the evacuation supporters. The proposed system image is shown in Fig. 2.

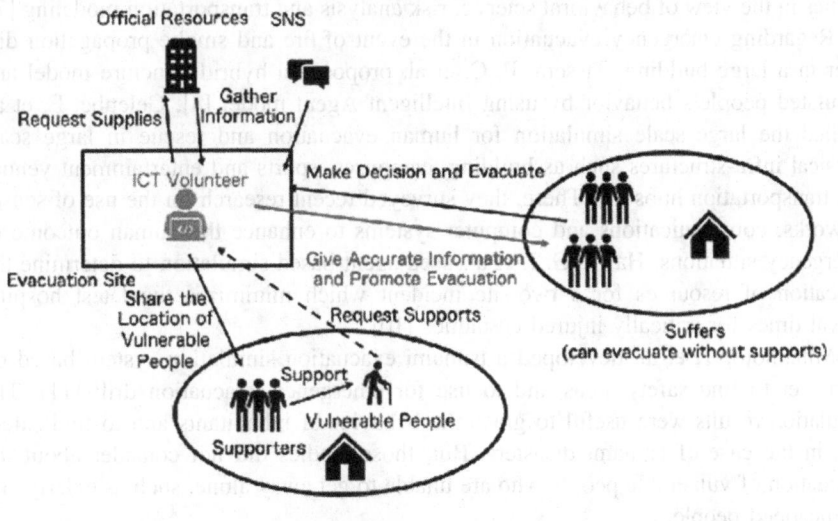

Fig. 2. Proposed system image

In the event of a disaster, the ICT volunteers gather at evacuation site (shelter) and register evacuation information and safety information for residents in the area by using a computer system. In addition, the information on the capacity of the shelter and the ratio of the number of evacuees is sent to all residents and evacuees via Social Network Service (SNS), etc. If the number of evacuees is worried to exceed to the capacity, the ICT volunteers recommend the other nearby and available evacuation site.

The supporters go to the registered Support Required Person. If two supporters have already arrived at the Support Required Person, they back to the evacuate site. This information can be confirmed by the supporter behavior information sharing system.

This proposed system is expected to solve the problem of changing the evacuation site because of the limited shelter capacity, the problem of late evacuation of the Support Required Person, and the problem of involving the supporters in the disaster. As we carried out a multi-agent simulation experiment to verify whether our proposed system has the expected effects, we describe it as a case study in the next chapter.

4 Evaluation

4.1 Case Study Field

In Japan, as there are many rains and typhoons, the river flood frequently occur from summer to autumn, and people often evacuate to shelters. We selected the Shirasawa area of Yahaba town in Iwate Prefecture which is a typical local area in Japan as the experimental field of the case study. Table 1 shows the condition of the Yahaba town and Shirasawa area, which is required data for the later described simulation.

Table 1. The condition of Yahaba town and Shirasawa area in 2018.

Items	Yahaba town	Shirasawa area
Population	27,340	626
Number of vulnerable people (Support Required People)	1,107 (4.05%)	25 (estimated)
Number of supporters (fire men)	308 (1.17%)	7 (estimated)

Figure 3 shows the hazard and the population distribution map of the Shirasawa area, where the size is approximately 2 km (from north to south) and 2.5 km (from east to west). This area has three official evacuation sites (shelters) of No. 38, 39 and 49 which are designated by the local government. They are used as a public hall (No. 38), a meeting place (No. 39) and a junior high school (No. 49) in a normal case. In the hazard map, the colors show the possibility of river flood, where yellow area is under 0.5 m of water and blue area shows under 2.0 m of water. This area has 14 districts and each population is opened by the government website. We estimated the number of vulnerable people (Support Required People) and supporters in each district by using the whole ratio (shown in Table 1) of those people presented by Yahaba town.

Table 2 shows the condition of the shelters. We calculated the capacity of evacuees by using the size of space and Sphere Standard (Humanitarian Charter and Minimum Standards in Humanitarian Response, 1998).

4.2 Evaluation Using Multi-agent Simulation

We simulated the behavior of evacuees when a disaster occurred in the above mentioned area by using multi-agent simulation. Table 3 shows the agent model. There are three types of agents, which are general evacuee, vulnerable person (Supporter Required Person) and Supporter. We assumed the simulation condition on the total number and moving speed for each agent type as Table 3. Ideally, it is desirable to rescue on vulnerable person by two or more people, but there is a possibility that the supporter may be a victim by late escape. For this reason, in this time simulation, we considered that one supporter could rescue one vulnerable person.

Figure 4 and Fig. 5 show the behavior model of each agent for a general evacuee (Fig. 4(a)), a vulnerable person (Fig. 4(b)) and a supporter (Fig. 5), respectively. The purpose of the simulation is to evaluate the effect of the proposed Evacuation Support

50   M. Kitsuya and J. Sasaki

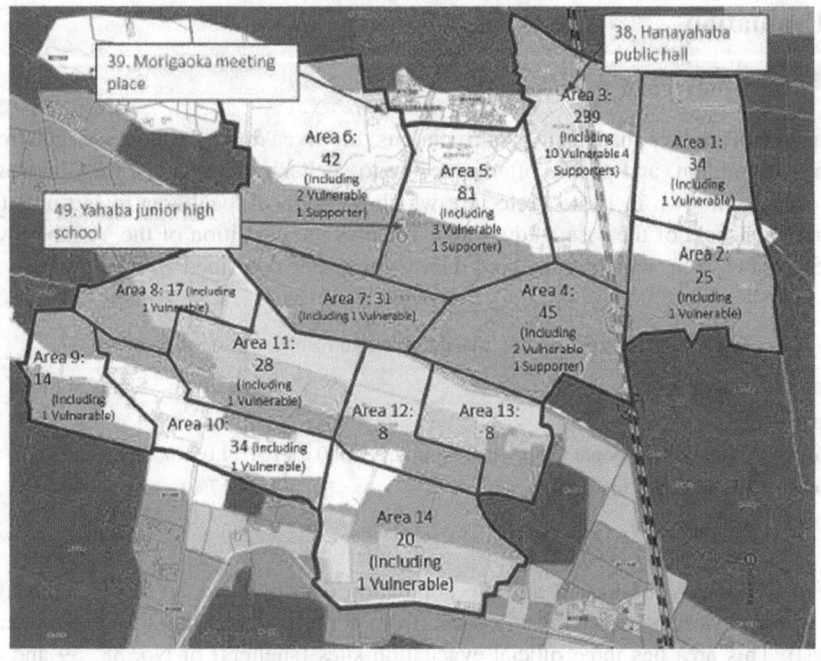

Fig. 3. Hazard and population distribution map around Shirasawa Area in Yahaba town.

Table 2. Conditions of shelters.

Evacuation sites (Shelters)	Size of space	Capacity of evacuees
No. 38 Hanayahaba public hall	300 m^2	85
No. 39 Morigaoka meeting place	80 m^2	22
No. 49 Yahaba junior high school	2,240 m^2	640

Table 3. Agent model.

Agents	Total number	Moving speed
General evacuee	586	Random (From 1.8 km/h to 7.2 km/h)
Vulnerable person (Supporter Required Person)	25	0 km/h or 1.8 km/h (with one supporter)
Supporter	7	7.2 km/h

System with ICT volunteers. The ICT volunteers give the shelter information and supporters' behavior information for general evacuees and the supporters by using information sharing system and SNS in the event of a disaster.

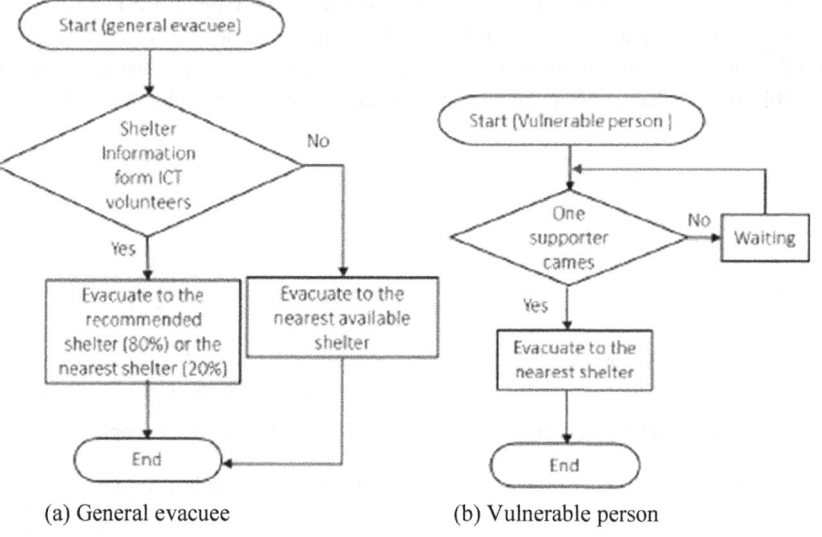

(a) General evacuee   (b) Vulnerable person

Fig. 4. Behavior model of a general evacuee and a vulnerable person

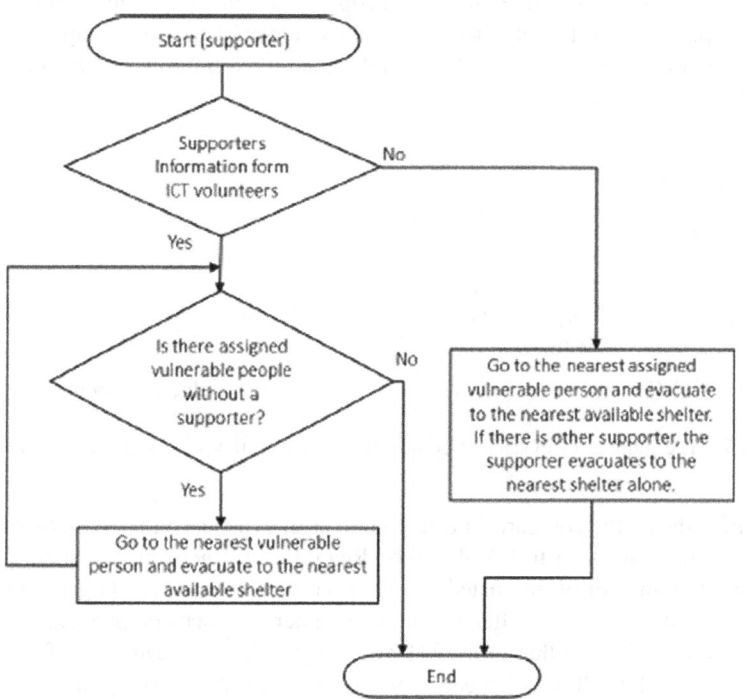

Fig. 5. Behavior model of a supporter.

Figure 6 shows the number of evacuated people in the case of no ICT volunteers, where (a) is for general evacuees and (b) is for vulnerable people. One hour after the start of evacuation, all of general evacuees could finish the evacuation but 20 of vulnerable people could not evacuate (evacuated vulnerable people was only 5).

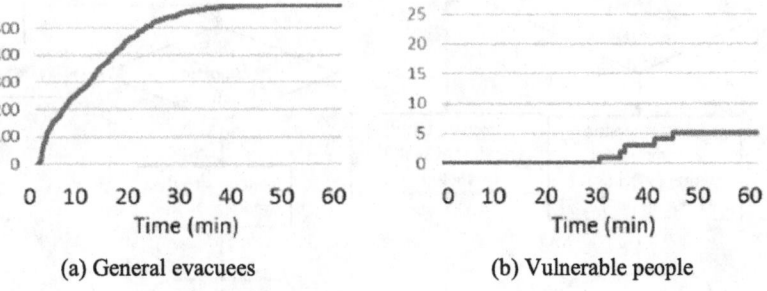

(a) General evacuees   (b) Vulnerable people

Fig. 6. The number of evacuated people in the case of no ICT volunteers.

Figure 7 shows the same meaning figure with Fig. 6 in the case of with ICT volunteers. One hour after the start of evacuation, all of general evacuees could finish the evacuation and only 5 of vulnerable people could not evacuate (evacuated vulnerable people was 20). The number of evacuated vulnerable people (Support Required People) increased to be four times by the information form the ICT volunteers.

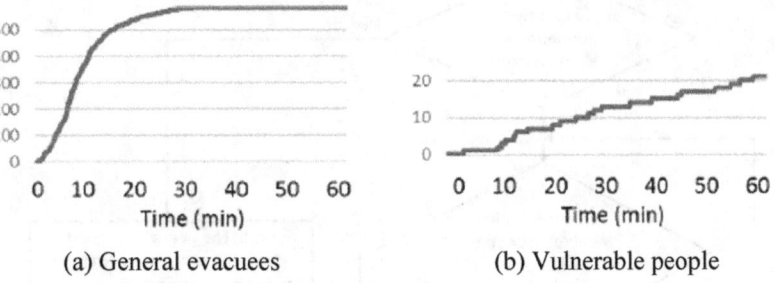

(a) General evacuees   (b) Vulnerable people

Fig. 7. The number of evacuated people in the case of the ICT volunteers existing.

Figure 8 shows the comparison of the number of evacuees in the case of with ICT Volunteers and that of no ICT Volunteers. Regarding (a) general evacuees, until the first 8 min, the number of evacuated people in no ICT volunteer is larger than that in with ICT volunteers. Though after 8 min, the number of evacuated people in with ICT volunteers increased than that in no ICT volunteers. This is because that freely evacuating people without ICT volunteers' information until the capacity of the shelter is filled would have better advantage than controlled evacuating by ICT volunteers. However, we could confirm that if we had longer time, it was more effective to evacuate by according to the information from ICT volunteers.

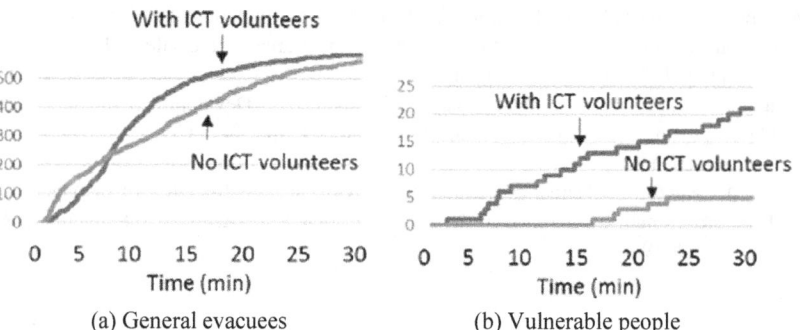

(a) General evacuees   (b) Vulnerable people

Fig. 8. The comparison of the number of evacuees in the case of with ICT volunteers and no ICT volunteers.

Acknowledgements. We would like to thank I-O DATA Foundation for support of this research.

References

1. Hilz, S.R., Van de Walle, B., Turoff, M.: The domain of emergency management information. In: Van de Walle, B., Turoff, M., Hiltz, S.R. (eds.) Information Systems for Emergency Management, pp. 3–20 (2009). The original figure was produced by Guy Weets

2. Weathernews Inc.: Tsunami investigation of the Great East Japan Earthquake (2011). http://weathernews.com/ja/nc/press/2011/pdf/20110908_1.pdf. (in Japanese)

3. Muraki, Y., Kanoh, H.: Multiagent model for wide-area disaster-evacuation simulations with local factors considered. J. Jpn. Soc. Artif. Intell. 2(4), 416–424 (2007). (in Japanese)

4. Liu, Y., Okada, N., Takeuchi, Y.: Dynamic route decision model-based multi-agent evacuation simulation – case study of Nagata Ward, Kobe. J. Nat. Disaster Sci. 28(2), 91–98 (2008)

5. Lie, Y., Okada, N., Shen, D., Li, S.: Agent-based flood evacuation simulation of life-threatening conditions using vitae system model. J. Nat. Disaster Sci. 31(2), 69–78 (2009)

6. Uno, K., Kashiyama, K.: Development of simulation system for the disaster evacuation based on multi-agent model using GIS, Tsinghua Science and Technology, ISSN 1007-0214 56/67, vol. 13, no. S1, pp. 348–353 (2008)

7. Lim, H., Lim, M.B., Piantanakulchai, M.: A review of recent studies on flood evacuation planning. J. Eastern Asia Soc. Transp. Stud. 10, 143–162 (2013)

8. Tissera, P.C., Castro, A., Printista, A.M., Luque, E.: Evacuation simulation supporting high level behavior-based agents. In: Proceeding of International Conference on Computational Science ICCS 2013, vol. 18, pp. 1495–1504. Elsevier (2013)

9. Gelenbe, E., Wu, F.J.: Large scale simulation for human evacuation and rescue. Comput. Math. Appl. 64, 3869–3880 (2012)

10. Hawe, G.I., Coates, G., Wilson, D.T., Crouch, R.S.: Agent-based simulation of emergency response to plan the allocation of resources for a hypothetical two-site major incident. Eng. Appl. Artif. Intell. 46, 336–345 (2015)

11. Minamoto, T., Nariyuki, Y., Fujiwara, Y., Mikami, A.: Development of tsunami evacuation simulation system and its application to assessment of area refuge safety. J. Jpn. Soc. Civ. Eng. **65**(1), 757–767 (2009). (in Japanese)

12. Futagami, T., Akizuki, K., Matsuyama, Y., Kunikata, Y.: Development of the vulnerable people supporting system for a tsunami refuge area. J. Jpn. Soc. Civ. Eng. **69**(2), I_1–I_6 (2013). (in Japanese)

13. Kawai, Y., Kaizu, Y.: Tsunami evacuation behavior and identification of damaged agents. In: The 33rd Annual Conference of the Japanese Society for Artificial Intelligence, 4Rin 1-34, pp. 1–4 (2019)

Environmental Monitoring and Population Protection from Environmental Factors

Tetiana Kovaliuk[1](✉), Nataliya Kobets[2], Dmytro Ivashchenko[3], and Valerii Kushnarov[4]

[1] Taras Shevchenko National University of Kyiv, Kyiv, Ukraine
tetyana.kovalyuk@gmail.com
[2] Borys Grinchenko Kyiv University, Kyiv, Ukraine
nmkobets@gmail.com
[3] National Technical University of Ukraine "Igor Sikorsky Kyiv Polytechnic Institute", Kyiv, Ukraine
ivas-90@mail.ru
[4] Kyiv National University of Culture and Arts, Kyiv, Ukraine
raketa1975@ukr.net

Abstract. The paper deals with the problem of providing users with information on optimal environmental protection means that guarantees safe stay in a given region. Problem statement of choosing optimal environmental protection means is given. A method to receive safety recommendations for general public based on information regarding available protection means, known thresholds of harmful emissions and hazardous substances impact on humans and environmental situation in a given region is considered.

Keywords: Environmental factors · Environmental protection equipment · Genetic algorithm · Branch and bound algorithm · Dynamic programming

1 Introduction

Ukraine is painted black on the UN map due to its environmental deterioration. It is the color of a country where the population is dying out. Ukraine ranks first in the world by death to birth rate [1]. According to Ptoukha Institute for Demography and Social Studies of the National Academy of Sciences of Ukraine the South and the East of Ukraine – the so-called "Black Belt" – is dying out at a record pace. Environmental problems contribute in no small part to this shocking statistics.

According to the Ministry of Health of Ukraine and the Ministry of Ecology and Natural Resources of Ukraine there are more than 3 million people living in more than 2000 settlements on radionuclide-contaminated territories only. Due to environmental deterioration, over the last 10 years medical incidence rate has increased by 25% on average. According to World Health Organization data, 80% of environmentally induced deceases are severe and practically incurable illnesses. Information on environmental conditions such as air pollution, water contamination, epidemiological situation, radiological hazards level etc. has become vital.

Y. Murayama et al. (Eds.): ITDRR 2019, IFIP AICT 575, pp. 55–66, 2020.
https://doi.org/10.1007/978-3-030-48939-7_6

However where and how to get such information promptly? Can the received information be trusted? These are the questions that the authors attempt to answer with their EcoSpotter project.

One of important functions of the EcoSpotter project is providing its users recommendations on protection from environmental factors. The relevant task is to develop means for a person to receive safety recommendations based on information regarding current environmental situation, known thresholds of harmful emissions and hazardous substances impact on humans and environmental situation in a given region and available protection means. Every person has right to be aware of all changes in ecological situation that take place both locally and country-wide, to know everything about the food consumed, quality of water drunk and to understand existing dangers and to act accordingly [2].

2 Analysis of Existing Web Resources and Services Regarding Environmental Situation

Analysis of accessible to public information resources and services that provide data on current environmental situation shows that obtaining reliable and up-to-date information is not an easy task. Following is an overview of some information resources that provide environmental monitoring data.

Environmental Interactive Maps [3] offers a list of interactive environmental maps of Europe. Water and soil pollution are represented best. Indisputable advantage of this resource is the variety of information. However, user-specified search for environmental data is complicated due to necessity to separate different forms of data representation.

Wireless Environmental Monitoring Systems (EMS) [4] provides data on the most reliable, consistent and accurate wireless environmental monitoring and control solutions by Hanwell Solutions Ltd. The Hanwell EMS software takes environmental monitoring data display to another level. The top-level displays a general overview of site sensor activity, with subsequent levels enabling customizable data groups for individual user requirements. Full data collection with interactive graphs, tables and plan views enable users to slice historical environmental data in multiple ways for more advanced analysis.

The Baltic Sea Region GIS, Maps and Statistical Database [5] is a result of the Baltic Drainage Basin Project, a multi-disciplinary research project under the EU. The datasets and maps have been combined into one interactive on-line map service. Database has become the most popular and pertinent environmental information resource about the transboundary Baltic Sea Region.

Lakes Environmental Company [6] offers a wide range of environmental software products. The Company provides a wide variety of services in the areas of air dispersion modeling, human health and ecological risk assessment, emissions inventory, compliance, as well as emergency release.

Climate Interactive Company [7] creates simulation models, interactive tools and programs for environmental and sustainability planning and education in such areas as climate change, energy, sustainability, environment, and disaster risk reduction.

Environmental Performance Index (EPI) [8] scores 180 countries on 24 performance indicators across ten issue categories covering environmental health and ecosystem vitality. The overall EPI rankings indicate which countries are doing best against the array of environmental pressures that every nation faces. Ukraine is on the 109th place (out of 180) in the 2018 EPI Country Rank.

Main Center of the Special Monitoring website [9] manages data of seismic, radionuclide, electromagnetic, infrasound monitoring, monitoring of nuclear tests and space weather, on both global and local scale, providing the state central government structures, which are responsible for the national security and defense, as well as other interested ministries and departments with all the required information.

Analysis of existing information resources that provide data on environmental situation and parameters leads to the following conclusions:

- Existing information services do not possess adequate degree of interactivity: the data is provide either as static maps or interactive maps with complicated and not user-friendly interface and limited functionality;
- Existing information services do not possess ecological monitoring data search tools;
- Information services software requires lengthy and complicated installation and
- configuration process;
- Information resources are narrowly focused on certain territories and/or provided data type;
- Information resources provide no recommendations on lessening or negating
- environmental hazards impact on human health and ways to improve environmental security.

3 Problem Statement

Within the context of environmental problems which society faces, development of ecological monitoring systems to provide timely, complete and reliable information on environmental state and civil protection from environmental hazards activities is a pressing challenge.

The goal of this work is to build mathematical model of choosing environmental protection means and to analyze performance of algorithms solving this task.

4 Mathematical Model of Choosing Environmental Protection Means

Suppose in a given region a person is influenced by a set of environmental hazards (radioactivity, water contamination with heavy metals salts, electromagnetic fields, hazardous air emissions from moving sources, hazardous chemical substances etc.). We consider that harmful emissions and hazardous substances exposure not exceeding government-approved thresholds causes no harm to human health. Suppose there is a set of protective equipment available with each item lessening negative impact of certain factors by a certain degree. The goal is to define the most affordable set of protective items that provides for person's safety.

A person is influenced by a set of hazardous environmental factors F. Every i-th environmental factor is characterized by its degree of influence upon a person's health $f_i : F = \{f_i, i = \overline{1, m}\}$.

Let boundary values of environmental factors lie within a_i in b_i in accordance with government-approved norms. This gives us boundary system (1):

$$\begin{cases} a_1 \leq f_1 \leq b_1 \\ a_2 \leq f_2 \leq b_2 \\ \ldots \\ a_m \leq f_m \leq b_m \end{cases} \tag{1}$$

A person has a set of protective means $D = \{d_{ij}, i = \overline{1, m}, j = \overline{1, n}\}$ available. For each j-th protective mean its cost $c_j, j = \overline{1, n}$, and degree of lessening negative impact $d_{ij}, i = \overline{1, m}$ of i-th environmental factor with j-th protective mean are known. Then the negative impact of i-th environmental factor upon a person can be defined as $f_i - \sum_{j=1}^{n} d_{ij} x_j$, where components of $X = \{x_1, x_2, \ldots, x_n\}$ vector acquire discrete values from [0, 1] range according to (2):

$$x_j = \begin{cases} 1, & \text{if a person uses protective means.} \\ 0, & \text{otherwise} \end{cases} \tag{2}$$

To define most the most affordable environmental hazards protection items objective function (3) is set:

$$\sum_{j=1}^{n} c_j x_j \rightarrow \min \tag{3}$$

Function (3) minimization is performed on a set of constraints (4):

$$a_i \leq f_i - \sum_{j=1}^{n} d_{ij} x_j \leq b_i, i = \overline{1, m} \tag{4}$$
$$x_j \in \{0, 1\}, j = \overline{1, n}$$

Let's reduce problem to the canonical form. To do it we apply to each i-th $i = \overline{1, m}$ system (4) constraint elementary operations, which gives us (5):

$$a_i - f_i \leq -\sum_{j=1}^{n} d_{ij} x_j \leq b_i - f_1, i = \overline{1, m} \tag{5}$$

Let's represent each of constraints (5) with two, introduce free variables $s_i, i = \overline{1, m}$ convert inequalities into equalities and come to a canonical form (6):

$$\begin{cases} \sum_{j=1}^{n} d_{ij}x_j + s_i = f_i - a_i \\ \\ \sum_{j=1}^{n} d_{ij}x_j + s_i = f_i - b_i \end{cases} \quad (6)$$

$$x_j \in \{0, 1\}, j = \overline{1,n}; \ i = \overline{1,m}.$$

The problem (2), (3), (6) is a Boolean programming problem. The solution lies in determining vector $X = \{x_j | x \in [0,1], j = \overline{1,n}\}$ minimizing (3) on constraints set (6). Problem can be solved using exact or heuristic algorithms.

Model Flexibility
Problem model (3), (6) is built accounting for certain range of environmental factors levels in accordance with government sanitary norms. It is known that government authorities periodically implement changes and additions to such norms to ensure adequacy of civil protection measures. In some instances, there is only upper boundary of environmental factor level. For instance, radiation level is considered safe up to 30 μR/h. To account for changes in model parameters and their range the second constraint (6) is made infinitely small (if it is a lower boundary) $-\infty \leq f_i \leq b_i, i \in I, I \subset N, N = \{1,\dots,n\}$ or infinitely big (in case of an upper boundary) $a_i \leq f_i \leq \infty, i \in I', I' \subset N, N = \{1,\dots,n\}$. For example, in case of radiation level constriction we have $-\infty \leq f_1 \leq 30$. If some of protective devices are unavailable their cost has to be set infinite, for example $c_j = \infty, j \in J, J \subset M, M = \{1,\dots,m\}$. This way flexibility of the model is implemented.

5 Solution Algorithm for the Problem of Choosing Optimal Environmental Protection Means

In this paper use of genetic algorithm (GA), branch and bound algorithm and dynamic programming to solve the problem (2) (3) (6) were analyzed. Time complexity assessment was performed and problem solving results were compared.

GA is intended to solve problems of combinatorial optimization, that is optimization of structures determined by vectors, components of which acquire discrete values. Since genetic algorithm uses some encoding of set of parameters instead parameters itself during search, it can be effectively used to solve discrete optimization problems.

If solutions of the problem of choosing optimal environmental protection means are to be presented as a decision tree, where on each level branching of sets of solutions is performed and estimation of approximation to the optimal solution is given, feasibility of branch and bound method is obvious.

Choosing optimal environmental protection means can be interpreted as a step-by-step process. On each step a category or set of items is chosen and eventually a certain item is chosen. This is the way problems are solved with dynamic programming.

Thus, to compare accuracy of calculations exact methods of solving discrete programming integer problem, such as branches and boundaries and dynamic programming.

5.1 Implementation of Genetic Algorithm for the Problem of Choosing Optimal Environmental Protection Means

To implement genetic algorithm the problem should be given in such form that its solution was presented as an array, contents of which are similar to a chromosome [10].

In our case set of individual environmental protection equipment is given as a vector with dimension n, where n is a quantity of individual environmental protection equipment. Vector elements are bits. Bit 1 corresponds to a chosen protective item that is a part of the solution, bit 0 means that the item was not chosen.

Several starting elements are designated in the array randomly, that is starting population is determined. Elements of this population are estimated using adaptation function, and as a result, each element gets certain adaptation value, that determines possibility of its survival. After that, selection of elements for the crossover is performed based on these values. Genetic operators are used on the element: crossover and mutation, thus creating next generation of elements. Genetic operators are used on the next generation again. This way, evolution process is simulated that goes on for several iterations (generation lifecycles), until stop criterion of the algorithm is met:

- A global or close to optimal solution is found;
- Number of generations designated for evolution is exhausted;
- Time given for evolution is over.

Generalized structure of genetic algorithm can be presented as such [6]:

Step 1. Starting population P_0 numbering n is initialized. In order to do that:
- Set current population number $t = 0$;
- Generate random chromosome set of n string encodings with fixed length L, where Hamming distance between any pair of encodings does not equal zero;
- Estimate each string of the chromosome set with adaptation function.

Step 2. Producing offspring with inherited parental genetic properties. In order to do that:
- Randomly choose from current population P_t two parents that make "wedding couple", according to encoding crossover scheme;
- Generate for the chosen "wedding couple" with probability p_c one or several offspring encodings that inherit parental genetic properties with the crossover operation;
- Assess each offspring encoding with adaptation function;
- Repeat all step two operations until predetermined number N_c of "wedding couples" is processed.

Step 3. Creation of mutants with genetic properties different from parental. In order to do that:
- Randomly choose encoding that inherits genetic properties form one or both parents from set of parents and offspring;

- Generate with probability p_m mutant code with the mutation operation for chosen encoding, ensuring variability of parental genetic properties;
- Assess mutant encoding with adaptation function;
- Repeat all step three operations until predetermined number of mutants N_m.is generated.

Step 4. Change current population P_t with new population P_{t+1}. In order to do that:

- Choose population P_{t+1} creation strategy;
- Build reproductive set of encodings that differ from each other by Hamming distance out of parents and offspring;
- Copy encodings that carry out population P_{t+1} creation strategy out of reproductive set with selection operation.

Step 5. Checking for condition of iterative cycle termination. Change the number of current generation $t = t + 1$ and repeat all operations of step 2 if genetic search ending condition is not met (for example evolution of population P_t is considered complete if it has exhausted its lifecycle, that is $t > T$).

5.2 Implementation of Branch and Bound Method for the Problem of Choosing Optimal Environmental Protection Means

Branch and bound is based on the idea of successive partitioning of current possible solutions set into branching subsets [12]. On each step, these subsets are checked for optimal solution presence. To do that, target function value assessment is performed on a given subset and the result is compared with the current record. Record is the target function value for the best current solution. If target function value assessment on the solutions subset is not less (or more) than the record this subset can be eliminated. Solution subset that is being checked can also be eliminated if at some point a solution was found that is better than target function assessment on this subset. If the target function value for the solution found is less than the previous record, the record value is changed to the found value of target function. When at some step all solution subsets can be eliminated, the record is the optimal solution of the problem. Otherwise, the most promising of the remaining subsets is chosen and undergoes partitioning. New subsets are checked again. Upon the completion of algorithm calculation, current record is optimal target function value and corresponding solution is the optimal problem solution [13].

Let's review branch and bound scheme that is used to solve the problem of choosing optimal environmental protection means [11].

Branching

The problem is partitioned into two sub problems on each algorithm step. Let there be a rule β, that matches any set $\overline{X} \subset X$ with finite number of subsets $X_j, j \in J$ such that $X_i \cup X_i = \overline{X}, \forall i, \forall j; X_j \cap X_i \neq \varnothing$. Partitioning of set $\overline{X}$ is designated $\beta(\overline{X}) = \{X_j\}$. Let's designate $|\overline{X}|$ the cardinality of $\overline{X}$. Let rules $\beta(\overline{X})$ of set $\overline{X}$ partitioning meet (7) and (8):

$$|\overline{X}| > |X_j|, \; if |\overline{X}| > 1, \; \forall j \in J \qquad (7)$$

$$\beta(\overline{X}) = \varnothing, \; if \; |\overline{X}| = 1 \qquad (8)$$

Subsets X_j, that are found during $\overline{X}$ branching can be normalized by branching and this connection can be shown as a tree (V, U) of solution subsets, where V – set of vertices, U – set of edges. The root of the tree corresponds to the set X, and leaves are singleton sets. Condition (7) guarantees that any route from the root to a leaf contains no more than $|X|$ edges. Condition (8) attests that it is impossible to partition singleton sets.

For each specific problem, there are many ways to branch set of its solutions into a tree (V, U). Considering the fact that all variables in problem (3), (6) of choosing optimal environmental protection means are Boolean, it is practical to use binary partitioning. For the problem under study, the partitioning means that for each j-th protective mean all possible solutions containing this mean are included in one set and possible solutions without this mean are included in another set.

Assessment Procedure

For each of subsets X_j of possible solution set of the given problem an assessment $\gamma(X_j)$ of target function $f(x)$ that corresponds to (9)–(11) is given:

$$\gamma(X_j) \leq f(x), \; \forall x \in X_j, \; \text{as a minimum target} \qquad (9)$$

$$\gamma(X_j) = f(\tilde{x}), \; if |X_j| = 1, X_j = \{\tilde{x}\} \qquad (10)$$

$$\gamma(X_j) = +\infty, \; if \; X_j = \varnothing, \; \text{as a maximum target} \qquad (11)$$

To calculate assessment $\gamma(X_j)$ of the target function $f(x)$ of the given problem another simple optimization problem can be solved that we shall call evaluative problem. Let there be problem (12):

$$f(x) \rightarrow \min, \; x \in X_j, \; \forall j \in J \qquad (12)$$

For the problem (12) evaluative problem (13) is considered:

$$\phi(x) \rightarrow \min, x \in \tilde{X}_j \supset X_j, \forall j \in J \qquad (13)$$

Evaluative problem (13) has to meet the following conditions:

- If evaluative problem (13) has no possible solutions than the problem (12) has no possible solutions also;
- Target function value for the problem (12) solutions is not worse the target function value for the problem (13) solution.

For the given problem, target function (3) assessment is defined according to (14) and (15) [13]:

$$\gamma(X_j) = \gamma(\overline{X}) + c_j \tag{14}$$

$$\gamma(X_j) = \gamma(\overline{X}) \tag{15}$$

Expression (14) attests that assessment $\gamma(X_j)$ of subsets X_j of possible solutions that contains j-th environmental protection item is equal to assessment $\gamma(\overline{X})$ of branched set of solutions, increased by the cost of this item. Assessment value of the solutions set that does not contain the j-th protective item equals to assessment value of branched set (15).

Testing Procedure
In the process of successive partitioning of solutions set X those subsets, which do not contain possible solutions better than the record, are eliminated. Elimination is performed with a test that is based on calculating assessment values and comparing them with the record. Let the current record value be f^*. Let's make a test: if for some set X_j the expression $\gamma(X_j) \geq f^*$ is true then set X_j is eliminated.

The Record
For the problem under study the following record notion is used: the best problem target function value that is achieved on the set of found possible solutions.

5.3 Implementation of Dynamic Programming for the Problem of Choosing Optimal Environmental Protection Means

Dynamic programming is based on Bellman's principle of optimality, according to which at any given step out of several possible solutions the one where gain at this step plus optimal total gain on all subsequent steps is maximal [14, 15].

This method is used for problems that fulfill following requirements:

- Optimization problem is interpreted as an n-stepped process of decision making;
- Target function of the problem equals the sum of each step's target functions;
- Choice of solution on the k-th step depend on the system state at current step and does not influence previous steps (no feedback);
- State s_k after k-th decision making step depends only on the previous state s_{k-1} and solutions x_k (no after-action);
- At each decision, making step x_k depends on finite number of control variables and state s_k – on finite number of parameters.

In accordance with provisions of the given problem let's split protective items into sets, each of which contains mutually exclusive items. For example several protective suits or gas masks cannot be used simultaneously. Given task can be interpreted as a multistage decision making if protective items from each set are chosen (or not chosen) sequentially one by one.

Let the system state to be defined by $\langle j, y_j \rangle$, where j – index of the protective items set currently being processed, $y_j = (y_{1j}, y_{2j}, .., y_{mj})^T, j = \overline{1,n}$ is the vector, components of which define lessening of negative impact of i-th environmental factor $i = \overline{1,m}$ due to use of j-th protective item.

Given task can be made into a task of finding the shortest path in a directed acyclic network, where each layer represents choice of certain protective items set and each vertice is a choice (or its absence) of a certain protective item from this set. Recursive nature of defining optimality principle brings recurrent ratios. Let's review creation of recurrent ratio for our problem.

Let there be protective items chosen from a set $k = \overline{1,j}$, that lessen harmful factors impact by $y_j = (y_{1j}, y_{2j}, \ldots, y_{ik}, \ldots, y_{mj})^T, j = \overline{1,n}$, where y_{ik} defines lessening of harmful effects of i-th environmental factor $i = \overline{1,m}$ due to use of k-th protective item. The problem requires choosing such protective items that guarantee human vital functions that is harmful factors impact has to be lessened by at least (16):

$$P = (f_1 - b_1, f_2 - b_2, \ldots, f_m - b_m)^T \tag{16}$$

Then y_j can be defined as $0 \leq y_j \leq P$.

Let's denote $f_i(y_j)$ as the minimal cost of protective items from the set $k = \overline{1,j}$, that lessens impact of the i-th environmental factor by at least y_j. Let's consider that choice of protective item x_j from the j-th set is possible if uncompensated impact of harmful factors after this item's use can be lessened with protective items from the remaining sets. The condition of environmental factors impact compensation is (17):

$$y_{ij} - p_{ij}(x_j) \leq \sum_{k=1}^{j-1} \max(p_{ij}(x_j)), i = \overline{1,m}, \forall j \in J \tag{17}$$

where $p_{ij}(x_j)$ – degree of protection from i-th environmental factor impact that is provided with the choice of x_j-th protection item from the j-th set.

If x_j-th protective item is chosen from the j-th set, it lessens environmental factors impact by $p_j(x_j)$, then items from the remaining sets have to lessen environmental factors impact by $y_j - p_j(x_j)$. Then the minimal costs of protective items from sets $k = \overline{1,j}$, that lessen environmental factors impact by y_j, on condition that from the j-th set item x_j was chosen is defined (18):

$$c_j(x_j) + f_{i-1}(y_j) = p_j(x_j) \tag{18}$$

Protection provided by choice of items from sets $k = \overline{1,j-1}$ by definition of $f_i(y_j)$ function is performed optimally thus, the sum (18) is conditionally minimal cost.

Let's minimize expression (3) with possible values of x_j, which we denote as x_j^v. According to (4) we get expressions (19) and (20):

$$x_j^v = x_j / \left(y_j^i - p_j^i(x_j) \leq \sum_{k=1}^{j-1} \max(p_j^i(\cdot)), i = \overline{1,M} \right) \tag{19}$$

$$f_j(y_j) = \min_{x_j^v} \{ c_j(x_j) + f_{j-1}(y_j - p_j(x_j)) \} \tag{20}$$

Expression (20) is true with $j = 1$, if $f_0(\cdot) = 0$. The result is the value of $f_n(P)$, where P corresponds to (16).

6 Testing Results

In this paper, the problem statement of choosing optimal environmental protection means was solved using genetic algorithm (GA), branches and boundaries method and dynamic programming.

The settings for GA were chosen as follows: maximum number of iterations – 5 lifecycles; probability of crossover 0.5; probability of mutation 0.2; population size 100 individuals; stop criterion – achieving maximum number of iterations (5 lifecycles); parental choice scheme – the best with random selection; mutation based on random change of one bit in the genotype (one protective item is added or removed); the crossover is standard. Runtime results are shown in Fig. 1.

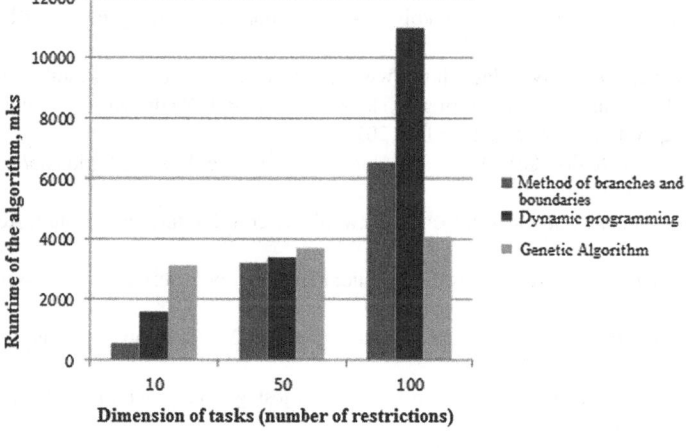

Fig. 1. Runtime results

Comparison of the algorithms runtime results showed that exact algorithms perform well in small-dimensional problems (10 constraints). Thus, the task execution time using the branch and bound method is 520 µs, the dynamic programming method is 1580 µs, and the genetic algorithm is 3120 µs. In medium-sized problems (50 constraints), the algorithms show almost the same results in terms of speed: the task execution time by the branch and bound method is 3200 µs, by dynamic programming 3400 µs, and the genetic algorithm 3700 µs. In large-scale problems, the 4100 µs genetic algorithm performs well, while the branch and bound method requires 6540 µs, and dynamic programming 11000 µs. So, it is advisable to use the branch and bound method, as well as the dynamic programming method, for problems with the number of constraints up to 50, and the genetic algorithm in large-dimensional problems (>50 constraints).

7 Conclusion

Authors have analyzed current state of population environmental awareness and protection from hazardous environmental factors impact, formalized the problem of choosing optimal personal environmental protection means. The problem was described in terms of Boolean programming. Methods of solving given task were reviewed and testing performed on tasks with low and high dimensionality. Further research prospects lie in inclusion of fuzzy logic elements due to imprecision of data regarding pollution parameters and protective gear availability or small data samples. The reviewed elements of algorithmic tools and software were implemented in one of real estate agencies in Kiev (Ukraine).

References

1. Ukraina vymirayet. V chom prichina demograficheskoy katastrofy? https://life.ru/1188481. Accessed 14 July 2019
2. Zakon Ukrayiny: Pro okhoronu navkolyshn'oho pryrodnoho seredovyshcha, vid 12.10.2018, No 1264-XII
3. Environmental Interactive Maps. http://www.eea.europa.eu. Accessed 14 July 2019
4. Wireless Environmental Monitoring Systems. https://hanwell.com/wireless-environmental-monitoring-systems/. Accessed 20 July 2019
5. The Baltic Sea Region GIS, Maps and Statistical Database. http://old.grida.no/baltic/index.htm. Accessed 20 July 2019
6. Meteorological Data Services. https://www.weblakes.com/products/index.html. Accessed 20 July 2019
7. Climate Interactive. https://www.climateinteractive.org/about/services/. Accessed 20 July 2019
8. EPI Results. https://epi.envirocenter.yale.edu/epi-report-2018/executive-summary. Accessed 20 July 2019
9. Holovnyy tsentr spetsial'noho kontrolyu. https://gcsk.gov.ua/programi.html. Accessed 20 July 2019
10. Haupt, R.L., Haupt, S.E.: Practical Genetic Algorithms. Wiley, New York (2004)
11. Batishchev, D.I., Neymark, Ye.A., Starostin, N.V.: Primeneniye geneticheskikh algoritmov k resheniyu zadach diskretnoy optimizatsii, Nizhniy Novgorod (2007)
12. Papadimitriou, C.H., Steiglitz, K.: Combinatorial Optimization: Algorithm and Complexity. Prentice Hall Inc., Englewood Cliff (1982)
13. Wagner, H.M.: Principles of Operations Research. Prentice Hall Inc., Englewood Cliff (1969)
14. Bellman, R.: Dynamic Programming. Princeton University Press, Princeton (1957)
15. Lew, A., Mauch, H.: Dynamic Programming: A Computational Tool. Springer, Heidelberg (2007). https://doi.org/10.1007/978-3-540-37014-7

Ecological Internet Resource as a Tool for Information Control of the Harmful Effects of Environmental Pollution

Tetiana Kovaliuk[1]([✉]), Nataliya Kobets[2], Olena Chaikovska[3], and Dmytro Ivashchenko[4]

[1] Taras Shevchenko National University of Kyiv, Kyiv, Ukraine
tetyana.kovalyuk@gmail.com
[2] Borys Grinchenko Kyiv University, Kyiv, Ukraine
nmkobets@gmail.com
[3] Kyiv National University of Culture and Arts, Kyiv, Ukraine
lena@knukim.edu.ua
[4] National Technical University of Ukraine "Igor Sikorsky Kyiv Polytechnic Institute", Kyiv, Ukraine
ivas-90@mail.ru

Abstract. The authors consider the feasibility of creating publicly available information resources and services that provide data about an ecological situation and degree of ecological contamination of concrete region. An Internet resource for information support of users on environmental pollution issues, which is based on the Microsoft Bing Maps map service and Silverlight plugin, is described. There was shown that application of given technologies allows to use multimedia, graphic arts, animation and interactivity in one software platform. Text, contained in the Silverlight applications, is accessible for the searching systems. The described application collects data on the ecological state of the environment in a specific region in the amount necessary for its analysis and decision-making on environmental issue.

Keywords: Ecological state · Environmental · Internet resource · Environmental information · Environmental pollution

1 Introduction

Ukraine is painted black on the UN map due to its environmental deterioration. It is the color of a country where the population is dying out [1]. According to Institute for Demography and Social Studies of the National Academy of Sciences of Ukraine the South and the East of Ukraine – the so-called "Black Belt" – is dying out at a record pace. Environmental problems contribute in no small part to this shocking statistics. According to the State Statistics Service, 72 kg of pollutants fall on each Ukrainian per year [2]. As of 2016, Ukraine is ranked 4th in the world and 3rd in Europe in terms of mortality [3].

The April 1986 explosion and core meltdown of a reactor at the Chernobyl' nuclear power plant in northern Ukraine had an enormous impact on the region's environment.

© IFIP International Federation for Information Processing 2020
Published by Springer Nature Switzerland AG 2020
Y. Murayama et al. (Eds.): ITDRR 2019, IFIP AICT 575, pp. 67–77, 2020.
https://doi.org/10.1007/978-3-030-48939-7_7

Radioactive materials from the accident seeped into the ground, contaminating farmland and the water supply. From 1992 to 2002 in Belarus, Russia and Ukraine, more than 40003 cases of thyroid cancer were diagnosed among those who were children and adolescents (0–18 years) at the time of the accident, the age group 0–14 years being most affected (Fig. 1) [4]. The long-term impact on human health and the environment is still being assessed.

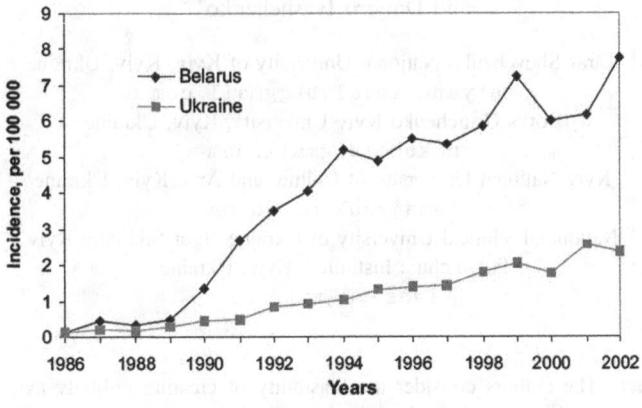

Fig. 1. Incidence rate of thyroid cancer in children and adolescents exposed to Iodine-131 as a result of the Chernobyl accident

Armed conflicts affect lands and terrain, surface and ground waters, vegetation and wildlife in a number of ways. Hostilities significantly increase the risks of incidents at industrial and infrastructure facilities. Especially hazardous for the environment are conflicts that take place in industrialized regions possessing a large concentration of environmentally hazardous installations and facilities, as is the case in the Donetsk and Luhansk regions. Soil pollution in conflict-affected areas are shown in Fig. 2 [5].

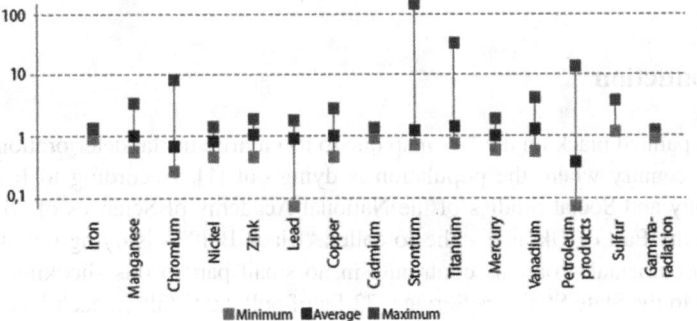

Fig. 2. Relative difference of soil pollution in conflict-affected areas vs. the background level.

According to the Ministry of Health of Ukraine and the Ministry of Ecology and Natural Resources of Ukraine there are more than 3 million people living in more than 2000 settlements on radionuclide-contaminated territories only. Due to environmental deterioration, over the last 10 years medical incidence rate has increased by 25% on average. According to World Health Organization data, 80% of environmentally induced deceases are severe and practically incurable illnesses. Information on environmental conditions such as air pollution, water contamination, epidemiological situation, radiological hazards level etc. has become vital.

Information as a special kind of resources and a factor of social development becomes a special type of product with all the properties of a product inherent to it. Ecological information (on the state of the environment, air pollution, water resources, epidemiological situations, the level of radiological danger, etc.) is especially valuable because it is vital for humans. Ecological information is necessary for all people, but its customers are those payable individuals and organizations that are at risk – money, reputation, health, life, etc. Moreover, the degree of risk and the possible price of information are directly dependent.

The existing environmental problems are relevant for humanity and raise the level of environmental awareness among the population requires the creation of new tools for organizing, storing, disseminating and updating environmental information resources [6]. However where and how to get such information promptly? Can the received information be trusted? These are the questions that the authors attempt to answer with their EcoSpotter project.

2 Analysis of Research and Existing Solutions

Analysis of accessible to public information resources and services that provide data on current environmental situation shows that obtaining reliable and up-to-date information is not an easy task. Following is an overview of some information resources that provide environmental monitoring data.

Environmental Interactive Maps [7] offers a list of interactive environmental maps of Europe. Water and soil pollution are represented best. Indisputable advantage of this resource is the variety of information. However, user-specified search for environmental data is complicated due to necessity to separate different forms of data representation.

Wireless Environmental Monitoring Systems (EMS) [8] provides data on the most reliable, consistent and accurate wireless environmental monitoring and control solutions by Hanwell Solutions Ltd. The Hanwell EMS software takes environmental monitoring data display to another level. The top-level displays a general overview of site sensor activity, with subsequent levels enabling customizable data groups for individual user requirements. Full data collection with interactive graphs, tables and plan views enable users to slice historical environmental data in multiple ways for more advanced analysis.

The Baltic Sea Region GIS, Maps and Statistical Database [9] is a result of the Baltic Drainage Basin Project, a multi-disciplinary research project under the EU. The datasets and maps have been combined into one interactive on-line map service.

Database has become the most popular and pertinent environmental information resource about the transboundary Baltic Sea Region.

Lakes Environmental Company [10] offers a wide range of environmental software products. The Company provides a wide variety of services in the areas of air dispersion modeling, human health and ecological risk assessment, emissions inventory, compliance, as well as emergency release.

Climate Interactive Company [11] creates simulation models, interactive tools and programs for environmental and sustainability planning and education in such areas: climate change, energy, sustainability, environment, and disaster risk reduction.

Environmental Performance Index (EPI) [12] scores 180 countries on 24 performance indicators across ten issue categories covering environmental health and ecosystem vitality. The overall EPI rankings indicate which countries are doing best against the array of environmental pressures that every nation faces. Ukraine is on the 109th place (out of 180) in the 2018 EPI Country Rank.

Main Center of the Special Monitoring website [13] manages data of seismic, radionuclide, electromagnetic, infrasound monitoring, monitoring of nuclear tests and space weather, on both global and local scale, providing the state central government structures, which are responsible for the national security and defense, as well as other interested ministries and departments with all the required information.

Analysis of existing information resources that provide data on environmental situation and parameters leads to the following conclusions:

- Existing information services do not possess adequate degree of interactivity: the data is provide either as static maps or interactive maps with complicated and not user-friendly interface and limited functionality;
- Existing information services do not possess ecological monitoring data search tools;
- Information services software requires lengthy and complicated installation and configuration process;
- Information resources are narrowly focused on certain territories and/or provided data type;
- Information resources provide no recommendations on lessening or negating environmental hazards impact on human health and ways to improve environmental security.

3   Consumers of Environmental Information

Consumers of reliable and timely environmental information were identified in the process of researching the problem. Such categories of environmental information consumers were considered:

- Real estate market;
- Agricultural business;
- Tourist industry;
- Recreational business.

The real estate market is inseparable from environmental issues that are relevant to people who want to improve the quality of their life. For example, information of the environmental impact assessment of housing and its location, analysis of the state of drinking water, harmful emissions that pollute the air in the place chosen by the buyer of real estate is an expensive item.

Problems of food security, environmental protection and conservation of natural resources are relevant for the agricultural sector. Agriculture is increasingly feeling the pressure of consumers, who need to increase not only the environmental safety of the products produced, but also the production itself in terms of its impact on the environment, and, consequently, the quality of life.

The implementation of the concept of sustainable tourism development provides for a close connection of natural and tourist resources. Eco-friendly regions attract tourists. There they can get a healthy rest and aesthetic impressions of communication with nature. Obtaining detailed and timely environmental information on the tourist route will help a potential tourist to make a decision regarding his resting place.

A person spends own physical and mental efforts through its work. Therefore, it should be able to maintain and correct the physiological state of the body during rest and recovery. To organize effective human recreation, it is necessary to take into account the ecological state of natural systems and the quality of the environment as a determining factor in recreational activities. Accounting, natural components (climate, water, balneological and mud reserves, phytotherapeutic factors, sea and beach resources) in the recreational process requires obtaining the necessary information about the environmental quality characteristics [2].

In conditions when the information becomes a commodity, you can get income and profit from its sale. Ecological information of a general nature should be available to users for free access. In order to allow market regulation of the demand for information, it should not be freely available. For efficiency, completeness, detail, exclusivity of data the consumer must pay.

A sociological survey conducted in Kiev on a sample of 1000 respondents showed that citizens are willing to pay for timely and reliable environmental data when property purchase (Fig. 3).

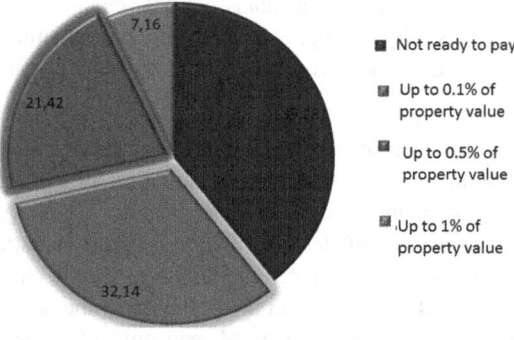

Fig. 3. The results of a sociological survey on the willingness of the population to pay for timely and reliable environmental data.

4   Problem Statement

Within the context of environmental problems which society faces, development of ecological monitoring systems to provide timely, complete and reliable information on environmental state and civil protection from environmental hazards activities is a pressing challenge.

The goal of this work is to analyze the possibility of using the Microsoft Bing Maps cartographic service in a client-server application to provide quick and convenient access to data on the environmental situation in the region, presented in an interactive, intuitive form.

5   Functionalities of the Web-Resource

The web-resource has been developed to achieve this goal. The web-resource provides the necessary information on the environment in the user's locations. It forms recommendations on environmental protection and reducing the consequences of the harmful effects of environmental pollution on humans.

The developed software system implements such business processes.

- Collection of primary data by measuring devices of environmental quality such as gas analyzers, smoke meters, sound level meters, dosimeters and other devices, including those based at terrestrial means of obtaining environmental information;
- Data transmission using GSM-channels, radio channels or the Internet;
- Storing environmental data in a database: attributive (directories, objects of observation, measurements of environmental parameters), cartographic (terrain maps, thematic maps—radiological, chemical, and other types of pollution);
- Statistical data processing for the purpose of modeling and forecasting environmental situations;
- Expert analysis and expert assessment of environmental hazards, the choice of the best solution among the existing ones, forecasting the development of the process;
- Statistical analysis of environmental impact assessment; development of recommendations for management decisions-making in emergency situations;
- Visual display of environmental data (maps, graphs, charts);
- Reporting on the results of modeling, prediction of environmental situations, expert assessment, and preparation of advisory recommendations for minimizing harmful effects on humans.

The user can go to the web resource and chooses regions interested for him. The user receives information on the environmental situation in the area, indicating the corresponding label on the map. He can view video images, read general recommendations on reducing the impact of negative factors, obtain statistics on changes in pollution indicators, and move to a forum for discussions on the environmental issues.

The application loads polygons, data on the pollution of the area and displays them on an electronic map to view the parameters of environmental pollution. If a specific section on an electronic map is selected, the application calculates the polygon on

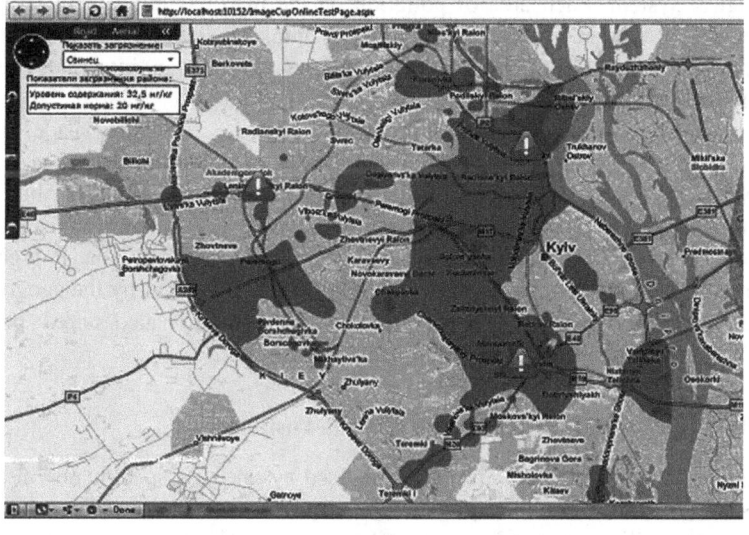

Fig. 4. An example of the EcoSpotter e-map of Ukraine's lead pollution.

which the selection was made, requests specific values for the section from the database, and displays them to the user (Fig. 4).

The mobile version of the project is intended for user registration of environmental data at the location of their measurement. The user does not need to record the coordinates of each measurement; all that is needed is to send data to the server by mobile phone from the place of their measurement. Data processing, expert assessment, and issuing recommendations to the user regarding environmental hazards are performed according to the base scenario of the EcoSpotter system

6   Interactive Maps with Silverlight and Bing Maps

6.1   Bing Maps Geometrical Object

Bing Maps offers access to rich map imagery and data as well as robust search, location, and routing services. Silverlight based Bing Maps allows to choose the map view: a two-dimensional road map, a satellite view and a bird's eye view (axonometric). There is also an automatic mode that switches the views when you change the scale: initially a simple map is displayed, then the surface of the earth begins to turn and a three-dimensional view appears. Laser scanning used to form three-dimensional images of objects [14].

Bing Maps can assign multimedia objects, such as video, images, photos, tags, to specific regions and coordinates on a map. The EcoSpotter project implemented the ability to link a graphic object, which is represented as a region of a locality on an electronic map, with a semantic object – a representation of the subject area in terms of an ecological system. Each area of pollution on the map has relevant image, which characterizes the type and level of danger, for example, radiation. The addition video content, multimedia objects and comments allows creating an integral system for displaying environmental information.

Working with a map is based on a polygon system, i.e. geometric shapes mapped and used to display polluted regions. The Bing Maps Silverlight SDK component allows you to apply such objects to a map on-line, which makes it possible to edit regions quickly. Each region is characterized by a danger level, which is visualized on the map in a certain color. The region is defined as a convex polygon. Polygons are stored in a database as a set of segments, each of which is defined by the geographical coordinates of its beginning and end. Regional information is also stored: pollution degree, hazard level, and other environmental parameters.

6.2   The Problem of Determining the User's Positioning

User requests for environmental data are processed by selecting specific regions. To do this, it is necessary to determine a point on the map by its coordinates. This point on the electronic map will correspond to a specific location. The task is to determine the belonging of a particular point on the map to a specific region displayed by a convex polygon. To solve this problem, two algorithms were considered.

The first algorithm is based on splitting a convex polygon that represents a region of locality into triangles and verifying that a user-defined point belongs to triangles.

To determine whether a point is a convex polygon, its vertices are sequentially numbered from 1 to n. Line segments to all other vertices of the polygon connect the vertex 1. As a result $n - 2$ triangles with number of vertices $\{\overline{1,n}; 3 \leq i \leq n\}$ are formed. Verification of the belonging a given point to at least one of these triangles is carried out. Splitting a polygon into triangles and checking the belonging of a given point to triangles is performed for vertices with subsequent numbers until one of the conditions is satisfied:

- a splitting convex polygon into triangles, in which the point does not belong to any of the triangles, and, consequently, the point does not belong to the selected polygon;
- all vertices of the polygon are scanned, and the condition of the point's belonging to the triangle is checked for each vertex, therefore, the point belongs to the selected polygon;

The second algorithm is based on the idea of counting the number of intersections of a ray emanating from a given point in the direction of the horizontal axis with the sides of a polygon. If the number of such intersections is even, the point does not belong to the polygon.

As the experiments showed, the speed of the second algorithm is 10 times higher with the number of segments forming the boundary of the polygon, more than 20 thousand. Therefore, to solve this problem in this project, in order to increase efficiency, the most recent algorithm was used.

7   The EcoSpotter System Architecture

The EcoSpotter system has three principal layers. Presentation logic is about how to handle the interaction between the user and the software. The primary responsibilities of the presentation layer are to display information to the user and to interpret commands from the user into actions upon the domain and data source. The presentation layer is implemented as a web client [15].

Data source logic is transaction monitors, other applications, messaging systems, and so forth. For EcoSpotter system the biggest piece of data source logic is a database that is primarily responsible for storing persistent data.

The domain logic, also referred to as business logic is the work that EcoSpotter system needs to do. It involves calculations based on inputs and stored data, validation of any data that comes in from the presentation logic, and figuring out exactly what data source logic to dispatch, depending on commands received from the presentation logic.

The EcoSpotter software system includes the following components (Fig. 5):

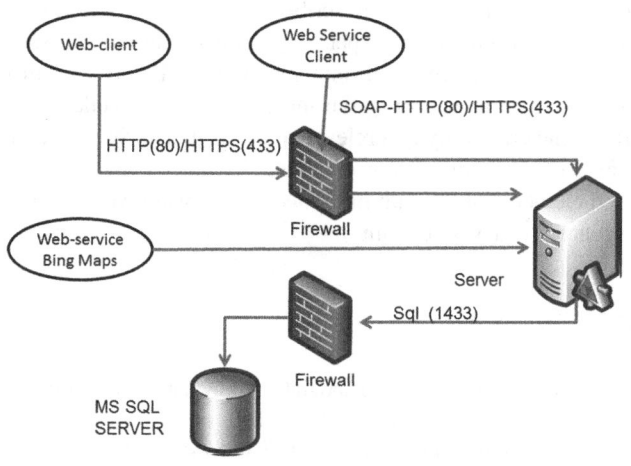

Fig. 5. The EcoSpotter system architecture.

- Database server running MS SQL Server. The database contains data on environmental pollution parameters (region name, type of pollution, degree of pollution, environmental pollution);
- XML Web Service Microsoft Bing Maps. The service provides management of the coordinates of the points on the map and determinates the latitude and longitude of the marked point of the map;
- Microsoft Bing Maps Silverlight SDK. Silverlight is a user interface component that allows to put on a map the polygons and geometric shapes, change its appearance, and process coordinates to calculate the location of objects [16];
- ASP.NET application for creating a Web interface and displaying the Silverlight component;

- Microsoft IIS Web Server is the environment for the functioning of the Web application;
- Expert System is a component that develops and evaluates the possible solution alternatives. The decision is limited to choosing one of the proposed alternatives. The component of the expert system uses the Bayesian system of logical output. It is intended for the user consultation with the expert in the field of environmental safety in order to determine the probabilities of possible events and uses for this the assessment of the probability of environmental hazards [17].

8 Conclusion

Authors have analyzed current state of population environmental awareness and protection from hazardous environmental factors impact. The authors consider the feasibility of creating publicly available information resources and services that provide data about an ecological situation and degree of ecological contamination of concrete region. The use of the Microsoft Bing Maps service opens up a wide range of possibilities for creating applications. The described application collects data on the ecological state of the environment in a specific region in the amount necessary for its analysis and decision-making on environmental issues. The environmental database uses mobile systems, instrumentation, environmental sensors and devices. The program provides control of the credibility and relevance of the data through the involvement of experts in the field of environmental protection.

The reviewed elements of algorithmic tools and software were implemented in one of real estate agencies in Kyiv (Ukraine).

References

1. Ukraina vymirayet. V chom prichina demograficheskoy katastrofy? https://life.ru/1188481. Accessed 14 July 2019
2. Vesti: Where is the dirtiest air in Ukraine. https://vesti-ukr.com/strana/286621-chem-teplee-tem-tjazhelee-dyshat-hde-v-ukraine-samyj-hrjaznyj-vozdukh. Accessed 10 July 2019
3. The World Factbook: The World Factbook—Central Intelligence Agency. Accessed 10 July 2019
4. Chernobyl's Legacy: Health, Environmental and Socio-Economic Impacts and Recommendations to the Governments of Belarus, the Russian Federation and Ukraine. The Chernobyl Forum: 2003–2005. IAEA (2006)
5. Environmental Assessment and Recovery Priorities for Eastern Ukraine. VAITE, Kyiv (2017)
6. Zakon Ukrayiny «Pro okhoronu navkolyshn'oho pryrodnoho seredovyshcha» vid 12.10.2018. No. 1264-XII
7. Environmental Interactive Maps. http://www.eea.europa.eu. Accessed 14 July 2019
8. Wireless Environmental Monitoring Systems. https://hanwell.com/wireless-environmental-monitoring-systems. Accessed 20 July 2019
9. The Baltic Sea Region GIS: Maps and Statistical Database. http://old.grida.no/baltic/index.htm. Accessed 20 July 2019

10. Meteorological Data Services. https://www.weblakes.com/products/index.html. Accessed 20 July 2019
11. Climate Interactive. https://www.climateinteractive.org/about/services. Accessed 20 July 2019
12. EPI Results. https://epi.envirocenter.yale.edu/epi-report-2018/executive-summary. Accessed 20 July 2019
13. Holovnyy tsentr spetsial'noho kontrolyu. https://gcsk.gov.ua/programi.html. Accessed 20 July 2019
14. Bing Maps Documentation. https://docs.microsoft.com/en-us/bingmaps/. Accessed 10 Feb 2019
15. Fowler, M.: Patterns of Enterprise Application Architecture. Addison-Wesley Publishing Company, Boston (2003)
16. Baydachny, S.S.: Silverlight 4: Build Rich Web Applications. Solon-Press, Berlin (2010)
17. Jackson, P.: Introduction to Expert Systems. Addison-Wesley Publishing Company, Boston (1986)

Building Resilient Community by Public Private Partnership – From Science to Action in Developing Countries

Wei-Sen Li[(⊠)], Yanling Lee, Yi-Chung Liu, Ke-Hui Chen,
and Chi-Ling Chang

National Science and Technology Center for Disaster Reduction, Taipei, Taiwan
li.weisen.ncdr@gmail.com

Abstract. The abstract should summarize the contents of the paper in short terms. In order to mitigate possible risks at community level in developing countries, it requires activations of all key stakeholders, especially contributions by public-private partnership. To engage two sides co-working on disaster risk management, there must be clear targets and strategies to gather synergies. Therefore, based on risk maps, social vulnerabilities, investments, tailor-made "smart" disaster risk management could be implemented through regional collaboration. By the definition of "smart risk management", it requires creative and innovative ideas from collecting data to offering better display that should satisfy different situations met by the general public and decision makers. At information ear, according to the base practices in Taiwan, an end-to-end operational model has been operating to produce information intelligence for efficient and effective responses. "Information intelligence" should be the future guidance on value of outputs by information system which must not just be limited in displaying scientific results, but also readable and actionable suggestions to follow. Within the paper, besides introduction on strategic developments, examples of small-scale pilot projects are also illustrated to perform as a pathfinder for setting a new model which meets demands in developing countries. And a systemic approach for developing countries is proposed to enhance capacity and capability of disaster risk management.

Keywords: Smart Disaster Risk Management (Smart DRM) · Public-Private Partnership (PPP) · Information-and-Communication Technology (ICT)

1 Challenges of Disaster Risk Management in Developing Countries First Section

In 2014, Maplecroft published the Natural Hazards Risk Atlas which states Japan, the United States, Taiwan, China, India, Mexico, the Philippines, Italy, Australia and Indonesia round out the top 10 countries with the highest economic exposure to natural disasters [1]. Figure 1 shows the world-wide evaluation. "Economic exposure" is a common terminology which can sever a vehicle commuting demand and supply of disaster risk management (DRM) between public and private sectors because it highly addresses societal interests. Major goals of DRM are set to protect lives, reduce losses

Y. Murayama et al. (Eds.): ITDRR 2019, IFIP AICT 575, pp. 78–84, 2020.
https://doi.org/10.1007/978-3-030-48939-7_8

and enhance resilience. In developing countries, small and medium enterprises (SMEs) occupy most portion of business and are vulnerable to natural hazards compared with global or large enterprises. Among all factors that might be key challenges of DRM in developing countries, the following ones could be essential for improvement:

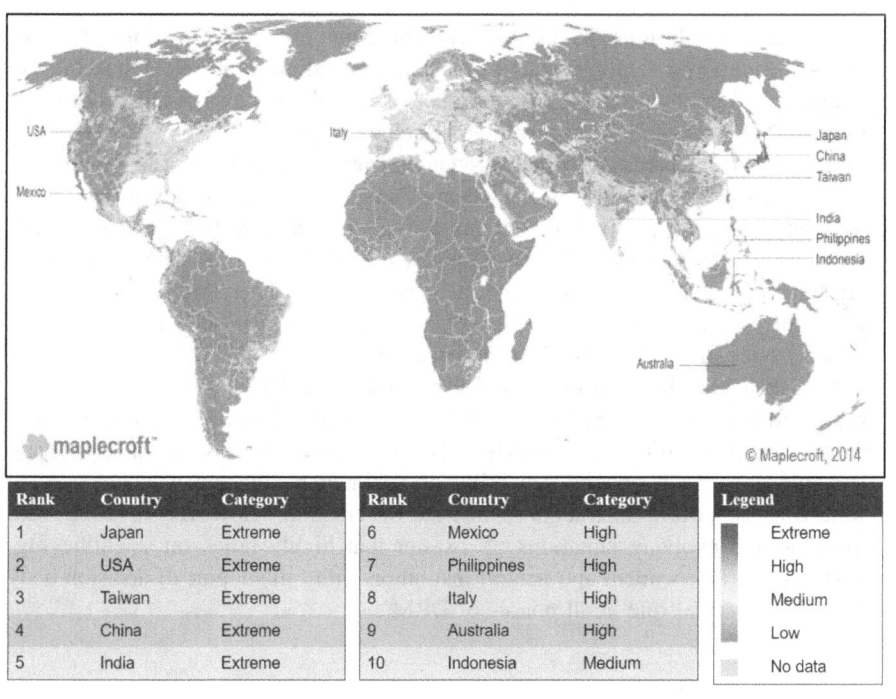

Rank	Country	Category	Rank	Country	Category	Legend	
1	Japan	Extreme	6	Mexico	High		Extreme
2	USA	Extreme	7	Philippines	High		High
3	Taiwan	Extreme	8	Italy	High		Medium
4	China	Extreme	9	Australia	High		Low
5	India	Extreme	10	Indonesia	Medium		No data

Fig. 1. Maplecroft absolute economic exposure index 2014 [1]

1. **Inter- and intra-government collaboration:** Nowadays, much more data has been produced by individual agencies which should be important for digitalizing preparedness for emergency response or disaster risk reduction, but due to bureaucracy or inertia reluctancy, low information sharing and exchange among government agencies is a major barrier preventing information integration. It is recommended to have a high-level plan to do inventory surveys on national database and assign clear operational functions to related agencies [2]. By doing so, it is the initial step for building up "smart disaster risk management" (Smart DRM).
2. **Risk maps of physical vulnerabilities:** After collecting basic datasets, production and overlapping of potential maps help to highlight areas with high or multiple risk. Based on the maps, appropriate early warning system and alert messages could be deployed and disseminated accordingly. About equipment of waring warning system and channels to disseminate alerts, possible solutions could be very high-end devices or traditional technology. No matter advanced or old-faction ones, efficiency and reliability decide true performance of the system [3].

3. **Understanding social vulnerabilities:** Evaluation of social vulnerabilities is aimed at measuring the whole society's resilience through identifying the insufficiencies of different aspects such like relevant issues of gender inequity, aging population, risk perception, social status, etc. Being paired with physical vulnerability, social vulnerabilities assist in pinpointing vulnerable minor groups which demand specific cares.

4. **Laws and regulations to enable environment for collaboration:** A well-established environment to regulate rights and obligation of all DRM stakeholders requires legal ground to implement a framework to follow. Laws of DRM can guide direction for inter- and intra- government collaboration.

5. **Setting up all-hazards approach for emergency preparedness and emergency response:** Considering limited capital and human resources in developing countries, an appropriate setup for operations during emergency is a keystone to succeed DRM agenda. Especially, emergency operation could be the most direct way to win credits from top decision makers and the general public. Therefore, a system which can offer operational information intelligence is highly requested is s shortcut to connect scientific community with decision body.

6. **Establish a high-level think-tank for consultancy:** Science-based or evidence-based DRM is a global trend and several best practices of Taiwan and Japan proved it helps quality decisions and saves lives [4–7]. To make the most use of science and technology is much beyond capability of bureaucratic officers who are used to following superior's instructions, instead of creation. However to cope with dynamic and evolving situations of disaster that highly relies on scientific suggestions. An independent and neutral institution with full support of decision body will play a critical role at all phases of DRM.

2   Mission-Oriented Design of Investment in Science and Technology for DRM

Investment in science and technology will make a direct link between research community and government administration. Though pure researches do help to accumulate scientific knowledge by publishing papers or journals, but usually these papers can't be directly applied for practical implementation, if without certain procedures to make them feasible. On contract to pure researches, mission-oriented investment first requires clear goals – "improvement" to specify what could be improved, changed or upgraded though filling up gaps, as shown in Fig. 2.

For example, to achieve the scheduled milestone of improving Earthquake Early Warning System (EEWS), before real investment, clear targets, like enhancement of accuracy or efficiency, need dialogues among all stakeholders to exchange ideas in developing measure of co-design, co-work and co-implementation. Other jobs required to be done include pre-disaster preparedness plan which will offer guidelines for both emergency responders and citizens to follow just in case of large-scale earthquake; and impacts assessment system provides scientific evidences for exploring vulnerabilities to mitigate in advance or identifying disaster hotspots after a major shock.

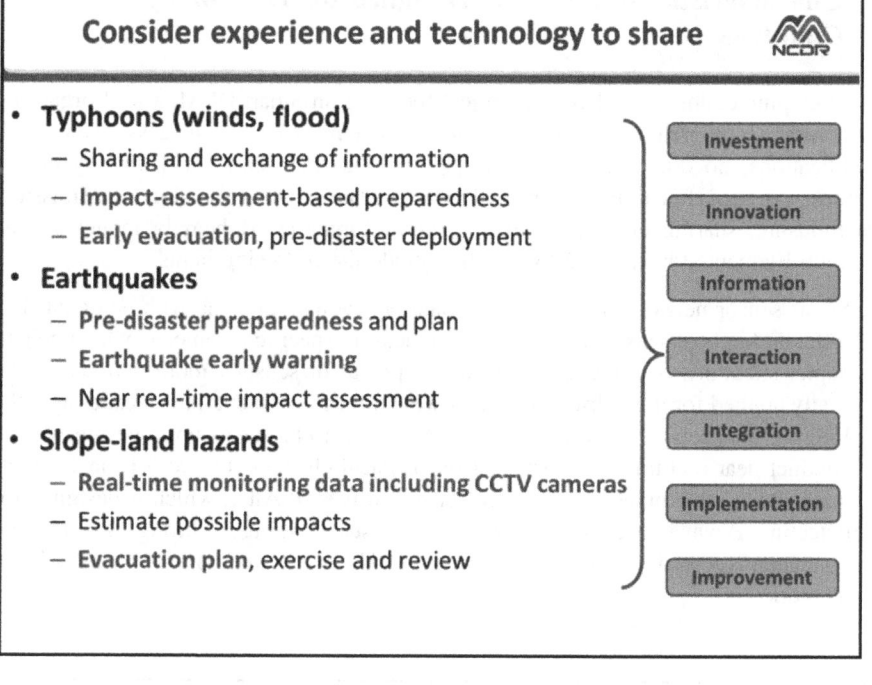

Fig. 2. Improvement-oriented investment on DRM

All ingredients to make an improvement-oriented investment on DRM are composed of:

1. Innovation: To revitalize existing technology or develop new one for filling gaps at real operations or satisfying people's demands is the ultimate purpose to introduce science and technology for DRM.
2. Information: To enhance collections and coverage of DRM information is aimed at better risk understanding. As mentioned previously, unselfish information sharing is the solid foundation to build up an information backbone for DRM.
3. Interaction: To routinely call meetings or discussions helps to form consensus through open-minded dialogues. Participation to the meetings should be not limited to any single background. Diversity at meetings, such members from government, scientific community, NGO and NPO, assists in broadening DRM scopes to cover end users' demands.
4. Integration: To integrate all stakeholder as a team, addition to information integration, that supports operations for mitigation, preparedness, response and recovery. And resources, capacity and social network of NGOs or NPOs should be considered, but with full communication first.
5. Implementation: To make good things happen for DRM, it demands real implementation of DRM science and technology to finds out both advantages and disadvantages.

3   Characteristics of a Project Designed for Developing Countries

In developing countries to deliver a project focusing on Smart DRM, a well-organized plan with a comprehensive capacity survey is a must-be for success. Among all qualifications, no doubts, quality and speed of Internet access will directly decide performance and functions of Smart DRM. Because data collection, transmission, warehousing, sharing or display, every part of Smart DRM heavily replies on the Internet. Elements for Smart DRM might include the following items:

1. Smart sensor network: For collecting data or readings in areas with potential risk, different kinds of sensors are designed to measure specific parameters which help to depict situations on sites. By rapid development of sensors, more options can be easily applied for filed observations. However, much different than decades ago, the Internet connects sensors as network and gives a chance to improve the way to conduct near real-time measurement on physical changes. Figure 3 is an Internet-connected accelerometer to measure seismic waves, P-Alter, which is designed for detecting P-wave to estimate S-wave and issue warnings. Through the Internet connections, certain number of individual P-Alerts can function as a local seismic network.

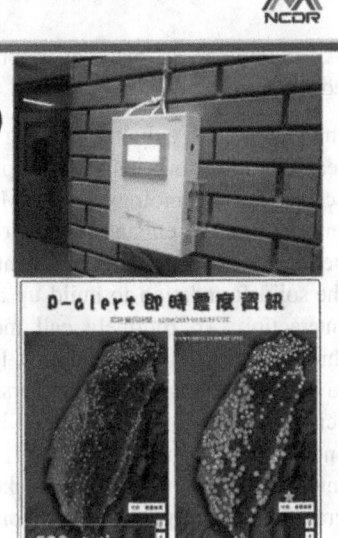

Fig. 3. An Internet-connected accelerometer to measure seismic waves, P-Alter

- To use IoT to collect real-time data: Internet of Things (IoT) is reshaping the way of real-time measurement on physical vulnerabilities. By applying IoT, the amount of data is increasing at exponential rate that demands new approaches to deal with.
- To collect and analyze basic data for pilot site: It is realistic to choose a pilot site for a small-scale deployment of sensors. Besides testing stability of Internet connection, the pilot project also can offer inputs before large-scale installation.
- To enable a disaster-resilient foundation for a smart city: Now most cities are doing their best efforts for becoming a smart city. Disaster risk management is an index for disaster-prone cites to achieve. So Smart DRM will be emphasized by both officials of central and local levels.

2. Cloud-based decision supporting system: Traditionally, central server at computer room is a typical setup for decision supporting system. But considering redundancy and readiness of the system, cloud technology provides ideal solutions to developing countries. Reasons to embrace cloud-based system: 1) The configuration can reduce loading to establish facilities for high-performance computing and storage; 2) The technology also offers easy assesses to all end users; 3) The environment is mature for cross-platform operation.

- To offer easy access for all users: Since the system can be applied for difference platform, Windows, macOS, IOS or Android, most of users can execute the system anywhere.
- To enhance system's readiness and redundancy: Compared with traditional setups, no matter public or private clouds are able to maintain very stable operation that meet the demands of emergency operation.
- To provide a platform connecting offsite stakeholders: In case of emergency operation, users might access the system anywhere by difference devices. Therefore, decision supporting system operated by cloud technology will also connect users operating at emergency operation centers or on sites.

3. Capacity building for information intelligence: Training qualified personnel to produce and interpret scientific information is an essential part of capacity building in developing countries. With appropriate and understandable interpretation, it will help both decision makers and the general public to take right actions.

- To co-produce tailor-made information for specific users- citizens, decision makers and private sectors: To meet demands of diverse end users, trainees must clearly identify right and in-time information.
- To engage more resources through public-private partnership: Nowadays, private sector also owns and produces big dada which is valuable for DRM. For example, social media and mobile companies can provide informative data, but all application must strictly follow personal privacy.

4   Conclusions

1. To have good teamwork by integrating government, research community, NGOs and NPOs, it needs linkages like mission-oriented projects which focus on demand and supply and encourages constant dialogues among stakeholders.
2. To establish a knowledge-and-technology center, that should function as a facilitator and coordinator and provide professional consultancy.
3. To build network between the knowledge-and-technology Center and local universities, through the process, it will both empower local governments and fill information gaps.

References

1. Maplecroft Homepage. https://www.maplecroft.com/insights/analysis/uks-economic-exposure-to-flooding-among-worlds-highest/. Accessed 20 Feb 2014
2. Hsieh, S.H.: Achievements and outputs of the program on applying science and technology for disaster reduction, 2011–2014 (2015)
3. Tasy, C.Y.: From academic research to policy making - a case of Taiwan effort in disaster reduction (2009)
4. Chen, L.C., Yen, C.L., Loh, C.H., Wei, L.Y., Lee, W.C., Ho, H.Y.: Development and implementation of disaster reduction technology in Taiwan. Nat. Hazards 37(1), 2–21 (2006)
5. Chen, L.C., Liu, Y.C., Chan, K.C.: Integrated community-based disaster management program in Taiwan: a case study of Shang-An village. Nat. Hazards 37(1), 209–223 (2006)
6. Hsu, H.H., Chou, C., Wu, Y.C., Lu, M.M., Chen C.T., Chen, Y.M.: Climate change in Taiwan: scientific report 2011 (Summary). National Science Council (2001)
7. Morakot Post-Disaster Reconstruction Council: Rebuilding a Sustainable Homeland with Innovation and United Efforts, Executive Yuan, Taiwan (2011)

Building Resilient Community Through Plant Back Better Initiative – Guiding Principles and Best Practices

Yanling Lee[1(✉)], Wei-Sen Li[1], Yi-Ching Liu[2], Ke-Hui Chen[1], Chi-Ling Chang[1], and Kenji Watanabe[3]

[1] APEC Emergency Preparedness Capacity Building Center, National Science and Technology Center for Disaster Reduction, New Taipei City, Taiwan
sophiancdr@gmail.com
[2] National Science and Technology Center for Disaster Reduction, New Taipei City, Taiwan
[3] The Nagoya Institute of Technology, Nagoya, Japan

Abstract. The 2019 UN report on Sustainable Development Goals (SDGs) revealed the impact on climate-related disaster. From 1998 to 2017, seventy seven percent of the estimated direct economic losses (US$3 trillion) are from disasters. It is about a 1.5 time rise compared to the one from 1978 to 1997. Estimated 1.3 million death toll for climate related and geophysical disasters. Asia-Pacific Economic Cooperation (APEC) recognized the urgent need of resilient infrastructure, early warning systems, emergency-actionable plans and countermeasures for better preparedness and recovery to tackle constant threat of extreme events, earthquakes, floods and natural disasters. Thus, APEC called for climate adaptation countermeasures. "Plant Back Better" (PBB) initiative emerged to functioned on the countermeasure of food security over climate extremes to boost microeconomic momentum. The PBB project aimed at mitigating vulnerability and facilitating self-sufficiency through disaster-resilient plantation of vegetable and flowers. This research explored the feasible and applicable approaches on engaging key stakeholders to map out a pathway of sustainable and resilient developments through capacity building activities and risk communication tools. This paper incorporated: 1) the best practices, 2) holistic and extensive policies on natural disasters and climate extremes for enhancing emergency preparedness and resilience, 3) cross-fora collaboration under APEC for sustainable development and inclusive growth. To conclude the PBB project, five principles are available to navigate APEC Resilience Community (ARC) over climate extremes and facilitate Livelihood Continuity Planning (LCP) before or after disasters.

Keywords: United Nation (UN) · Sustainable Development Goals (SDGs) · Asia-Pacific Economic Cooperation (APEC) · Plant Back Better (PBB) · Food security · Resilience

Y. Murayama et al. (Eds.): ITDRR 2019, IFIP AICT 575, pp. 85–106, 2020.
https://doi.org/10.1007/978-3-030-48939-7_9

1 The Force Majeure

On September 9, 2018, nine active storms; Hurricane Florence, Helene, Isaac, Olivia, Tropical Storm Paul, Typhoon Mangkhut and etc.; appeared simultaneously in the Atlantic Ocean and the Pacific Ocean [1]. In 2018, at least 1,000 earthquakes hit the APEC region with magnitudes 5.0 and above [2]. The "new normal" shows its tremendous challenges to project timeline and threat the project deliverables. Environmental risk/natural disasters with its increasing frequency and intensive struck APEC region in the year of 2018 brought along with floods, earthquakes, wildfires, and etc. We are facing the significant increasing risk of natural disaster threats ranked higher than average for both likelihood and impact for the upcoming 10 years.

On the other hand the 2019 UN report on Sustainable Development Goals (SDGs) [3] indicated that "Extreme poverty today is concentrated and overwhelmingly affects rural populations. Increasingly, it is exacerbated by violent conflicts and climate change. The toll of climate-related disasters is rising, with the poorer countries most affected." Climate-related disaster accounted for 77% of the estimated total of $3 trillion direct economic losses from disasters from 1998 to 2017. It is about a 1.5 time rise compared to the direct economic losses from 1978 to 1997. For live losses, climate related and geophysical disasters claimed an estimated 1.3 million death toll. Over 90 percent of the disasters were floods, storms, droughts, heatwaves and climate extremes. The recent synchronous adoption of landmark UN agreements the Sendai Framework for Disaster Risk Reduction (SFDRR) [4], Sustainable Development Goals (SDGs), The 2015 United Nations Climate Change Conference (COP21's) Paris Climate Conference [5], World Humanitarian Summit [6] and Habitat III [7] for climate change and human wellbeing urge the global society to picture the blueprint for building coherence across different but overlapping policy areas. On a near complete resilience agenda as building resilience, it requires action spanning development, humanitarian, climate and disaster risk reduction areas. This coherence will serve to strengthen existing risk vulnerability and resilience frameworks for multi-hazard assessments, and aim to develop a dynamic, local, proactive, and adaptive urban governance system at the global, national, and local levels.

Economic development and sustainability can be severely impacted by natural disasters through extensive interruptions impact daily livelihood, lifeline systems, critical infrastructure or supply chain resilience. At facing impacts brought by natural disasters or climate change, food security is directly linked to emergency preparedness and economic livelihood, especially in affected agricultural communities. According to the 2016 Piura Declaration on APEC Food Security endorsed by the Fourth APEC Ministerial Meeting on Food Security, sixty percent or more food will be needed if the anticipated global population increase to 9.7 billion by 2050. Moreover, take the example of 2019, we suffer from the prolonged drought following by heavy rainfall and typhoons struck while implementing the 1st and 2nd phases of PBB project. The urgent needs emerged for us to look at the impacts brought by both population in hunger and in disasters while emergency happens. We soon utilized the art of change management [8] to intensified efforts to mitigate impacts of drought, flood and climate-related disasters on food production and food security to demonstrate the APEC successful story on PBB initiatives. We expand the scope and scale of the PBB project from flood solution to all hazard solutions to incorporate real scenarios for implementation. The capacity building program and "Home Garden" toolkits designed in terms of sharing local knowledge and synergizing regional resources for resilient community against disasters and cascading impact. In this context, the project received warm welcome and support from the APEC family. Thus, the PBB project initiated to deliver the goals of zero hunger or end hunger, achiever food security and improved nutrition to promote sustainable agriculture – growing your vegetables for dinning in your garden.

1.1   Take Climate Action to Partnership for the Goal

From scientific to action, the APEC Emergency Preparedness Capacity Building Center (EPCC) [9] called for cross-fora synergies among the APEC Emergency Preparedness Working Group (EPWG), Policy Partnership for Science, Technology and Innovation (PPSTI), Policy Partnership on Food Security (PPFS) and the National Science and Technology Center for Disaster Reduction (NCDR) to complete this research project on the "Plant Back Better" (PBB) initiatives [10]. It fully elaborate APEC agenda on human security and gender balance with vision, creativity, local knowledge and practical experiences across the border. The in-depth strong research and implementation guiding support resources from the World Vegetable Center (WV) and the Known-You (KY) contributed to the APEC community with fruitful outputs.

Meanwhile, APEC emphasized on smallholders since they are the majority of food producers in agricultural communities in most of the developing APEC member economies. These communities could be vulnerable to either natural disasters or climate extremes such as typhoons, floods or droughts. Considering the dynamics and diverse impacts of natural disasters, we promote the continuous investment on science, technology and innovation for "**APEC Resilient City**" based on "**APEC Resilient Community**" for better adaptation countermeasures in APEC region to echo the SDGs [11].

1.2   Exploring the Strategic Approaches in Support to Disaster Risk Governance for Public and Private Partnership (PPP) [12]

PBB project engaged government officials, experts, practitioners, Non-profit Organization (NPOs) and Non-Governmental Organization (NGOs) to brainstorm the feasible collaborations mechanism. In the three-phase intensive efforts, we appreciate the contributions from APEC member economies to the APEC PBB initiatives with sharing of best practices across the border for quality and resilient society against natural disasters. With significant outputs from the APEC member economies, the guiding principle developed to tackle climate extremes and natural disasters and provide rapidly growing global population with economic access to sufficient, safe, nutritious and quality food as well as better livelihoods of millions of rural people, mainly small farmers, particularly women on vegetable plantation. While implementation, female-oriented opinions highlighted from experts and speakers to ensure gender balance of preparedness, sourcing and accessibility to PBB and DRR information on user friendly aspects.

Resources of Expertise

The APEC Emergency Preparedness Capacity Building Center (EPCC) - With conviction to build a platform for APEC EPWG to strengthen innovation and capacity building for emergency preparedness to meet the demanding needs of APEC member economies, EPCC aims at all-hazards approaches for emergency preparedness in support of disaster risk reduction and emergency preparedness under APEC through hosting of well-structured capacity-building activities: to develop sustainable programs to promote disaster risk reduction and emergency preparedness in accordance with EPWG's mandate and guidance as well as the proposals and priorities of APEC member economies;

- Establishing knowledge database: collecting best experiences, science and technology to support policy and decision making;
- Enhancing public-private-people partnerships in disaster risk management by actively introducing new technology and concepts as well as highlighting contributions from experts and professionals of governments, academia and practitioners, where appropriate;

The World Vegetable Center (WV) [13], an international nonprofit research and development institute, is committed to alleviating poverty and malnutrition in the developing world through the increased production and consumption of nutritious and health-promoting vegetables. The Center mobilizes resources from the public and private sectors to disseminate improved varieties and production methods in developing countries. We help farmers increase vegetable harvests, raise incomes in poor rural and urban households, create jobs, and provide healthier, more nutritious diets for families and communities.

Known You Seed Co., Ltd. (KY) [14], a professional seed company engaging in breeding, production, and marketing of F1 hybrid vegetable varieties for more than 40 years. The main crops include cucurbit, solanaceae, and crucifer. Many of varieties are highly valued by global customers and have won the international prizes such as All-America Selections.

The National Science and Technology Center for Disaster Reduction (NCDR) [15], as the think-tank of EPCC in disaster risk management at the Cabinet level, NCDR coordinates and collaborates with public and private sectors to deliver the emergency preparedness synergies from science to action for decision making, policy reshuffle and R&D innovation under the Ministry of Science and Technology.

1.3 Partnerships Across the Border – Pubic Private Partnership Operational Model [16]

APEC Enhances Livelihoods through Planting Seeds, Planting Hope, Planting Friendship, Planting Linkage

– Connecting People for Resilience and Better Livelihood

How to provide rapid growing global population with economic access to sufficient, safe, nutritious and quality food as well as better livelihoods of millions of rural people, mainly small farmers, particularly women on vegetable plantation? We call upon the APEC member economies to stand shoulder to shoulder with us to implement the climate extremes adaptation countermeasures for sustainable and inclusive growth through PBB initiatives.

PBB engaged community-based capacity building and preparedness for quick recovery of microeconomic activities through public private partnership before or after disasters hit. The project incorporates the on-site implementation of the best practices and toolkits with sharing local knowledge and regional resources to facilitate Livelihood Continuity Plan (LCP) before or after disasters. To elaborate the climate adaptation countermeasures for food security, it is critical to promote PBB initiatives and call for actions on mitigating vulnerability to enhance self-sufficiency through disaster-resilient vegetables and flowers plantation to foster sustainable and inclusive growth under APEC.

The PBB project developed capacity building by adopting smarter and disaster-resistant plantation of flowers and vegetables. It also mainstreamed DRR for building up resilient city and community with respect to local knowledge over the local social networking.

The targeted goal is to revitalized local microeconomic activities efficiently and effectively as a learning organization [17]. The PBB pilot project in Iloilo City fully engaged the stakeholders in public and private sectors to build a good partnership networking for being resource partners. Base on "the Barangay Disaster Risk Reduction and Management Plan of Barangay Lanit, Jaro, Iloilo City for 2018–2020." (REPUBLIC OF THE PHILIPPINES, OFFICE OF THE PUNONG BARANGAY, BARANGAY LANIT), the project team leads the Public Private Partnership PPP) dialogue to network with the school, the church and the Barangay office via discussion to customized the workplan based on the local needs. From local governments, the agriculture department and the disaster risk reduction and management office in Iloilo City Government [18] contributed to harmonize the law and regulation for resource allocation and infrastructure sustainability that paved the concrete foundation for project implementation. Local technical supports in agriculture from the Know-You Seed Philippines (KYP) and the World Vegetable Center (WV) for providing advanced skillset and technology in smart agriculture is another key to succeed. The EPCC called for NCDR and Christian Aid Philippines to deliver the community-based capacity building efforts as the advocators for PBB project with concept of DRR towards SDGs.

1.4   Pilot Project Kick-off for PBB

To implement the PBB, EPCC has been working with the Philippines on public private partnership to conduct a pilot project-the Best Practice at Barangay Lanit, Jaro Iloilo City, the Philippines.

The ATI, the original inhabitants, suffered from severe disasters including drought in 2007, floods in decades since 2008 Typhoon Frank, drought in 2019 and annual monsoon from May or August to October. In Barangay Lanit, the resettlement site, the population reached 5,484 (1.22% of Iloilo city's) in 2015 and total of about 1,600 households as of April 2019 (40% are farmers).

The PBB initiatives in the Iloilo City aimed at community-based capacity building and preparedness for quick recovery of microeconomic activities through public private partnership to tackle climate extremes and natural disasters. Vegetables are cash crops with offering quality nutrition. Besides, flowers, sunflower chosen for the school gardening, are one of the direct sales and marketing business models for activating the MSMEs' and Small and Medium Enterprise (SMEs)' business cycle. With stories, the PBB pilot site caught attention of the general public and attracting tourist paying visits on-site. In this context, we promote the disaster resilient farming with economic returns on flowers and tickets sold as financial resources for sustainable plantation. PBB initiatives incorporate the implementation of the best practices and toolkits with sharing local knowledge and regional resources to facilitate Livelihood Continuity Planning before or after disasters (Figs. 1 and 2).

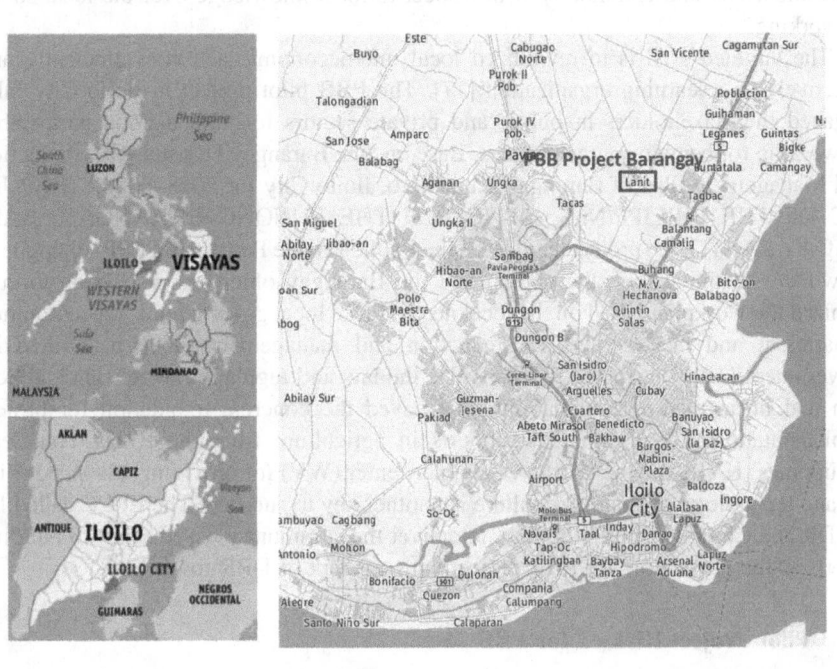

Fig. 1. Location of the pilot project at Barangay Lanit, Jaro Iloilo City, the Philippines [19]

Census date	Population	Growth rate
1990 May 1	823	–
1995 Sep 1	883	1.33% ▲
2000 May 1	1,251	7.76% ▲
2007 Aug 1	1,698	4.30% ▲
2010 May 1	2,658	17.72% ▲
2015 Aug 1	5,484	14.78% ▲

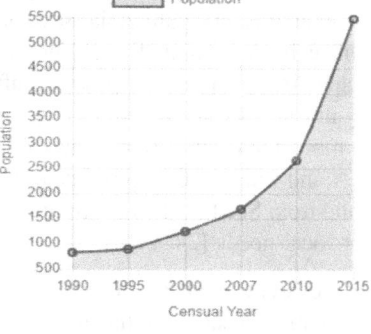

Fig. 2. Statistics of the pilot project at Barangay Lanit, Jaro Iloilo City, the Philippines [20]. Data Source: https://www.philatlas.com/visayas/r06/iloilo-city/lanit.html

To achieve the commitments of the APEC Food Security Road Map [21], we targeted the following agenda while delivering PBB in the Iloilo City:

- Enhancing self-sufficient food supply for low social status communities,
- Sharing the best practices and knowledge for APEC Resilient Community,
- Facilitating smart vegetable and flower plantation to mitigate disaster impacts and maximize sustainable economic benefits;
- Promoting on demands capacity building programs at community level;
- Empowering women leadership at all phases of implementation;
- Synergizing regional and local resources for coordinated planning and implementation,
- Conducting follow-up actions to sustain the project.

The above-mentioned project: 1) shared the best practices for APEC Resilient Community, 2) shared smart vegetable plantation; 3) promoted on demands capacity building program; 4) showcased female's contributions on Plant back better initiatives; 5) synergized regional resources for delivering assistance.

1.5   The PBB Workplan

The workplan as described below including developing Disaster Resilient Seed Kits and guiding principles focused on assisting the most vulnerable members at community level for formulating Livelihood Continuity Plan (LCP) and enhancing resilience over climate extremes and natural disaster for a sustainable food supply chain.

Home Garden Seed Kits for SMEs/MSMEs [22]

WV promotes home gardening in sub-Saharan Africa and South Asia with healthy diet gardening kits designed to improve family nutrition. The PBB project utilized the existing mechanism of the kits to deliver capacity building activities in the PBB pilot community to promote home gardening. Of a particular note, local food preferences and agronomic conditions are taken into account when seed is selected for the kits to ensure enough seeds to plant a home garden and provide a healthy diet for a family [23]. For example, in South Asia, several different kits containing seed of 7–26 vegetables have been used in Bangladesh and the Indian states of Punjab, Jharkhand, Odisha, and Assam. Most kits provide sufficient seed to plant a 6×6 m home garden to supply nutritious leafy vegetables year round. The more complex garden designs can produce more than 250 kg of vegetables per year and provide more than adequate vitamin A and vitamin C requirements for a family of four as well as supplementary protein and iron. Seed for kits is produced by partners who assemble home garden seed packs for local needs [24, 25].

Disaster Resilient Seed Kits for PBB

For more than 20 years WV has researched and developed vegetable production seed kits for farmer training programs. Meanwhile, **Disaster Relief Seed Kits** also serve an additional purpose: When natural disasters destroy food production systems, vegetables can help rebuild local food supplies and provide essential nutrition for survivors. Since 2000, WV has distributed more than 65,000 disaster seed kits through humanitarian agencies to the victims of major disasters in Africa and Asia. The kits include seed of locally adapted varieties of nutrient-rich, fast-growing vegetables, and technical information in local languages on vegetable production, food preparation and preservation methods. For facing the future challenge of climate extreme and natural disaster in the APEC region, EPCC works with WV to promote the value of PBB and develop **Disaster Resilient Seed Kits for PBB**. Vegetables selected for the kits are commonly grown in many tropical and subtropical areas with characteristics of nutritious, hardy, fast-growing with low input requirements, relatively free of pests and diseases. Each kit provides enough seed for one household to grow vegetables on 100 square meters of land to provide a balanced supply of protein and micronutrients during the initial months after a disaster. **Disaster Resilient Seed Kits for PBB** will be distributed mainly to farmers in potential–disaster-affected areas in conjunction with EPCC capacity building activity on PPP basis.

EPCC Deliver Changes in TCT School & The ATI Community [26]

EPCC delivered the PBB capacity building in the TCT Foundation Integrated School (TCT) as the Capacity Building Center, which is planned for PBB implementation and the flood-prone community including a church (the residential landownership) and 20 households (urban poverty immigration). Of particular note, the pilot project community suffered from drought while implementing the PBB project in May of 2019. This climate extreme reminded all the involved partners that the climatic impact is hampered the plantation in a great deal.

With EPCC's conviction and WV/KY's sustainable & organic agriculture skill-set, the project exercised gender balance planning with extremely limited resources. Under the good leadership of TCT principal, the PBB project blossom on people's courage, pupil and school faculty's passion, community practitioners' enthusiasm, experts' innovation and government's recognition. From the press briefing of Major's office in the Iloilo City, the PBB initiatives contribute to further promote the value of PPP collaboration on building "the City of Flowers" in the Iloilo City. The following photo showed the scope of work after the 1st and 2nd phases PBB capacity building activities as outputs:

The implementation of the PBB project followed a model similar to that developed by WV in Asia for household gardens aimed at nutrition but with contests of disaster resilience. The differences between two are: household gardens focused on fast growing highly nutritious vegetables combined with a limited selection of hardy perennial vegetables which are likely to survive and regrow quickly after the disaster.

For 1st phase of project implementation, the following activities prior to the proposed on-site assessment visit to Barangay Lanit, the City of Iloilo, the Philippines in April and August 2019 are to (Fig. 3):

Fig. 3. Workplan on the Map of School Project at Barangay Lanit, Jaro Iloilo City, the Philippines

1. **Select appropriate households and a pilot community [27].** It is important to note that rural households tend to be more vulnerable than urban households due to less access to societal resources, emergency or community services. It is important that the selected households joining the project must satisfy prerequisites and likewise for the local government. With the fully understanding, planning and assessment, the good start with the PBB plantation can be assured. The PBB initiative conducted as following plan turns out to be efficiently and effectively:

- Select households according to the following criteria:

– Vulnerable households: such as woman-led households; poor households with young children; elderly households with limited means in which to recover from a disaster

– Households generating the major income through rural activities either from production on small farming or labour on farming

– Households have a small land available for gardening, or just tenants.
– Households are willing to or actively participate in the capacity building activity for outputs and outcomes.

• Limit the number of households to a maximum of 20 within the Lanit Community

– The reasonable size for short lead time for introducing concepts of implementation.
– The households fit the appropriate selection criteria outlined above
– A local technical support availability Known-You Philippines (KYP) and The Office of Civil Defense, The Philippines (OCD) [28] in Iloilo City for implementing capacity building and resource allocation.

2. **Definition of appropriate vegetables:**

• WV and KY identify a list of vegetable species that would be suitable for Barangay Lanit, the City of Iloilo region. Through consultation and discussion with local proposed demands and needs, WV and KY assist project participants to identify what are the main fast-growing vegetables they consume on a regular basis and also explore the flowers chosen for better off the landscape and economic benefits.
• KY functions as a local source of seed supply for the proposed number of households. WV recommends the following vegetables for implementing in this project:

– Fast growing annuals for nutrition and cash crop purposes that have a crop duration between 20–40 days
– Fast growing perennials that have been identified as highly nutritious and tolerant of both dry conditions and short-term flooding.

3. **WV coordinate the local seed company, KYP**, to facilitate a technical person with knowledge of vegetables and flowers to be involved in the capacity building activities

• EPCC provided a capacity building package based on knowledge and skill-set of WV and KYP's household garden programs to implemented with rural households
• During the site visit in April, an assessment team conducted assessment on-site and discussed plans for implementing EPCC capacity building activity. The capacity building activity targeted the School, the Church, the Community households and government officials on succeeding the PBB plantation and conducted policy dialogue to team up EPCC, WV, KYP experts and pilot project involved partners including the school, the church and the households.
• Single Window of Contact – Networking the information for emergency preparedness and decision-making support through discussion amongst project partners.

The COMMUNITY Varieties

With consulting the local demand, the selection of the 1st batch for plantation are Lettuce- red & grand rapid, Sweet corn (bright jean), Cucumber (richmond & vantage), Squash (fairy) and Melon (jill). The 2nd batch are Okra-peter pan, Eggplant-fond may,

Sweetcorn - Bright jean, Sitao-Green pod kaoshiong, Lettuce-grand & red rapid, Hot pepper- KY sinigang, Cucumber- vantage, Tomato- Nina.

During implementation, the target plantation overcame the challenges of drought, severe storm and floods in 2019 which are the frequent or reoccurrence situation for the small scale agriculture nowadays. From three phase's implementation, we contribute the sharing on DRR and climate change adaptation to develop tools for smallholders and building APEC Resilient Community. We further engaged stakeholders' to brainstorming the guiding principles after on-site field assessment, implementation and capacity building activities. For real-time information flow of sharing, applied science and technology for actions in this project help formulating disaster-resilient plantation and ensure the quality harvests (Fig. 4).

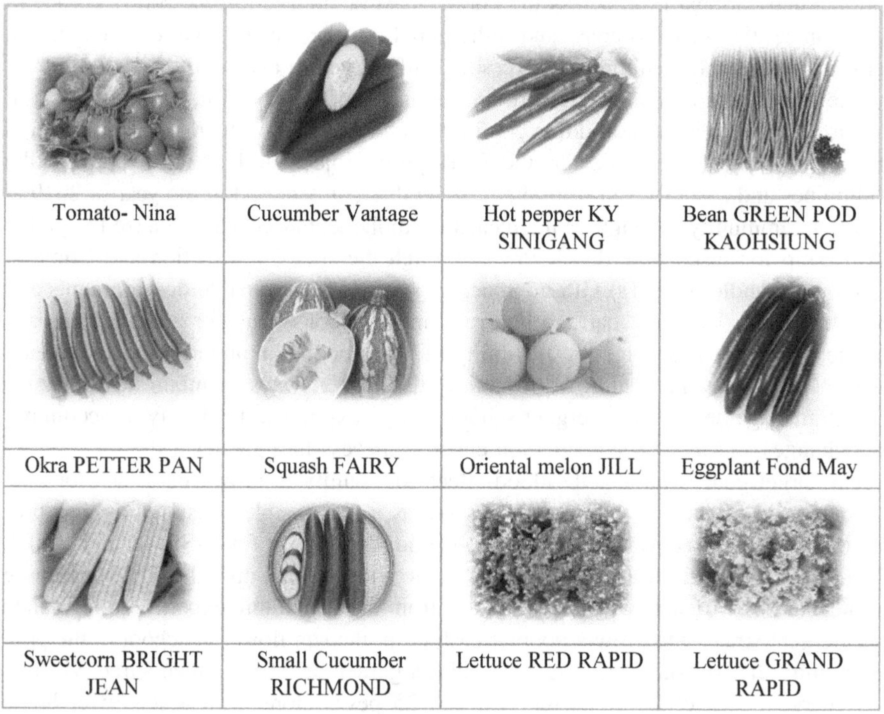

Tomato- Nina	Cucumber Vantage	Hot pepper KY SINIGANG	Bean GREEN POD KAOHSIUNG
Okra PETTER PAN	Squash FAIRY	Oriental melon JILL	Eggplant Fond May
Sweetcorn BRIGHT JEAN	Small Cucumber RICHMOND	Lettuce RED RAPID	Lettuce GRAND RAPID

Fig. 4. Vegetable Selection for plantation at the pilot community in Barangay Lanit, Jaro Iloilo City, the Philippines

2   Capacity Building

2.1   School Garden – Business Continuity Planning and Management

Enhancing Disaster Resilience through Effectiveness of PPP Model, EPCC is leading the development of PBB Gardening tool kits and Guiding Principles for APEC Resilient Community on PBB Initiatives. To facilitate the implementation of the APEC PBB,

EPCC will continue to promote food supply projects over climate extremes and natural disasters and identify challenges for providing capacity building programs through cross-fora collaboration on cross-cutting issues. From science to action, EPCC adopted smart ICTs approaches for PBB initiatives to connect APEC resilient community to improve food supply reliability in supporting the sustainability and competitiveness of business in the APEC region. EPCC promoted PBB initiatives for APEC resilient community through smart ICTs approach for real-time information connectivity.

Adopting Appropriate Public Private Partnership [29] on the Sustainable Development Goals (SDGs)

Human-centered, culture-orientated planning is the key approach to succeed the implementation of the PBB project. Self-sufficient, local demand first is the core value to sustain the project outcomes and deliverables in the long run. Partnership at global, regional and national level across the border must be engaged in the primary stage to synchronize the inconsistency and differential in the perspective of recognition, demand, deliverables, culture, resources and infrastructure availability.

The coherence of legal framework and harmony of the social networking, make it easy to achieve the goal of building confidence and moral when team up. Sun-flower is the symbolic strategic choice in the PBB pilot project. A high cash crop in the Philippines and can survived from the prolong draught occurred in the year of 2019 at the pilot community. Strengthen the means of implementation and revitalize the global partnership for sustainable development through the smart Information and Communication Technology (ICTs) GIS approach to sync with sustainable developments and to mitigate the language barrier. For reaching the consensus for short-term goals. Practical project tends to request flexibility of implementation under the force majeure event especially while dealing with natural disasters. Always maintain flexibility for change management - the emergent school garden expo. The flexibility to accommodate changes and unexpected situation ensured success in a greater deal.

The target goal is to help the flood-affect community to grow vegetables for self-sufficient and sell to the market if excessive as a responsible consumption and production for quick recovery of the Micro-economic activity for MSEMS and SMEs. However, the flood is no long a case but couple with prolong drought in the beginning of the year 2019. Hence, we take the advice from the agriculture expertise to formulate an emergent strategy to grow a popular cash crop, the sun flower at school in the pilot community. It turns out successfully to build a garden at school which attract visitors. An emergent idea of 20 pesos for visit and 25 pesos along with a sunflower home campaign sustain a miniature seeds purchasing funding to uphold the vegetable plantation following the raining season. After the sunflower harvest, it became a feasible PBB business continuity planning role model for circular economy. The emergent strategy adopted the core value of change management demonstrated the importance of flexibility while facing the uncertainty of climate extremes or natural disasters.

2.2   Empower Women and Community for Food Security on PBB Initiative

Women suffered the most at the community from the constant threat of extreme events, earthquakes, floods and natural disasters if the food supply chain interruption. The majority workforce in the rural/vulnerable areas are also women. They are critical human resource in community and the rural economy for keeping the family functioned and livelihood continuity. Facing the constraints of disaster and climate extremes that impact their productivity, we empowered women in disaster at community to develop easy 'PBB toolkits' to plant cash crops as self-sufficient nutritious foods on table and the excessive harvest trade in the market place for living. The direct beneficiaries of our outcomes include women and households at community level of developing economies.

2.3 Cultural Diversity and Disaster Resilience for Selection of Seeds for Sawing

Be a small-scale food producers and empowering gender capacity for equality to participate fully in development is critical to improving food security and solve the world hunger. Open the barrier of the limited access to the markets and services, empowering the family farmers and small-scale of production can help quick recovery after a disaster strike. Vegetables are quick harvest cash crop with nutrition. To strengthen the resilience and adaptive capacity of small-scale producers, it is important to help the disaster affected area to improve their agricultural productivity on natural resources sustainability perspective again climate extremes.

In order to strengthen the effectiveness of disaster risk reduction and resiliency of the whole society, this project will serve as a platform for sharing the best practices of PBB initiatives. For the medium-term impact, EPCC continued 1) supporting capacity building activity through smart ICTs approach to succeed a sustainable model on appropriate PPP, 2) learning the lesson for sharing on PBB project implementation as one of the best practices under APEC, 3) updating the living document "guiding principle for PBB" and 4) visiting pilot community on smart plantation for SME/MSMEs.

2.4 The Key Ingredients for the Successful Story in the Iloilo City

- **Strong Leadership** – conviction to lead for effective coordinated team efforts on the local needs and opinions. Needs driven mission can motivate the local practitioners and households as self-starters. It is critical to synergize the efforts among the stakeholders creatively while implementation in terms of engaging the whole community/society's participation in the process target on the common interests and goals.
- **Active Participation** – passion to take action to change for a better livelihood at community. The inclusive growth value is critical from sharing. Helping hands can make the world a better place. The coordinated efforts on-site contribute fruitful outputs and outcomes if constantly take turns to look out the whole process. With team efforts, we share work loading and knowledge for better harvests while implementation.
- **Determined Public Private Partnership** – collaboration on land ownerships neighborhood for vulnerable community from policy to strategy for action. Harmonized legislation for common practices at community is essential. For sustainable farming and livelihood continuity planning (LCP), it is a must to involved legal

assistance from the local government to identify the farmlands and resources availability while implementation.

- **Risk Awareness** – a multi-disciplinary approach for mitigation. For tackle climate extremes and natural disasters such as typhoon, flood and earthquakes, it is necessary to draw appropriate attention on multiple disciplines for solutions based on a new understanding of complex situations. For upgrade the local plantation skill-set on sharing dynamic disaster risk exposures, information dissemination through the information intelligence platform on smart agriculture helps risk communication.
- **Human Capacity Building** – building a learning organization for sustainable growth. Agriculture activities are labour intensive. For sustainable development toward the future, human capacity building for smart agriculture and disaster risk management through structure capacity building programs are critically important to maintain labour capacity with skill-set to gear towards the goals for LCP among the stakeholders.
- **Local Investment** – local knowledge and capacity benefit the in-time local needs and development in culture aspects. Both tangible (such as local funding and grants) and intangible (such as local knowledge and culture) are key to sustaining the long term development for PBB implementation. Reducing food miles and selling agriculture products to a more local rather than regional demography are environmental friendly approaches. Local investment from the stakeholders or business activities provide long-term community benefits in terms of satisfying in-time local needs. Local investment came from local consumer behavior (buying and selling) can self-sufficient the grass-root implementation of PBB and revitalize the local economic activities.

Meanwhile, the PBB Toolkit developed to provide for a single and easy-to-access gateway to various materials for a cross-border public private partnership to engage expertise among the EPCC, NCDR, WV, KY and APEC economies to offer best practices, guidance, capacity building, training materials and practitioners and other stakeholders in the areas of appropriate: 1) Emergency Preparedness Practices for PBB, 2) Agriculture Practices, 3) Community-based Capacity Building Practices, 4) Smart ICTs Practices and Digital Resilience, 5) Business Continuity Planning (BCP) Practices for Micro Small and Medium Enterprise (MSMEs) and Small and Medium Enterprise (SMEs), 5) LCP Practies for MSMEs, 6) Surveillance and Monitoring for In-time Support, and 7) Single Windows of Contact-Focal Point of Contact Mechanism.

3   ICTs on PBB

Synergized Capacity Among Expertise from Agriculture Technician, Disaster Manager, Community Practitioners and Government Officials for PPP on Science and Technology Sharing
Nowadays, almost everyone lives within scope of mobile-cellular networks. Coverage of mobile-cellular signals and mobile-broadband Internet has expanded rapidly. In 2018, 96% of the world population covered by third generation (3G) or higher-quality

network [3]. For the disadvantaged and at-risk population groups, it is a handy device to access innovative GIS information for risk communication through social media to take urgent action to combat climate extremes, disasters and its impacts. Smart ICTs approach help to facilitate the information intelligence networking on quality situation assessment for emergency on global synergy and partnership.

Local-Based Knowledge for Support, Grass-Root Community-Based Experience Sharing for Scenario-Based Strategy and Decision-Making Process over Resilience Community

While implementing the PBB initiative, EPCC engaged PPP policy dialogue among stakeholder of the Philippines and the expertise. The cross-border PPP built among the ATI community, the City of Iloilo, the Manila Observatory and the National Resilience Council, shortened the lead time of PBB implementation and information intelligence support for fruitful outputs and outcomes. Adopt appropriate technology approach is effective and efficient to lower the barrier of DRR scientific technology application on cost effective for easy access and maintain via the ICTs risk communications for climate/weather information. Centralized the situation assessment in EPCC and utilized the social media for situation feedback is the approach for synergy the capacity from High Developed Countries (HDCs) to Low Developed Countries (LDCs) to reduce the inequalities of development for sustainable cities and communities. It is a healthy flow to share the scientific outputs and outcomes to benefit learning organization at the pilot community for the good health and wellbeing on inclusive growth. The daily checkup and support from international expertise to the agriculture sector online became possible. The synergized capacity among expertise among agriculture technician, disaster manager, community practitioners and government officials for PPP on science and technology sharing is in operation daily to connect domestic and foreign sources to further sustain the deliverables in a long-term basis. Surfing the website to consistently look out the pilot community through social media for real time situation and feedback are critical to ensure the in-time situation assessment if needed for proactive emergency preparedness and recovery.

4 Guiding Principles for APEC Resilient Community on PBB Initiative

During implementation, we suffered from drought, severe storm and floods that required teamwork between expertise and local involvements to deliver emergency response to the dynamic situations especially for the prolong drought in 2019. In this context, the PPP is a corner stone of the PBB pilot project on team efforts as an excellent example deal with the emergencies first for sustainable growth. Thus, the project elaborated the value of EPWG's contribution in the long run. Overcome the impacts from the Mother Nature, the ATI community harvested flowers, melons and vegetables for a living for future sustainable reoccurring plantation. PPP has been highly valued and recognized by the local community and government. The plantation starts with the assistance of the Iloilo City Government and EPCC will expand in the near future for long term development.

The PBB Initiative extends grassroots support to those whose livelihoods depend on the agricultural sector and exposed to extreme weather and disasters at an economic and social level. When extreme events, typhoons or other natural disasters strike, the farmers are always hit hardest. The PBB initiative focused on "Enhancing agriculture's ability to adjust and mitigate the impact of climate change" to recover the SMEs/ MSMEs' economic activities with nutrition concept. The guiding principle aimed at providing guidance to tackle climate extremes and natural disasters and provide rapid growing global population with economic access to sufficient, safe, nutritious and quality food as well as better livelihoods of millions of rural people, mainly small farmers, particularly women on vegetable plantation (Fig. 5).

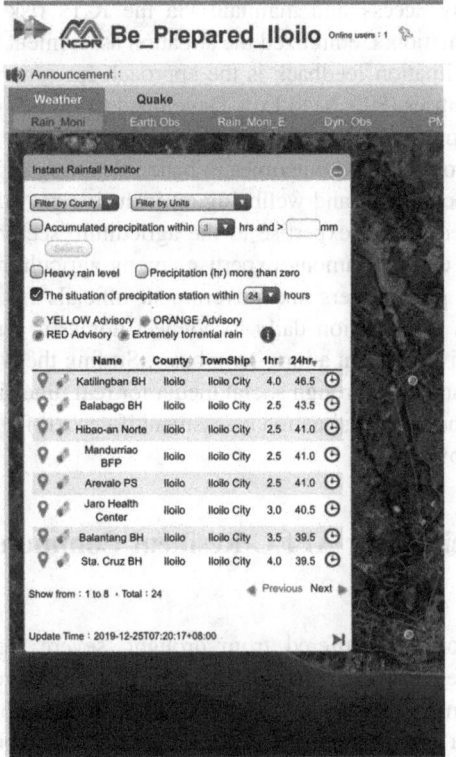

Fig. 5. Smart ICTs support on early warning of weather related disasters [30]

4.1 Strengthening Rural Development as a Place of Opportunities

To face impacts brought by natural disasters or climate extremes or food security at the community level, the PBB initiatives seek smart solutions for sustainability, inclusiveness and resilience in line with the spirit of the APEC Food Security Roadmap Towards 2020 and the UN 2030 Agenda for Sustainable Development for enhancing society's wellbeing and aims at community-based capacity building and preparedness for quick recovery of microeconomic activities through public private partnership if disasters hit. Echo to APEC Chile 2019 theme of "Connecting People, Building the Future" [31] on Sustainable Growth, Digital Society, Integration 4.0 and Women, SMEs and Inclusive Growth as well as APEC Ministers of Agriculture Joint Statement of "Towards Integrated Smart and Sustainable Food Systems" (Puerto Varas, Chile 24 August 2019 Issued by the 5th APEC Food Security Ministerial Meetings) [32] in the areas of fostering sustainable food systems and embracing emerging technologies, we seek to cooperate on strengthening PBB initiative and widely implementing better policies towards integrated, smart and sustainable food systems, public-private partnership for building APEC Resilient Community/City on the following Five Principles for APEC Resilient Community [33]:

1. Well-structured Policy Framework for Implementation

- To encourage policies that improve infrastructure, basic services and the quality of life of rural populations as well as strategies that help develop sustainable and market-based methods for added-value for promoting the integration through the PBB initiatives.
- To enhance infrastructure resilience for the economic performance, social inclusiveness and environmental sustainability through sharing best practices.
- To enable dialogue exchanges for extensive participations by key stakeholders such as community leaders, local governments, local NGOs, local experts and resource persons.

2. Applicable Financial Resilience [34]

To enhance financial resilience through innovative mechanisms in line with FMP-DRFI workplan for promoting the efforts on Disaster Risk Financing of FMP-DRFI as "Finance is a Shield in Times of Natural Disaster". Enhancing resilience to disasters became APEC priority for FMP and EPWG. EPWG promoted efficient and effective early warning systems and emergency-actionable plans or countermeasures for disaster risk reduction for years under APEC. The cross-fora collaboration synergy between FMP-DFRI and EPWG can be expected on introducing the best practices both at both economic and social level on APEC Resilient Community. With knowledge sharing in disaster risk financing from FMP, EPWG can further achieve disaster-resilient livelihoods of APEC Resilient City. For example, the pilot project in Iloilo City, limited seed grants can offer sufficient financial support to boost microeconomic activities and sustainable plantation.

3. Effective Public Private Partnership

To enhance public-private partnership on disaster resilience for PBB Initiative: Amid food production process, it requires risk understanding to build up resilience. More valuable disaster risk reduction knowledge sometimes offered by private sector. An appropriate network recommended as Network of Emergency Management Officials

(NEMO) designed for integration on infrastructure, agriculture and disaster resilience for APEC Resilient Community be as following:

- To encourage cross-fora collaborations and public private partnership to work out feasible solutions. The proposed project includes experiences and the best practices sharing on disaster risk management as well as climate change adaptation tools for smallholders and showcases handy tools for improving food security.
- To support strengthening regional cooperation with an aim at creating enabling conditions to face the challenges and leverage the opportunities brought by climate extremes to enhance resilience of our food systems to climate variability for our economies.
- To encourage the **public-private partnership with cross-fora collaborations** for food supply chain as part of disaster risk management in coping with future challenges if extreme event, natural disasters and climate change.
- To facilitate PBB **information and knowledge sharing** on best practices for enrooting food security awareness and good supply chain resilience at agricultural communities.
- To facilitate the APEC Capacity Building for Sustainable Development at APEC Resilient Communities if extreme events such as floods or drought impact.
- To intensify efforts to **mitigate impacts** of drought, flood and climate-related disasters on food production and food security.
- To boost microeconomic momentum to tackle future challenges on extreme events and climate change. PBB initiatives endorsed by EPWG for cross-fora supports from ATCWG, PPFS, PPSTI, PPWE and regional institutes to synergize the project deliverables and crosscutting outcomes. Within agendas, workshops and plans under APEC **ATCWG** and **PPFS**, the **APEC Food Security Road Map Towards 2020** and the APEC **Food Security Business Plan** (2014–2020) call for actions on cross-cutting collaboration on **disaster risk management** and **food security** issues to increase resilience to natural disaster and **global climate change**.
- To develop workplan in line with PBB toolkits for **APEC Resilient Community** on growing vegetables in the APEC disaster-prone areas.

4. Empower Human Capital and Gender Balance

- To empower women in disaster: The majority of rural or disaster community are women, children and the elderly population. PBB aimed at "Women leading capacity building" on "Home Garden" to better illustrate the important role of women in agriculture and disasters for sustainable and quality growth. To encourage the incorporation of gender into the design of the PBB initiative. Higher level of women participation in the economy is key to raising living standards and boosting economic growth in the disaster-prone areas. Recognizing the significant contribution and impact that women have in rural and coastal communities is key to success the implementation of PBB initiative.
- Leveraging associativity and enhancing food value chains and trade: Micro, small and medium enterprises (MSMEs), including small-scale farmers, indigenous peoples, and women in particular, face constraints to being competitive in food

value chains. Individually these actors may have limited capacity to negotiate and less access to the financial system, market information and new technologies, among other challenges. To strengthen their resilience and adaptive capacity, we support identifying new trading opportunities and promotion online (Online to Offline, O2O) to encourage well-functioning markets.

5. Efficient In-time Information Sharing

- Efficient Information Sharing through ICTs on best practices of value-added knowledge base on local demand for disaster-resilience food production
- To facilitate dialogues on formulating robust policies for supporting APEC cross-cutting issue and cross-fora cooperation in generating information and improving measurements; strengthening partnerships with the stakeholders; encouraging research, development and innovation, including information and communications technology (ICT); raising awareness and building capacity for APEC Resilience Community.
- **Embracing innovation, emerging technologies and digital opportunities:** Innovation, emerging technologies and digitalization are engines for sustainable productivity growth in the agriculture. To make innovation a priority, including through effective coordination with the stakeholders for appropriate adoption of new technologies.
- To digitalize agriculture impacts, identifying common approaches to promoting technology adoption, challenges and opportunities for human capital, and developing policy that targets local realities, effectively leveraging the opportunities from the digital transformation, sustainably and inclusively for digital resilience.
- To promote vegetables plantation: Vegetable are cash crops with offering quality nutrition which can help farmers in the affected area reclaim the productivity with healthier workforce.
- To incorporates real scenarios for implementation: Best practices and "Home Garden" toolkits designed with sharing local knowledge and regional resources to better fit in the real situation for planning before or after disasters. Take the example of 2019 pilot community (where is a frequent flood affected community suffered from prolong drought in 2019), the fruitful outcome of plantation activity can inspire and encourage the APEC economies to further promote food security and resilient food supply chain on PBB initiatives.
- To quick recovery after disasters – "Home Gardening". Healthier lives and more resilient livelihoods through greater diversity in what we grow and eat. Vegetables can **alleviate poverty** by creating new jobs and new sources of income for farmers and landless labourers, **improve health** by providing essential micronutrients lacking in diets, **enhance learning and working capacities of whole community through** improved diets and health, and improve the sustainability of food production practices by **diversifying cropping systems.**

5 Future Prospectives

Stocktaking the PBB project from assessment, implementation and harvests, the team efforts from grass-root support are the spine to sustain the PBB project with fruitful outcomes delivered. Among all factors assessed, women are the integral element to the health and growth of economies at community level. The PBB empowered women for strengthening the local resilience. In total, up to 56% expert and practitioners are female that demonstrates female potentials to make a change for sustainability future. The medium-term for developing the key findings from PBB initiatives are detailed as following:

- To **widely initiate projects** and **promote capacity building** on PBB disaster-resilient APEC community and encourage the **appropriate public-private partnership with cross-fora collaborations** for food supply chain as part of disaster risk management in coping with future challenges by natural disasters and climate change.
- To facilitate PBB **information and knowledge sharing** on best practices for enrooting disaster risk reduction at agricultural communities through **smart technology.**
- To widely share the PBB related publications for enhancing **APEC Resilient Communities and SMEs/MSMEs** for growing vegetables with **business continuity planning** (BCP) [35] for **food supply chain sustainability**.
- To promote adaptation countermeasures of weather related hazards on **socio-economic** impacts for inclusive and sustainable growth.
- To promote **digital preparedness** [36] for regional economic sustainability and human security.
- To empower women in disaster at agriculture and rural area with easy 'PBB toolkits'.

The future development on the PBB project will conclude here to: 1) Networking - Accumulation of Knowledge, Experience and Know-how of PBB upgrade, 2) Living PBB Community with LCP for better preparedness, 3) Updates or disseminate the involved partners for disaster information for PBB, 4) Synergies of Regional Collaborations for Human Well-being, and 5) Building APEC Resilience Partnership (ARP) Toward APEC Resilient City.

References

1. Science Alert. https://www.sciencealert.com/super-typhoon-mangkhut-north-atlantic-hurricane-florence-helene-isaac-shown-up-overnight. Accessed 01 Oct 2019
2. The USGS Earthquake Hazards Program. https://earthquake.usgs.gov/earthquakes/browse/significant.php. Accessed 01 Oct 2019
3. The Sustainable Development Goals Report 2019. https://unstats.un.org/sdgs/report/2019/The-Sustainable-Development-Goals-Report-2019.pdf. Accessed 01 Oct 2019
4. The Sendai Framework for Disaster Risk Reduction. https://www.undrr.org/implementing-sendai-framework/sendai-framework-action. Accessed 01 Oct 2019

5. United Nations Framework Convention on Climate Change. https://unfccc.int/process-and-meetings/the-paris-agreement/the-paris-agreement. Accessed 01 Oct 2019
6. Report of the Secretary-General for the World Humanitarian Summit. https://www.agendaforhumanity.org/sites/default/files/resources/2019/Jun/%5BA-70-709%5D%20Secretary-General%27s%20Report%20for%20WHS_0.pdf. Accessed 01 Oct 2019
7. Habitat III Issue Papers. http://habitat3.org/wp-content/uploads/Habitat-III-Issue-Paper-17_Cities-and-Climate-Change-and-Disaster-Risk-Management-2.0.pdf. Accessed 01 Oct 2019
8. Filicetti, J.: Project Management Dictionary. PM Hut, 20 August 2007. https://project-management.com/pmo-and-project-management-dictionary/. Accessed 01 Oct 2019/16 Nov 2009
9. The APEC Emergency Preparedness Capacity Building Center. https://www.apec-epcc.org/. Accessed 01 Oct 2019
10. EPWG 03 2017A - Capacity Building and Emergency Preparedness for Sustainable Development at Agricultural Communities through "Plant Back Better" (PBB) Initiatives PBB Toolkits
11. APEC Website. Building APEC Resilience Partnership (ARP) Toward APEC Resilient City. https://aimp2.apec.org/sites/PDB/Lists/Proposals/DispForm.aspx?ID=2152last. Accessed 01 Oct 2019
12. Lee, Y., Watanabe, K., Li, W.-S.: Exploring the strategic approaches in support to disaster risk governance for public and private partnership. In: Proceedings of the 23rd Pacific Science Congress (PSC-23), p. 323 (2016)
13. The World Vegetable Center. https://avrdc.org/. Accessed 01 Oct 2019
14. Known You Seed Co., Ltd. http://www.knownyou.com/en_index.jsp. Accessed 01 Oct 2019
15. The National Science and Technology Center for Disaster Reduction. https://ncdr.nat.gov.tw/oriNCDR/home.aspx?WebSiteID=873f5b27-b86d-4d5c-a356-c369768bffe9. Accessed 01 Oct 2019
16. Lee, Y., Watanabe, K., Li, W.-S.: Public private partnership operational model-a conceptual study on implementing scientific-evidence-based integrated risk management at regional level. J. Disaster Res. 14(4), 667–677 (2019)
17. Harvard Business Publishing. https://hbr.org/1993/07/building-a-learning-organization. Accessed 01 Oct 2019
18. Iloilo City Government FB. https://www.facebook.com/iloilocitygov/?_tn_=%2Cd%2CP-R&eid=ARAUuajA_yapeSGvZPLh_H5RCnUpZv4QQz_D15W_2XQ4UEzDrYa-9lJEhzrgvYUsvkBmLqrUxR4I9jRF. Accessed 01 Oct 2019
19. Location of the pilot project at Barangay Lanit, Jaro Iloilo City, the Philippines. www.google.com/map. Accessed 01 Oct 2019
20. PhilAtlas. https://www.philatlas.com/visayas/r06/iloilo-city/lanit.html. Accessed 01 Oct 2019
21. APEC Website. Food Security Road Map Towards 2020 and the APEC Food Security Business Plan (2014–2020). http://mddb.apec.org/Documents/2014/PPFS/PPFS/14_ppfs_008.pdf. Accessed 01 Oct 2019
22. World Vegetable Center, Home garden seed kits: a sustainable business model. https://avrdc.org/home-garden-seed-kits-a-sustainable-business-model/. Accessed 01 Oct 2019
23. World Vegetable Center, Entrepreneurs are quick to grasp the value of packing vegetable seed in small quantities for home use. https://avrdc.org/?s=Entrepreneurs+are+quick+to+grasp+the+value+of+packing+vegetable+seed+in+small+quantities+for+home+use. Accessed 01 Oct 2019
24. World Vegetable Center, Home garden seed kits pioneered by AVRDC – The World Vegetable Center four years ago in Jharkhand in eastern India have now stimulated entrepreneurs to supply growing demand for the kits. Accessed 01 Oct 2019

25. World Vegetable Center, Seed Kits. https://avrdc.org/seed/seed-kits/. Accessed 01 Oct 2019
26. FB Tiu Cho Teg-Ana Ros Foundation Integrated School. https://www.facebook.com/pages/ Tiu-Cho-Teg-Ana-Ros-Foundation-Integrated-School/390453294299833. Accessed 01 Oct 2019
27. APEC Website. Guiding principle on selecting a voluntary pilot community for Plant Back Better (PBB). https://aimp2.apec.org/sites/PDB/Lists/Proposals/DispForm.aspx?ID=2152. Accessed 01 Oct 2019
28. Iloilo City Disaster Risk Reduction and Management Office FB. https://www.facebook.com/ IloiloCityDRRMO/. Accessed 01 Oct 2019
29. Lee, Y.: Enhancing Disaster Resilience Through Public Private Partnership: From Collaborations, Integration to Practices for Business Continuity. https://nitech.repo.nii.ac. jp/?action=pages_view_main&active_action=repository_view_main_item_detail&item_id= 6467&item_no=1&page_id=13&block_id=21. Accessed 01 Oct 2019
30. NCDR, EPCC Website: BE_Prepared Illoilo. Accessed 01 Oct 2019
31. APEC Website. APEC Chile 2019 theme of "Connecting People, Building the Future" on Sustainable Growth, Digital Society, Integration 4.0 and Women, SMEs and Inclusive Growth as well as APEC Ministers of Agriculture Joint Statement. https://www.apec.org/ Meeting-Papers/Leaders-Declarations/2019/2019_aelm. Accessed 01 Oct 2019
32. APEC Website. Towards Integrated Smart and Sustainable Food Systems. https://www.apec. org/Meeting-Papers/Sectoral-Ministerial-Meetings/Food-Security/2019_food_security. Accessed 01 Oct 2019
33. APEC Website. EPWG 03 2017A - Capacity Building and Emergency Preparedness for Sustainable Development at Agricultural Communities through "Plant Back Better" (PBB) Initiatives Completion Report. https://aimp2.apec.org/sites/PDB/Lists/Proposals/ DispForm.aspx?ID=2152. Accessed 01 Oct 2019
34. APEC Website. Finance is a Shield in Times of Natural Disaster. https://www.apec.org/ Press/Features/2019/0613_risk. Accessed 01 Oct 2019
35. Lee, Y., Watanabe, K., Li, W.S.: Enhancing regional disaster resilient trade and investment – business continuity management. In: Murayama, Y., Velev, D., Zlateva, P. (eds.) ITDRR 2017. IAICT, vol. 516, pp. 108–122. Springer, Cham (2019). https://doi.org/10.1007/978-3- 030-18293-9_10
36. Lee, Y., Watanabe, K., Li, W.S.: Enhancing regional digital preparedness on natural hazards to safeguard business resilience in the Asia-Pacific. In: Murayama, Y., Velev, D., Zlateva, P., Gonzalez, J. (eds.) ITDRR 2016. IAICT, vol. 501, pp. 170–182. Springer, Cham (2017). https://doi.org/10.1007/978-3-319-68486-4_14

An Earth Coordinate System for Earthquake Forecasting Using SLHGN

Benny Benyamin Nasution[✉], Rahmat Widia Sembiring,
Muhammad Syahruddin, Nursiah Mustari,
Abdul Rahman Dalimunthe, Nisfan Bahri, Berta br Ginting,
and Zulkifli Lubis

Politeknik Negeri Medan, Medan, Indonesia
benny.nasution@polmed.ac.id

Abstract. An attempt for an earthquake forecasting has been challenged by the current earth coordinate system. The latest architecture of mHGN which is called SLHGN requires that the observed locations must be spread out regularly, that is within regular grid-like distances. Such a requirement would not be fulfilled, as within the current earth coordinate system a longitude-difference would produce different distances. The extreme examples are locations in equator compared to those on the earth poles. Therefore, an earth coordinate system has been developed to support the ongoing earthquake forecasting technology using SLHGN. Additionally, two important positive issues related to this earth coordinate system have been developed, they are: 1) each location is not represented through two-value (longitude and latitude), but only a single value. This value does not represent a point but an area; 2) the conversion of this earth coordinate system to the x-y Cartesian System requires no angular formulas, which is therefore fast. These issues have given positive support to the SLHGN in forecasting earthquakes. Although the accuracy and the performance are not yet ready to be analyzed properly, because local weather data at the time of an earthquake occurrence is not always available, the characteristics of the SLHGN experiments show very promising results

Keywords: Hierarchical Graph Neuron (HGN) · Multidimensional Hierarchical Graph Neuron (mHGN) · Single Layer Hierarchical Graph Neuron (SLHGN) · Natural disaster forecasting · Earthquake forecasting

1 Introduction

Despite some pessimistic opinions, there are still many researchers who are undertaking research on earthquake forecasting or predicting. The usual reasons of such pessimistic opinions among others are due to three obvious conditions. First: the location of an epicentre is changing, second: locations of faults are also changing, third: various assumed precursors have never been proven. The other important issues that also need to be discussed further are that most approaches that have worked on the ground motions and electromagnetic fields have never come up with proven formula.

Y. Murayama et al. (Eds.): ITDRR 2019, IFIP AICT 575, pp. 107–118, 2020.
https://doi.org/10.1007/978-3-030-48939-7_10

It is therefore quite acceptable that those researchers do not believe that the earthquake is predictable.

Some other problems that hinder the analysis is that the structure of SLHGN requires that the locations of measurements should be like a grid. It means that all the points of the measurement locations should be distributed evenly. Such a requirement would become more and more difficult when the observation takes place in the area of the poles of the earth. The reason to this is that the longitude value of either poles goes to a singularity. The other thing that also needs to be discussed further is that it is very unlikely to forecast an earthquake on particular coordinate (a point) on the earth. The more logical strategy would be that the forecasting would produce a coordinate of an area on the earth rather than a point. However, the current coordinate system does not have ways to represent the coordinate of a particular area. So, for our research we need to develop another coordinate system that would be useful for SLHGN and also for other earthquake researchers.

The following diagrams show that many researchers have difficulties to determine the coordinate of particular area on the earth (Fig. 1).

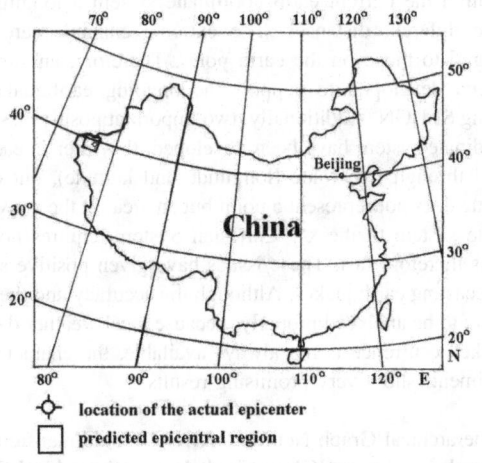

Fig. 1. Researchers focus on an area, not a point [1]

Some researchers also propose a grid-like measurement method. The following diagrams shows that.

Originally, an earth coordinate system was proposed for the first time in 1866 [4, 5]. Following that, a more precise coordinate system utilizing satellites has then been introduced in the 80 s. Until now, such a coordinate system is the only coordinate system that people are using worldwide. Within the system, each coordinate actually consists of three values, they are: latitude, longitude, and altitude. But, only latitude and longitude are required when a coordinate is on the earth surface.

In fact, the world is an oblate spheroid [4]. It means that it is difficult to calculate the distance between two points on the earth surface precisely using the usual coordinate system, as the area that makes the earth oblate is not publicly known.

The difficulty would increase when people need to work with distances on the earth surface. There are several algorithms available to be used to calculate a distance based on coordinates as parameters, but there is no appropriate algorithm to calculate coordinates based on distances as parameters (Figs. 2 and 3).

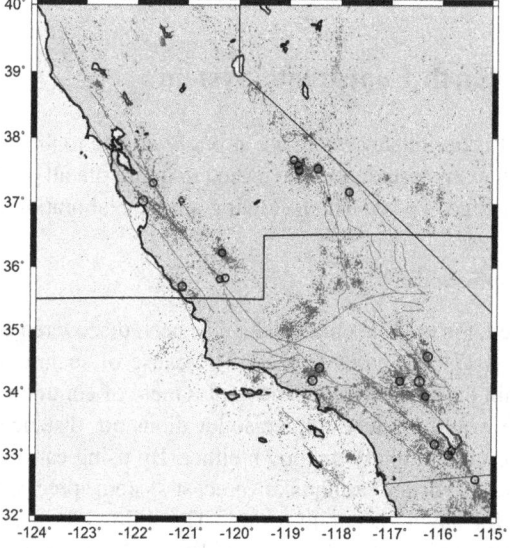

Fig. 2. So many coordinates need to be represented in the analysis [2]

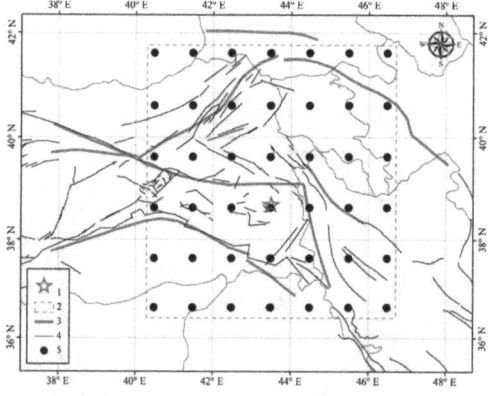

Fig. 3. Researchers propose grid-like measurement points [3]

The same difficulty will be apparent when earth coordinate system needs to be incorporated into an earthquake forecasting system using Single Layer Hierarchical Graph Neuron (SLHGN). The architecture of SLHGN requires that the positions of all neurons have to build a grid-like structure. Additionally, the earthquake forecasting system should be capable of being deployed on all parts of the earth surface, including those on both earth poles. To deal with those problems another coordinate system has been developed. This system is more appropriate to be incorporated with the ongoing earthquake forecasting system using SLHGN. Although more and thorough tests are still required, results taken from previous tests and analysis have shown promising capabilities.

2 Problems of Earth Coordinate System

The problems of earth coordinate system are strongly related to the problems within the earth itself. Although many researchers have tried to figure out all of those problems [6], the results are not satisfactory yet. The following are the elaboration of those problems.

2.1 The Oblate Spheroid

As already mentioned, the earth is oblate. This has been discovered by researchers who work with cosmology [7] and earth science. The cause of such a shape is due to the unknown force within the solar system. The deployment of common coordinate system on an oblate surface would produce imprecise locations nor distances. The exact areas of the oblate positions are publicly unknown either. By using earth surface, coordinate would be more precise. For an earthquake forecast system, precise locations and distances are essential for having accurate results. The following is an example how the oblate surface of earth inner core hinders researchers in having precise calculations for inner core of the earth (Fig. 4).

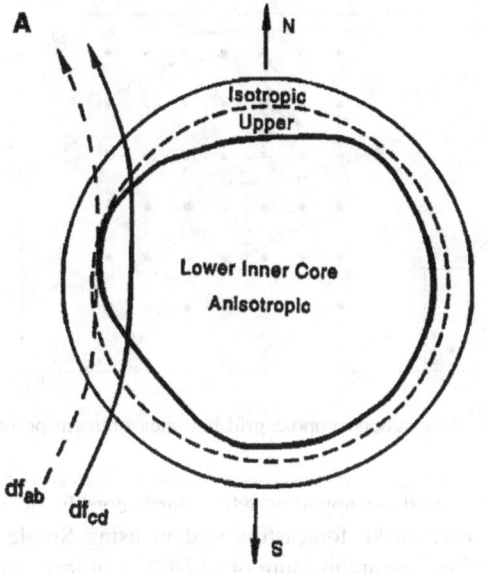

Fig. 4. The Oblate shape of earth inner core [8]

2.2 The Rotation and the Rotation Axis

The rotation axis is another problem within an earth that would affect the coordinate system. First, it is not clear what the cause of earth spinning is. When the cause of it is known, researchers would be more confident with analyzing the coordinate, since precise coordinate is important to measure correct time. Second, the spinning time is not entirely constant. The spinning time would be important to measure the time-series events that would lead to the discover patterns, for example earthquake patterns. Third, the spinning axis is not stable. Researchers have reported that the axis shifts (precession) and vibrates (perturbation). When the axis is not stable [9], then the poles have different positions either. The following figure shows the phenomenon (Fig. 5).

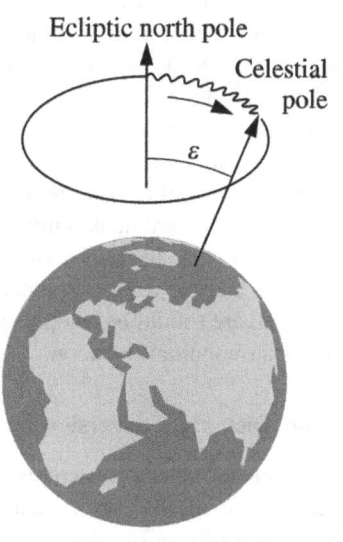

Fig. 5. The precession and perturbation of the earth axis [10]

2.3 Magnet Axis of the Earth

The planet's (earth) magnet field is generated within the core [8]. It is a result of thermal and chemical reaction between the core and its mantle. The substance between the outer core and the mantle is fluid. The magnet field is very important as it together with electric field builds the electromagnetic field that influence the earth rotation [8].

Again, based on long time measurements the axis of the magnet field is not constant either. It changes dynamically. Not only the axis, the rotation speed of inner core is not the same as the rotation speed of the mantle, sometimes faster sometimes slower. Due to fact that the magnet axis and the rotation axis of the earth are not stable, the calculation and the measurement using rotation axis and magnet axis are not very accurate. It is not surprising that the values of latitude and longitude, that are determined by GPS system using satellite, are not based on instrument measurements on the surface. Additionally, the accuracy of the coordinate will be within 100 m if the coordinate is provided by the unpaid GPS system, and the accuracy will be within 10 m if the coordinate is provided by the paid GPS system.

2.4   Malfunction of GPS Components

Until now, it is not common that people know the coordinate of a place or building. Only particular places such as airports and train stations have their coordinates been determined. Such a coordinate in those areas and buildings is not published broadly. The information about the coordinate is usually established through a metal plate in front of a building.

There are some questions related to the current coordinate system that need to be addressed. What is the benefit of knowing the coordinate of a place or a building? Is it possible for people without using GPS components to pinpoint a building if its coordinate is given? Can a GPS system—with 100 m accuracy—be used to measure land borders? What would happen to a GPS system when the connected satellites have troubles? What if the base stations on the earth surface have troubles as well? Would people still be able to determine or to calculate the coordinate?

All the answers of the above questions are very important for handling disasters such as earthquakes. They are also important for people who need to be aware of those during a disaster. For instance, during an earthquake, infrastructures are the first items that will be destructed, or even destroyed. In such a situation accurate coordinate is essential during recovery processes and for work coordination. Despite no equipment can be used during recovery state, there should be a sophisticated approach that can be utilised to find the coordinate of an important location.

2.5   Area and Coordinate for Distance Conversion and Vice Versa

The other problem in the current coordinate system is that it only generates the coordinate of a point on the surface of the earth. There is no option the current coordinate system can generate a coordinate of an area. For an earthquake forecaster like SLHGN it is difficult to obtain earthquake related data on an exact location, because the hit epicentre vary. Seismic data shows that earthquakes occur in particular areas, which are normally in areas of a fault. Using SLHGN, an area of the previous earthquake area should have data that does not describe a point, but an area. Therefore, the more suitable coordinate system for SLHGN is the one that can represent an area.

Not only that such a coordinate system should be able to represent an area, but it should also be easy to be used for converting a distance using the coordinate system. The conversion capability is required, because the SLHGN should have a grid-like structure, in which the distance between points (two coordinate data) plays a big role. Through various algorithm, the current coordinate system can be used for converting two points of coordinates to a distance, but unfortunately not the other way around.

3   Earthquake Forecasting Using SLHGN

SLHGN is the latest version of its predecessors of pattern recognizers. They are HGN, and mHGN. There are already several pattern recognition related problems that have been solved using SLHGN. As some problems depend on the sequence of data appearance, some of the implementations have utilized time-series data. As already mentioned, earthquake data is an example of time-series data. The convincing result of the previous pattern recognizer using time-series data indicates that the earthquake forecaster using SLHGN would produce convincing result as well. The description of HGN and mHGN can be found in [11–15].

3.1   Another Coordinate System

The beginning stage when developing this coordinate system is finding shapes and the structure that can cover the surface of the earth evenly. Based on mathematical analysis, only the combination of pentagons and hexagons will be the answer. The lowest number of them are: 12 pentagons and 20 hexagons. This combination is the same as of the one we have known for a long time, that is a football (soccer ball) (Fig. 6).

Fig. 6. A football consists of 12 pentagons and 20 hexagons

When required, each hexagon can be divided into 4 small hexagons and each pentagon can be divided into 1 pentagon and 2.5 hexagons. The following shows the divisions (Fig. 7).

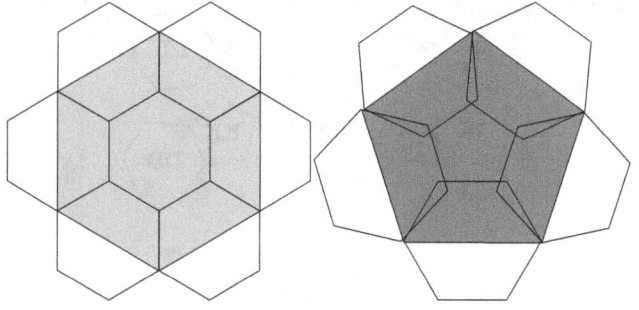

Fig. 7. The division of a hexagon and a pentagon

After dividing each pentagon and each hexagon, the number of hexagons will be $20 \times 4 + 12 \times 2.5 = 110$, and the number of pentagons remains the same, that is 21. In total, there are 122 faces on the surface of the ball. The following is the Fig. 8.

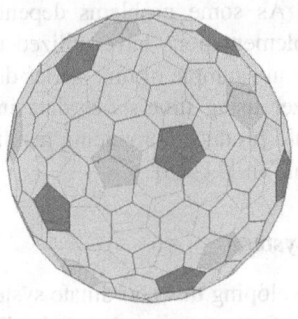

Fig. 8. A ball consists of 12 pentagons and 110 hexagons

The next step is to determine the position of a reference point. In this case, the coordinate latitude = 0 and longitude = 0 has been chosen as the reference point. In the following figure, the reference point is the corner between shape A, shape B, and shape C. To help identifying which pentagon or hexagon is under scrutiny, identities have been given to each shape. The shape AA is exactly on the other side of the ball if it is observed from the shape A. The shape BB is exactly on the other side of the ball if it is observed from the shape B, and so forth (Fig. 9).

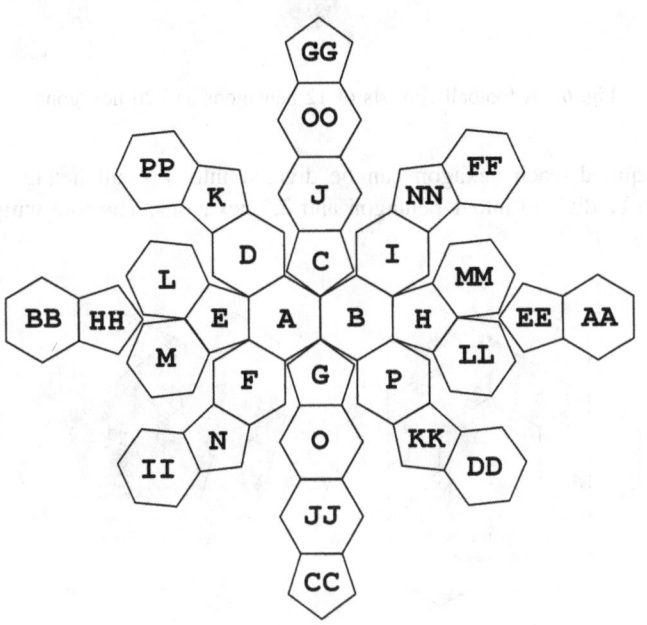

Fig. 9. Faces of the football lies on a flat surface

After all the shapes have been labeled with identities, an algorithm needs to be developed that will generate a coordinate for any face of the surface. The coordinate will be calculated from the reference point. By doing so, there will be three possible directions from the reference point. Each direction has an identity, either 1, or 2, or 3. After the first direction from the reference point, the next direction can only be 1, 2, 3, 5, or 6. The following figure shows those possible directions. The red color arrows would build all the directions to the destination before entering a face of the destination. When the face of the destination has been reached, the direction will be one of the blue color arrows (Fig. 10).

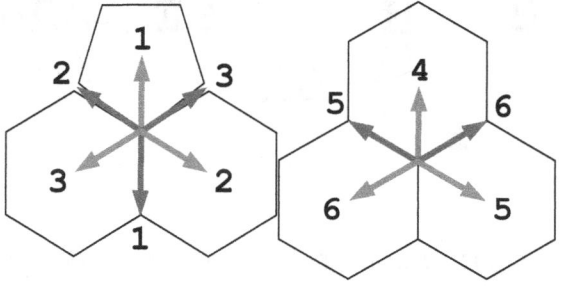

Fig. 10. All the possible directions (red) before entering (blue) (Color figure online)

The coordinate will look like the following: **Tabcdefghi+jklmno…**

The letter T means type, it can be 1, 2, 3, etc. The type shows which version of the ball the coordinate refers to. For the football, the version would be 1. The other letters a, b, until i shows the identity of the direction starting from the reference point. The letter j shows the direction to the middle of the shape of the destination (blue colour arrow). The letter k shows the area of triangle within the face. If the shape is a pentagon, the value of j would be: 0 till 4, whereas if the shape is a hexagon, the value of j: 0 till 5. The following figure shows the division of the face into triangles (Fig. 11).

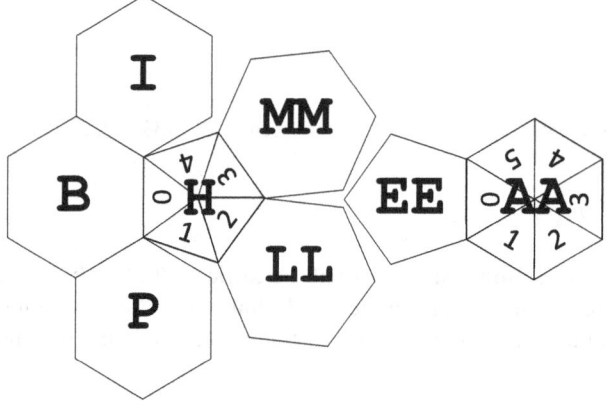

Fig. 11. Divisions of a face into triangles

When the destination area is smaller than a triangle of a face, then a triangle can be divided into four smaller triangles. The process continues until the appropriate area has been reached (Fig. 12).

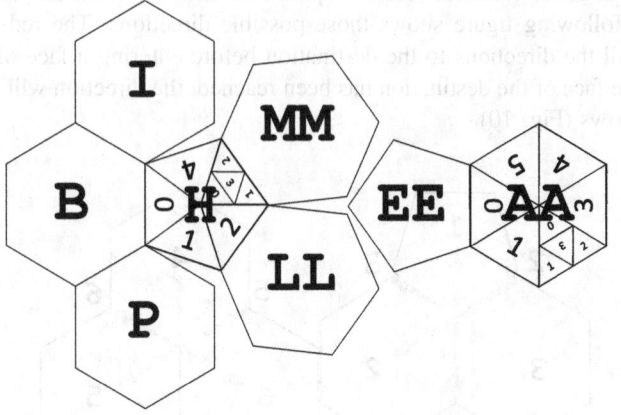

Fig. 12. Divisions of a triangle into four triangles

The following figure shows some coordinates of particular faces (Fig. 13).

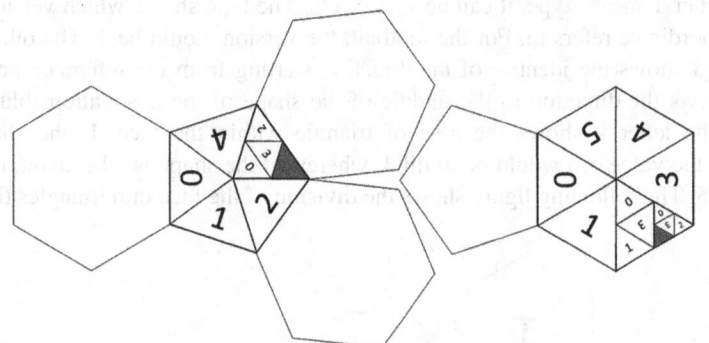

Fig. 13. The coordinate for red: 131 + 131, for green: 13122133 + 2221 (Color figure online)

4   Further Steps

The following are the further steps that will be carried out after the coordinate system has been finalized. The steps are basically dealing with other problems, such as the scarcity of earthquake data, how the forecasting is prepared, and remaining issues.

4.1 Collecting Data Strategies

Although additional and various data will be required, we are lucky that the seismic data of earthquakes happening from around the world are recorded and publicly available. The data will then be collected according to the time of the occurrence, for instance every one hour, every day, every month, every year. Collecting data based on the time of the occurrence would be known as time-series-data. This time series data of strong earthquakes will be prepared as patterns that will be fed to SLHGN. Weather-related data will also be collected, including various data related to galaxy components (Fig. 14).

```
A    →  1+3
B    →  1+2  .
C    →  1+1
G    →  11+1
D    →  12+3
E    →  121+1
F    →  113+2
J    →  122+3 or 133+2
O    →  1133+2 or 1122+3
AA   →  13122122+3 or 13122133+2 or 13121312+3
BB   →  12133133+2 or 12133122+3 or 12131213+2
```

Fig. 14. Some samples of coordinates

4.2 Forecasting Strategies

The common earthquake forecasting approach researchers have develop is named as now-casting. The time window of now-casting is short, for instance: 20 min, or up to an hour. Although this approach has been utilised for long time, such earthquake now-casting has not yet produced satisfactory results. The number of casualties and trau-matized people is still high. Not only now-casting, other earthquake technologies have produced location and the time, they are not yet able to provide data about when? how long? which part? More specific and detailed data of an earthquake is important for many people.

4.3 Remaining Forecasting Issues

Due to the devastation caused by an earthquake, important data such as weather data before, during, and after an earthquake is often very difficult to be gathered. For this research, historical data must be gathered from the location of the affected area. Temporal and spatial data is important for an earthquake forecasting through a pattern recognition. The remaining steps that need to be worked out in the future are: 1) How can time series data related to earthquakes build patterns? 2) How can seismic and weather data be fed to SLHGN architecture? 3) How can it be proven that it is effective?

References

1. Li, J.Z., Bai, Z.Q., Chen, W.S., Xia, Y.Q., Liu, Y.R., Ren, Z.Q.: Strong earthquakes can be predicted: a multidisciplinary method for strong earthquake prediction. Nat. Hazards Earth Syst. Sci. **3**(1), 703–712 (2003)
2. Holliday, J.R., Rundle, J.B., Tiampo, K.F., Turcotte, D.L.: Using earthquake intensities to forecast earthquake occurrence times. Nonlinear Process. Geophys. **13**(1), 585–593 (2006)
3. Mojarab, M., Kossobokov, V., Memarian, H., Zare, M.: An application of earthquake prediction algorithm M8 in eastern Anatolia at the approach of the 2011 Van earthquake. J. Earth Syst. Sci. **124**(5), 1047–1062 (2015)
4. Vleux, B.E.: Distributed Hydrologic Modeling Using GIS. Kluwer Academic Publishers, Oklahoma (2001)
5. Dutton, G.H.: A Hierarchical Coordinate System for Geoprocessing and Cartography. Springer, Heidelberg (1999). https://doi.org/10.1007/BFb0011617
6. Harvey, F.: A Primer of GIS: Fundamental Geographic and Cartographic. The Guilford Press, New York (2008)
7. Biari, P.D.: Cosmology and the Early Universe. CRC Press, Boca Raton (2018)
8. Dehant, V., Creager, K., Karato, S.-I., Zatman, S.: Earth's Core: Dynamics, Structure, Rotation. American Geophysical Union, Washington, DC (2003)
9. Lambeck, K.: The Earth's Variable Rotation: Geophysical Causes and Consequences. Combridge University Press, New York (2005)
10. Karttunen, H., Kröger, P., Oja, H., Poutanen, M., Donner, K.J.: Fundamental Astronomy. Springer, Heidelberg (2017). https://doi.org/10.1007/978-3-662-53045-0
11. Nasution, B.B., Khan, A.I.: A hierarchical graph neuron scheme for real-time pattern recognition. IEEE Trans. Neural Netw. **19**, 212–229 (2008)
12. Nasution, B.B.: Towards real time multidimensional hierarchical graph neuron (mHGN). In: The 2nd International Conference on Computer and Information Sciences 2014 (ICCOINS 2014), Kuala Lumpur, Malaysia (2014)
13. Nasution, B.B., et al.: Realtime weather forecasting using multidimenssional hierarchical graph neuron (mHGN). In: The 16th International Conference on Neural Networks (NN 2015), Rome, Italy (2015)
14. Nasution, B.B., et al.: Forecasting natural disasters of tornados using mHGN. In: Murayama, Y., Velev, D., Zlateva, P., Gonzalez, J. (eds.) ITDRR 2016. IFIPAICT, vol. 501, pp. 155–169. Springer, Cham (2017). https://doi.org/10.1007/978-3-319-68486-4_13
15. Nasution, B.B., et al.: Weather data handlings for tornado recognition using mHGN. In: Murayama, Y., Velev, D., Zlateva, P. (eds.) ITDRR 2017. IFIPAICT, vol. 516, pp. 36–54. Springer, Cham (2019). https://doi.org/10.1007/978-3-030-18293-9_5

ImpactMap: A Collaborative Environment to Support Impact Projection of Complex Decision

Juliana Baptista dos Santos França[1]([⊠]), André Viana Tardelli[2],
Raffael Siqueira de Souza[2], Angélica Fonseca da Silva Dias[2],
and Marcos Roberto da Silva Borges[2,3]

[1] Federal Rural University of Rio de Janeiro (UFRRJ), Seropédica, Brazil
julibsf@gmail.com
[2] Federal University of Rio de Janeiro (UFRJ), Rio de Janeiro, Brazil
andretardelli@gmail.com, raffael.siqueira94@gmail.com,
{angelica.dias,mborges}@ppgi.ufrj.br
[3] TECNUN, University of Navarra, Donostia/San Sebastián, Spain

Abstract. In emergency domain, specialists must make complex decisions to solve problems. Complex decisions are characterized as a complex dynamic system composed of interrelated variables. Complex decisions are made up of actions, and their complexity arises from the surrounding environment, including the context and the behaviors of the individuals involved. It is difficult to isolate the elements that influence such a decision. These decisions lead to unpredictable impacts, causing the need to deal with impacts mitigation in the earlier phases of the decision process and the emergency management cycle. To reach a consensus and solve complex decision problems, collaborative strategies are being used. The general knowledge and different experiences, acquired from the experts through collaborative approaches, is crucial to identify and discuss the impacts (consequences) of decisions actions in a broader way. This paper presents ImpactMap approach, a collaborative environment that allows exchange of ideas and perspectives to discuss and project impacts of complex decisions. This research was evaluated in an emergency simulation and the results achieved showed that this research approach is able to create an interactive environment and supports the impact projection needs of a decision team.

Keywords: Complex decisions · Emergency management · Impact projection · Collaborative decision-making

1 Introduction

Emergency management is a discipline that deals with risk. Risk represents a broad range of issues and includes a diverse set of players and the necessity to discuss the impacts of their actions on the environment. Emergence management is concerned to the security of everyone and should be consider in everyday situations, not only in disasters situation [1]. According to [2], the emergency management is characterized as the entire rescue planning and intervention process to reduce the impact of emergencies, as well as

Y. Murayama et al. (Eds.): ITDRR 2019, IFIP AICT 575, pp. 119–134, 2020.
https://doi.org/10.1007/978-3-030-48939-7_11

response and recovery measures to mitigate significant social, economic and environmental consequences for the community.

Emergency management should be comprehensive, progressive and not just reactive. Its process should include risk and impact analysis, besides need to consider all phases of the emergency cycle, prioritize actions to minimize present and future impacts on the scenario [3]. Good emergency management should always consider the impact of decisions made on the environment and on the lives reached or attainable.

Within the emergency cycle, there will always be decision making ranging from a high-level individual to a field responder who needs to decide within seconds due to the present risks. In the occurrence of a disaster, specialists, volunteers and government agencies do their best to supply quick and effective responses to the dwelling problem that immediately arises [4]. In such scenario complex decisions are present, and in this research, the definition of complex decision is based on Naturalistic Decision-Making [5] because it describes how decision-makers work in real life problems [6, 7]. Besides it, collaborative aspects are also present and act as resources to support decision-making during emergency management through communication, cooperation and coordination [8] actions.

Decisions with high complexity can be understood as a complex dynamic system [9]. Complex decisions are composed of actions, and those deal with uncertainty [10]. Their impacts (consequences) are interdependent, and the environment in which they exist generates constant change in the decision [11].

The analysis of impact projection of complex decisions is a way to minimize unexpected consequences [3, 12] inside an emergency management, after the decision taken. To enable a broader share of exchanged information, it is necessary to establish a collaborative interaction between decision-makers and specialists in an environment suited for it.

To support decision-makers to analyze complex decisions and project its futures impacts, a research was conducted for the development of an approach materialized into ImpactMap technological environment. Based on fundamentals discussed in [3, 12, 13], this environment is the first version of a collaborative and virtual tool where decision-makers can be part of a group and discuss, analyze and project impacts still in the planning phase of a decision making process. According to [14], collaborative initiatives support decision making process during an emergency response situation.

The first version of ImpactMap proposes also a different visualizations of projection information such as maps, textual descriptions and graphics. Therefore, this tool allows the development of collaborative maps along with communication resources such as instant messages and videoconferences. This research main goal is an approach to support decision makers project complex decision impacts in the environment, especially considering emergency domains. This goal will attend the phases mitigation and preparedness of emergency management cycle.

In literature, is hard to find works that discuss the impact of a complex decision before the decision's execution in an emergency domain. Based on these arguments, this research will provide a technological and interactive environment able to share ideas, points of view and experiences, supporting decision-makers groups to structure their thoughts.

If a collaborative environment that supports impact projection of complex decision is available, decision-makers will be able to project impact maps, making their thoughts and experiences externalized in a structured way. Furthermore, it is expected that this environment promotes further interactions between decision-makers. To evaluate this work, a simulation was made based on a real-life emergency problem, and groups of experienced decision-makers conducted the impact projection using the ImpactMap environment.

This paper is structured through five sections. Section 2 presents related concepts and work. Section 3 presents the ImpactMap approach with its fundamentals, functions and characteristics. Following it, Sect. 4 presents the research evaluation and Sect. 5 presents and discusses the results achieved. To finish this paper, Sect. 6 presents our conclusions highlights the goals achieved and the limitations of this research.

2 Related Concepts and Works

2.1 Decision Impacts Investigation

The word Impact is understood as the measure of tangible and intangible consequences of something upon another. According to Hammond [15], to achieve intelligent choices, it is necessary to compare the merits of the known alternatives, assessing how well each one satisfies the decision's fundamental goal, and analyze the consequences of each decision executed. Some authors defend the possibility to analyze the impact of a decision implemented through its process monitoring. However, it is necessary to wait on the occurrence of the decisions actions' impact to introduce solutions for the damage or improvements on the environment and its components.

It is possible to find on literature other works that support an impact analysis beyond inference and quantitative results. Others discuss that the decision impact is still at the beginning of decision analyses – like those on the decision-planning phase [16]. However, most research in this area does not highlights details about how effectively the impact is projected in practice, not showing how to systematize these projections [17–19]. Most of the authors deal with impacts projected in a subjective way. That is why complex domain had shown difficulty in anticipating the secondary effect of decision actions. As was discussed in this section, project impact of complex decisions is an action performed by decision makers to minimize unexpected consequences after the decision implementation.

Regarding emergency domain, tools to support projected impacts usually use geographic information systems to combine the relevant data and overlay the impact of the disaster [20]. Regarding this combination, it is possible to identify population, infrastructure and resources affected by the disaster.

2.2 Collaborative Decision Making

The concept of collaboration considers that two or more individuals working together can reach an equilibrium situation [21]. In it, ideas can be exchanged between the participants of the group, generating new knowledge fruits of the collective work.

In contrast to the task-sharing model, the collaboration aims for teamwork establishment, focusing on synchronous activities of continuous efforts that help maintain a shared conception of the problem.

Implementing collaboration in an environment allows for increased processing power of information. In a collaborative environment, more participants deal with problem-solving. This promotes the sharing of different points of view, intuition and experiences about the same problem.

In collaborative decision making, the definition of decision groups is an activity to be considered. According to Sommers [22], there is a greater sharing of knowledge in decision making when the group is formed by members of different characteristics. Factors such as the diversity of personalities, values, and cognitive abilities lead to a greater use of the information obtained inside the team.

It must also be considered that not every collaborative decision-making process is beneficial. One of the major challenges of group activities is interpersonal conflicts [20]. Often discussions involving conflict of opinions, inability to obtain consensus, or shyness among participants leads to unsuccessful discussions to resolve problems. Therefore, it is necessary to analyze groups that have greater compatibility of interpersonal communication and complementation of cognitive and emotional attributes, thus guaranteeing better performance in the results of the tasks [23].

Considering the concepts and works discussed in this section, this paper proposes the development of a collaborative environment, capable to promote impacts projection of a complex decision based on interactions between decision-makers. In this environment, decision-makers are encouraged to construct projection models based on their shared knowledge and experiences. Consequently, projected impacts may support new decision-making groups and individual decision-makers in complex decision-making.

3 ImpactMap Approach

The four phases model of emergency management encompasses mitigation, preparedness, response and recovery. Mitigation involves deciding what to do where a risk to the health or safety has been identified. Mitigation is a sustained action to reduce or eliminate risk to people or hazards and their effects. Preparedness is a continuous cycle of planning, organizing, training, evaluating the actions to be applied to solve an emergency decision problem. Response is the management of resources including personnel, equipment, and supplies. The response phase is a reaction to the occurrence of a catastrophic disaster. To finish, recovery involve activities focus on restoring critical functions to stabilize operations. This phase goal is to bring the affected area back to some degree of normality as soon as possible [24]. The approach proposed by the technological tool (ImpactMap) will be able to support the mitigation and preparedness phases.

In each phase of an emergency management cycle, complex decisions can be made. This research is concerned in supporting decision makers team, to project impacts of complex decisions in the environment. The tasks involved in the decision-making process are not trivial, especially when decisions are complex. This happens because decision-makers need to consider the lack of clarity in defining the decision's problems and objectives and analyze the external influences of the environment. Besides, find a way to work collaboratively in a scenario where specialists need decision's information details and orientation about what they must discuss.

Information and communication technologies can assist a group decision-making process through tools that promote collaboration and interaction among participants. ImpactMap is a collaborative web-based decision support tool. It has as main objective to provide a collaborative environment that is able to stimulate the exchange of experiences and knowledge between decision-makers participating in the session. Because of these interactions, ImpactMap aims to support the mapping of impact projections before executing an alternative decision.

Kirikihira and Shimada [19] proposed a tool for supporting consensus-building beyond a discuss map development, called "Discussion Map with Assistant (DMA)". This tool considers in its consensus map two main constructors that are: alternatives and criteria. Although this proposal supports a decision question discussion as ImpactMap, it does not promote the complex decision impacts discovery and analyses in a collaborative way.

The main language implemented on ImpactMap's development was Javascript, along with base libraries such as JQuery and Bootstrap to create the interface, with NodeJS and MongoDB to store the maps and send requests to the server. This tool presents three basic structures: Model structures, Collaborative strategies (collaborative environment), Projections management (reuse, cloud, and store), and Descriptions (Fig. 1).

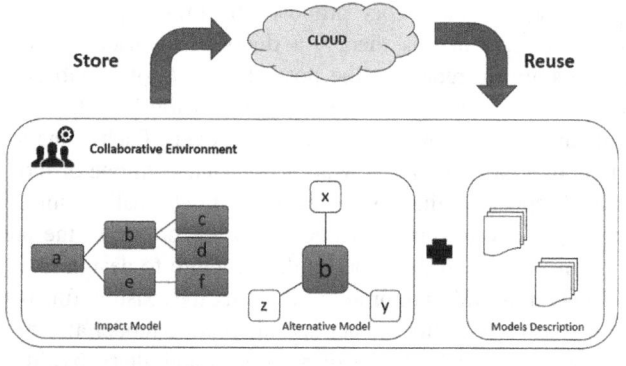

Fig. 1. ImpactMap structure.

Table 1 shows the set of functionalities provided by ImpactMap. Each one is associated with a structure previously mentioned.

ImpactMap is an environment that provides impact projection maps development in a collaborative session and stored by different URL's. This tool allows data persistence and the URL associated with the collaborative projection session is sent as an invitation to other decision-makers to attend the session. All maps and constructs' descriptions in ImpactMap are stored in the cloud and can be view and edit by those with an access profile to their decisions. The ImpactMap environment allows knowledge sharing, joint analysis and impact projections still in the planning phase of the decision-making process.

Table 1. ImpactMap functions

ImpactMap structure	Function
Models	Impact model, alternative model, graphics
Collaborative strategies	Chat, videoconference, collaborative map construction, shared actions in real time by socket
Description	Models descriptions, export description as PDF, invite to collaborate, export history chat, tutorial screen
Projection management	Cloud environment

The impact and alternative models are the core maps of ImpactMap. This tool is based on the development of impact maps that are like mental maps [25]. The use of mental maps is constantly diffused as a solution for the resolution of complex decisions, since it is seen as a cognitive facilitator of decision-makers. The main difference between common mental models and the models proposed by ImpactMap is the definition of its constructs and the hierarchy of these elements for the composition of impacts projection. The maps proposed by ImpactMap allows the conduction of an orientation process to perform impact projections.

ImpactMap is based on the theory proposed by França [13] that deals with the evolution of [3] and [12]. In this theory, a **decision** is made up of one or more scenarios. **Scenarios** aim to represent the possible effects of variables that affect the decision and to classify the areas of action of the decision in a domain. They are an integral part of the hierarchy to build the situation analysis. Each scenario can be made up of one or more **alternatives**, and they are associated with one or more impacts. At the end, the **impact** represents the consequences of an alternative, since it has not yet been implemented. To develop the projection maps according to the predicted structure, the tool presents a tutorial that teaches the structure to design it (Fig. 2).

Figure 2 presents ImpactMap tutorial highlighting the existing functionalities and a glossary with the constructs of the impact and alternative model also provided by the tool. Figure 3 presents a draft hierarchy of an impact and alternative models.

The alternative model view is activated by selecting an alternative previously presented in the impact model. In the on-screen expansion of the alternative model, the alternative characterization elements created and evaluated by the decision-maker group are presented. The values imputed in each characterizer can be analyzed in a radar chart.

The graphs created for each alternative allow the analysis of the decision not only by the projection group, but also by new groups or individual decision-makers who will reuse this information. To support the impact projections, some collaboration resources were introduced in ImpactMap, like communication (via videoconferences and chat – Fig. 4), cooperation and coordination strategies.

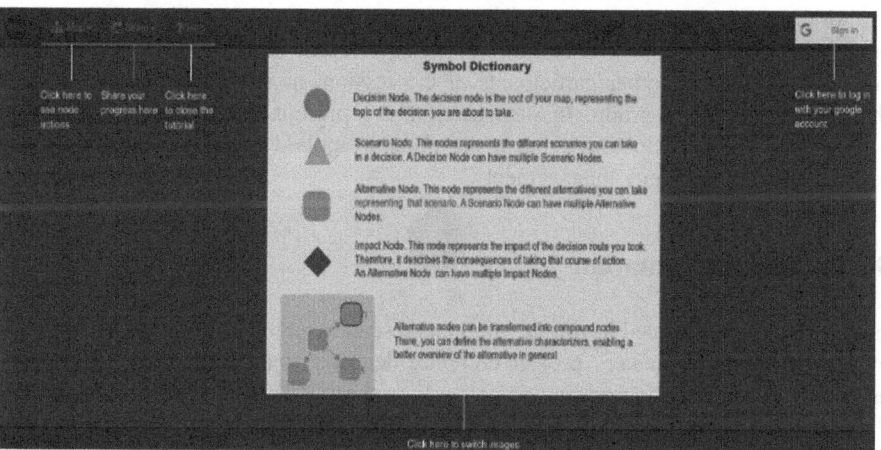

Fig. 2. Tutorial ImpactMap.

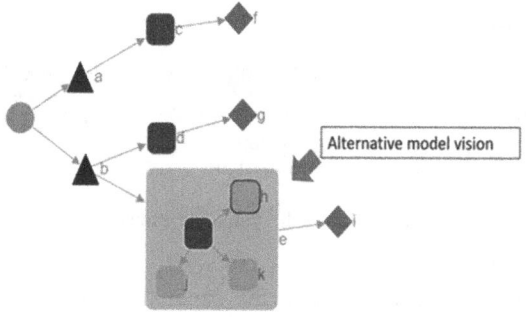

Fig. 3. Impact model and alternative model vision.

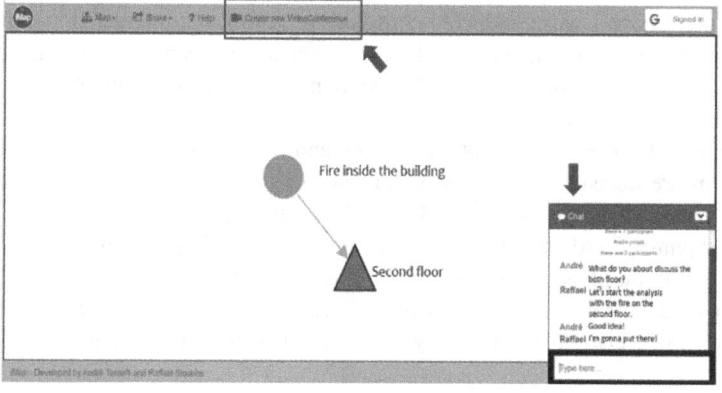

Fig. 4. Communication resource.

All actions taken on impact and alternative models are monitored in real time by all components of the projection section. When an element is updated or created, these actions appear to the other participants of the session, maintaining the new changes throughout the entire group. In next section, we present our approach evaluation, highlighting the participating groups, the domain applied and the influence of this research in an emergency management.

4   Research Evaluation

ImpactMap was evaluated having in mind this research main goal stated as an approach to support decision makers project complex decision impacts in the environment, especially considering emergency domains. In order to provide a simple and easy tool that encourages collaboration between decision-makers, this study was divided into two phases: a pilot experiment (an exploratory study) and a remote experiment (Fig. 5).

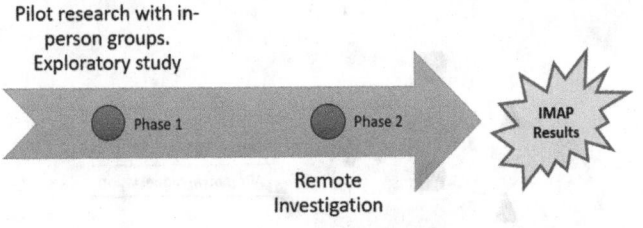

Fig. 5. Research evaluation phases.

Each phase was planned considering the simulation of an emergency domain, considering the mitigation phase of the emergency management cycle. To conduct this evaluation, it was necessary to form decision-makers groups. The following Figure (Fig. 6) presents the process that oriented this evaluation. This process was used in both phases.

However, Phase 1 was conducted considering groups that interacted in person (but using ImpactMap environment – each participant in one computer, but at the same virtual session), while phase 2 considered remote interaction with group members geographically dispersed.

Phase 1 had three groups with two, three and four decision-makers, respectively. All of them are decision maker and specialist in software usability, trained as emergency responder in their enterprise. Phase 2 had two groups with the same characteristics as phase 1. All groups projected impacts using ImpactMap tool simulating: (i) Phase 1: the building where they work was invaded by an immense shooting and they must save their live and as many other lives as possible. (ii) Phase 2: the building where they work caught fire and they must save his life and as many other lives as possible.

All groups attended the tutorial session, where the tool and features were presented. After it, all groups had a period of time to finish their impacts projections. During the evaluation, all groups were observed, and these data were collected by notes. In Phase 1 the observation occurred in person, while in Phase 2, occurred inside the ImpactMap session (virtual session).

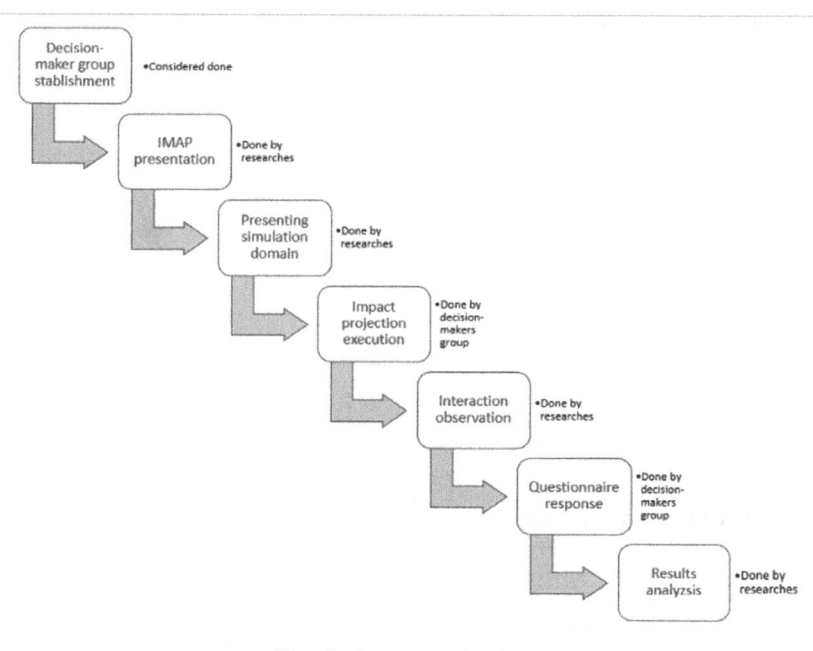

Fig. 6. Process evaluation.

Another way to investigate the applicability of this technological environment to project impact of complex decisions attending the mitigation and preparedness phases of emergency management cycle were the answers collected beyond a questionnaire. These answers presented the specialists view about the real applicability of this proposal simulated in this study. This instrument was prepared considering two main aspects: (a) capability to project decisions impacts in a collaborative way in the previous phases of decision making process and emergency management cycle, and (b) tool usability (utility, efficiency, effectiveness, learnability, and satisfaction) to verify if the technological problems could be the reasons to evaluate the tool as unsuitable to discuss a decision problem and project its impacts in a collaborative way [26]. The questionnaire was applied in both phases, however, Phase 2 had specific questions related to the communicative functions of ImpactMap. The next section presents the results achieved by both phases of experiments and discuss it considering the main goals of this research.

5 Results Presentation and Discussion

All groups projected impacts of the simulation proposed (i and ii). They developed impact and alternative models, besides each elements' description.

Figure 7 shows the impact map produced by group III during the experiment. All groups produced a similar structure. In Phase 1, we have three groups. Table 2, 3 and 4 present a summary of these groups' experiences and report some technical problem faced during the experiment.

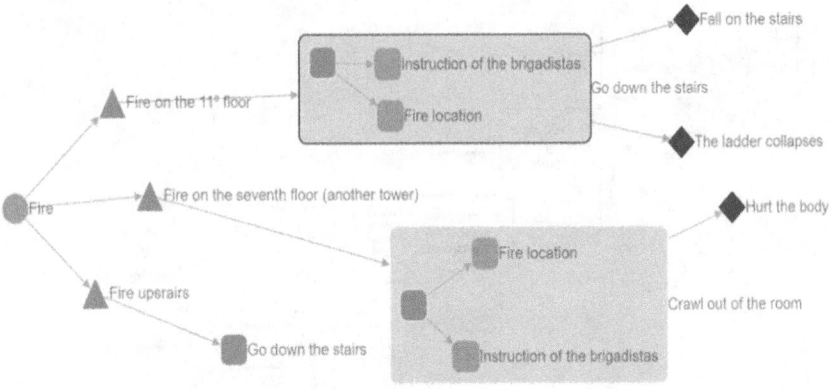

Fig. 7. Impact projection using impact and alternative model. Example produced by Group III - phase 2.

Table 2. Group I participation – phase 1

Aspects	Description
Participants number	2
Duration	13 min
Technical problems faced	After deleting a node, the model presented problems in the hierarchy

Table 3. Group II participation – phase 1

Aspects	Description
Participants number	3
Duration	15 min
Technical problems faced	Alternative characterizers were not intuitive

Table 4. Group III participation – phase 1

Aspects	Description
Participants number	4
Duration	45 min
Technical problems faced	Node description doesn't allow editing
	Absence of a function to undo actions
	Removal of compound alternative to return
	to common alternative unstable

In phase 2 the experiment was conducted considering a new version of ImpactMap, with the technological problems faced in phase 1 solved. The solution's evolution is relevant for this study because we can isolate the technical influences and analyze the main strategy to support decision making and emergency management.

Phase 2 main goal focus on the investigation of the same aspects discussed in phase 1, but now the participants considered another simulation domain and analyzed the communication resources made available by ImpactMap.

Table 5. Group I participation – phase 2

Aspects	Description
Participants number	4
Duration	17 min
Technical problems faced	Video conferencing functionality does not work for those who need to use the microphone without a camera

Table 6. Group II participation – phase 2

Aspects	Description
Participants number	2
Duration	24 min
Technical problems faced	Alert messages appear to all users in the session

Tables 5 and 6 summarizes the participation in Phase 2. Some problems were faced but the collaborative environment (ImpactMap) was enough to investigate the potentials of the approach proposed (as will be discussed below considering the usability aspects - utility, efficiency, effectiveness, learnability, and satisfaction). The groups activity observations and the answers collected by the questionnaire led us to some conclusions.

In both phases, groups with more participants developed impact projections in more detailed but required more time to do so. As was observed, larger groups can promote conflicts in peer interactions.

ImpactMap and the approach related can provide detailed information, however it could be a problem if an emergency demands a short period of time as few minutes or

130   J. B. dos Santos França et al.

seconds for the specialist project and analyze the decisions impacts in the early stages of an emergency management cycle. In this case, this approach is not recommended. But it is able to support decisions team in their impact's projection and decision analysis in emergency situations considering geographically disperse specialists.

During phase 1, all participants informed that it is possible to play more than one collaboration pattern using ImpactMap to project impacts. Figure 8 shows the numbers considering: (a) Member which sought consensus in conflict situations; (b) Member more focused on organization and description of model elements; (c) Member which led the discussions between the group; and (d) Which proposed creative ideas for solving situations. Phase 2 showed a similar result in all the usability aspects.

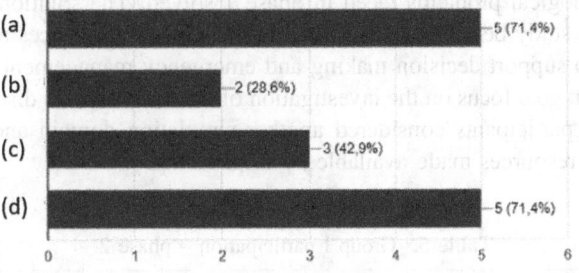

Fig. 8. Collaboration pattern applied during the impact projection section.

For more than 70% of participants in phase 1, ImpactMap supported the impacts projection and its discussion (Fig. 9), and more than 65% were satisfied with the impact projection results. These results were the same in Phase 2 and shows that ImpactMap is useful. So, **utility** and **satisfaction** aspect are observed in this tool.

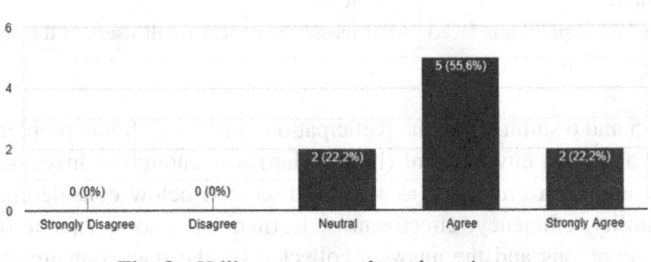

Fig. 9. Utility aspect result – phase 1.

The **Efficiency** aspect was inconclusive. There are different kind of variables that influence this aspect. The complexity of the decision and the numbers of the participant in each group affect the time of impact projections.

The tool helped keeping track of relevant informations about the decision.

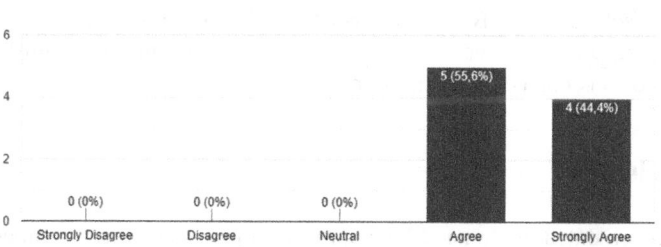

Fig. 10. Effectiveness results – phase 1.

For all the experiment participants, ImpactMap supported decision-makers, showing the concepts that must be analyzed in an impact projection. For that, ImpactMap strongly shows **effectiveness** in its functions (Fig. 10).

Learnability was a usability aspect that generated controversy. Figure 11 shows that 11,1% answered that the functionalities are not intuitive, while 33,3% defined as neutral, 33,3% intuitive, and 22,2% strongly intuitive. This difference occurred because some participants tried to evaluate functions that are useful in another step of the decision-making process, like the radar graphics. These graphics bring a different and summarized visualization to support new decision-makers with details about a complex decision already analyzed. The functions related to support impact map construction and description were evaluated as easy to learn.

The tool's functionalities were very easy and intuitive to use.

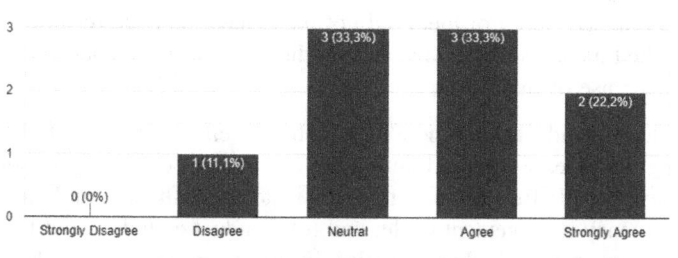

Fig. 11. Learning results – phase 1.

These results show that ImpactMap is an environment prepared to support decision-makers and specialists analyze a decision problem and project its impact in a collaborative way. This tool allows specialists work together even they are not present in the same place, i.e. dispersed geographically.

As were discussed in this paper, the phases mitigation and preparedness can be supported by ImpactMap. Mitigation phases is concerned deciding what to do in a problem identify. So, the approach delivered by ImpactMap tool is capable to orient specialists analyze the problem and project the impacts before the solution proposed by the team be implemented. Preparedness is worried to plan, organize, train and evaluate the actions selected to solve an emergency problem. Know the actions' (alternative construct) impacts will give more resources to decision-makers team to analyze the influences of this choice in the environment.

6   Conclusion

This paper presented the ImpactMap approach. It provided an environment to sup-port decision-maker projecting impacts of complex decision in a collaborative way. Another important quality of ImpactMap is its capability to orient decision-makers in how to externalize and share tacit knowledge.

The main goal of this paper was to provide an approach through the ImpactMap tool able to support decision makers project complex decision impacts in the environment, especially considering emergency domains. This goal will attend the phases mitigation and preparedness of emergency management cycle. This tool provided an environment able to share ideas and experiences, in order to support decision-makers groups structure their knowledge into impacts map. This research presented an environment that encourage collaboration between decision-makers disperse geographically. This research argued that if a collaborative environment to support impact projection of complex decision is available, decision-makers will be able to project impact maps, making their thoughts and experiences externalized in a structured way.

This research was evaluated in a study divided into two phases, both using ImpactMap environment. The first one was conducted in person and the second was conducted remotely. This evaluation showed that ImpactMap is a technological resource able to support decision makers analyze a complex decision and project its impacts. During this evaluation some technical limitations were faced (concerned to the tool development), but all of them did not influenced the main result of this research. However, the time available to analyze and discuss a decision question is important to decide for the use of ImpactMap.

The next steps include: (a) run more tests with different group sizes; (b) Evolve the tool considering the aspects observed during the evaluation; (c) Make the tool available in mobiles devices; (d) Run a study to investigate the influence of ImpactMap in the whole emergency management cycle; and (e) Conduct a study about the influence of decision-makers personal characteristics inside a group responsible to projecting impacts of complex decisions.

Acknowledgements. This research was supported by National Council for Scientific and Technological Development (CNPQ) in Brazil. Marcos R. S. Borges was partially supported by the National Council for Scientific and Technological Development (CNPQ) under grant # 308149/2015-7, and by Rio de Janeiro Research Support Foundation (FAPERJ) under grant # E-26/202.876/2018.

References

1. Haddow, G.D., Bullock, J.A.: Introduction to Emergency Management. Butterworth-Heinemann, Newton (2003)
2. Nimpuno, K., Hilman, R.: United Nations Centre for Human Settlements. Technische Hogeschool Delft: Disaster management glossary. United Nations Centre for Human Settlements (Habitat), Nairobi, Kenya (1998)
3. França, J.B.S., Neiva, F.W., Dias, A.F.S., Borges, M.R.S.: Towards projected impacts on emergency domains through a conceptual framework. In: International Conference on Information Systems for Crisis Response and Management, Albi, France. XIV International Conference on Information Systems for Crisis Response and Management, (2017). http://idl.iscram.org/files/julianabsfranca/2017/1467_JulianaB.S.Franca_etal2017.pdf
4. Lederman, E., Chimenz, L.: Supporting decision making in disasters: the DiMas tool. In: Murayama, Y., Velev, D., Zlateva, P. (eds.) ITDRR 2017. IAICT, vol. 516, pp. 25–35. Springer, Cham (2019). https://doi.org/10.1007/978-3-030-18293-9_4
5. Klein, G.A., Orasanu, J., Caldewood, R., Zsambok, E. (eds.): Decision Making in Action: Models and Methods, pp. 138–147. Ablex Publishing Corporation Norwood, New Jersey (1993)
6. Klein, G.A., Calderwood, R.: Decision models: some lessons from the field. IEEE Trans. Syst. Man Cybern. **21**, 1018–1026 (1991)
7. Orasanu, J., Connolly, T.: The reinvention of decision making. In: Klein, G.A., Orasanu, J., Caldewood, R., Zsambok, E. (eds.) Decision Making in action: Models and Methods, pp. 3–20. Ablex Publishing Corporation Norwood, New Jersey (1993)
8. Fuks, H., Raposo, A., Gerosa, M.A., Pimentel, M., Lucena, C.J.P.: The 3C Collaboration Model. The Encyclopedia of E-Collaboration, pp. 637—644. Ned Kock (org) (2007). ISBN 978-1-59904-000-4
9. Qudrat-Ullah, H.: Better Decision Making in Complex, Dynamic Tasks. Training with Human-Facilitated. Interactive Learning Environments. School of Administrative Studies. York University, Toronto (2015)
10. Yang, L., Xu, Y.: Decision making with uncertainty information based on lattice-valued fuzzy concept lattice. J. Univ. Comput. Sci. **16**(1), 159–177 (2010)
11. Doyle, J.K., Radzicki, M.J., Trees, W.S.: Measuring change in mental models of complex dynamic systems. In: Qudrat-Ullah, H., Spector, J.M., Davidsen, P.I. (eds.) Complex Decision Making. Theory and Practice, Cambridge, Massachusetts, pp. 269–294 (2008)
12. França, J.B.S., Neiva, F.W., Dias, A.F.S., Borges, M.R.S.: Toward impact projection characterization of complex decisions. In: IEEE International Conference on Systems, Man, and Cybernetics, Banff, vol. 1 (2017). https://ieeexplore.ieee.org/document/8123003/
13. França, J.B.S.: EPIDRÓ: An Approach to Guide a Collaborative Impacts Projection of Complex Decisions. Post-Graduation Program in Informatics, Mathematics Institute, Tércio Pacitti Institute of applications and Computational Research, Federal University of Rio de Janeiro. Rio de Janeiro, Brazil (2018). (in Portuguese)
14. Padilha, R.P., Borges, R.M.S., Gomes, J.O., Canós, J.H.: The design of collaboration support between command and operation teams during emergency response. In: The 2010 14th International Conference on Computer Supported Cooperative Work in Design. In: 2010 14th International Conference on Computer Supported Cooperative Work in Design (CSCWD), Shanghai, China. IEEE (2010). http://ieeexplore.ieee.org/lpdocs/epic03/wrapper.htm?arnumber=5471873
15. Hammond, J.S., Keeney, R.L., Raiffa, H.: Smart Choices: A Practical Guide to Making Better Life Decisions. Broadway Books, New York (2002)

16. Shattuck, L.G., Miller, N.L.: Extending naturalistic decision making to complex organizations: a dynamic model of situated cognition. Organ. Stud. **27**, 989–1009 (2006)
17. Aldea, A., Bañares-Alcántara, R., Skrzypczak, S.: Managing information to support the decision making process. J. Inf. Knowl. Manag. **11**(3), 1250016 (2012)
18. Ayyub, B.M.: Risk Analysis in Engineering and Economics, 2nd edn. Chapman & Hall/CRC (2014). ISBN 1-58488-395-2
19. Kirikihira, R., Shimada, K.: Discussion map with an assistant function for decision-making: a tool for supporting consensus-building. Collaboration technologies and social computing. In: 10th International Conference, CollabTech 2018, Costa de Caparica, Portugal, 5–7 September 2018 (2018)
20. De Dreu, C.K.W., Weingart, L.R.: Task versus relationship conflict, team performance, and team member satisfaction: a metaanalysis. Res. Appl. Psychol. **88**(4), 741–749 (2003)
21. Dillenbourg, P., Baker, M., Blaye, A., O'Malley, C.: The evolution of research on collaborative learning. In: Spada, E., Reiman, P. (eds.) Learning in Humans and Machine: Towards an Interdisciplinary Learning Science, pp. 189–211. Elsevier, Oxford (1996)
22. Sommers, S.R.: On racial diversity and group decision making: Identifying multiple effects of racial composition on jury deliberations. J. Pers. Soc. Psychol. **90**(4), 597–612 (2006). https://doi.org/10.1037/0022-3514.90.4.597
23. Van Knippenberg, D., Schippers, M.C.: Work group diversity. Ann. Rev. Psychol. (2007). https://doi.org/10.1146/annurev.psych.58.110405.085546
24. Sylves, R.: Disaster Policy and Politics: Emergency Management and Homeland Security. CQ Press, Washington, DC (2008)
25. Qudrat-Ullah, H., Spector, J.M., Davidsen, P.I. (eds.): Complex Decision Making. Springer, New York (2007). https://doi.org/10.1007/978-3-540-73665-3
26. Jeff, R. (ed.): Handbook of Usability Testing. 2A (2008)

Ad-Hoc Architecture of Systems for Disaster Risk Management

Oleksii Kovalenko[1(✉)] and Dimiter Velev[2(✉)]

[1] Institute of Mathematical Machines and Systems Problems NAS of Ukraine,
Kiev, Ukraine
`Kovalenko.O.E@nas.gov.ua`
[2] University of National and World Economy, Sofia, Bulgaria
`dgvelev@unwe.bg`

Abstract. The essence of functioning of present-day systems of disasters risk management is information processing for decision making in target domain of risk management. Risk management is the specific field of situational management. Disasters is a result of evolution of situations concerned with different environment natural, technogenic, and human activity processes. The main purpose of disasters risks management (DRM) systems is to provide organizational and technological services to participants in risk management processes to perform the functions assigned to them. DRM system is a complex organizational and technical system. The result of its configuration should be accorded with the architectural model of the organization and cover all levels of organizational and technical means that ensure its operation. Ad-hoc architectural views should reflect point of views concerted with situation context (semantics), stakeholders' positions and available required management means. Organization of DRM system based on ad-hoc architecture approach is proposed in the paper.

Keywords: Disasters risk management · Information technologies · Ad-hoc architecture

1 Introduction

By United Nations Office for Disaster Risk Reduction (UNISDR) definition disaster is '*a serious disruption of the functioning of a community or a society at any scale due to hazardous events interacting with conditions of exposure, vulnerability and capacity, leading to one or more of the following: human, material, economic and environmental losses and impacts.*' [1]. Disaster risk management according to the terminology of UNISDR [2] '*is the application of disaster risk reduction policies and strategies to prevent new disaster risk, reduce existing disaster risk and manage residual risk, contributing to the strengthening of resilience and reduction of disaster losses. <> Disaster risk management actions can be distinguished between prospective disaster risk management, corrective disaster risk management and compensatory disaster risk management, also called residual risk management.*' The first phase of disaster risk management is disasters awareness.

© IFIP International Federation for Information Processing 2020
Published by Springer Nature Switzerland AG 2020
Y. Murayama et al. (Eds.): ITDRR 2019, IFIP AICT 575, pp. 135–145, 2020.
https://doi.org/10.1007/978-3-030-48939-7_12

Disasters is a result of evolution of situations concerned with different environment natural, technogenic, and human activity processes. We can say that disaster is some catastrophic situation caused by different factors. Situation, in general sense, defined as all of the facts, conditions, and events that affect someone or something at a particular time and in a particular place [3]. The situation notion could be defined as a conscious knowledge of the individual (-s) about the dynamics of the environment, represented by certain types of information messages that is the basis for constructing a substantiated interpretation of the sequence of changes in states (dynamics) of the world (subject area) from a certain point of view [4]. In situational management information presents as assessment on a state of a target domain through the formal logical treatment of knowledge and beliefs in the context of information theory, results of questionnaires, or propagation of general messaging. Semantic information theory [5] defines semantic information as well formed, meaningful, useful and (it is desirably) truthful information.

Situation awareness is one of important elements in the complex problem of situation management [6, 7]. Situation management is considered "as a framework of concepts, models and enabling technologies for recognizing, reasoning about, affecting on, and predicting situations that are happening or might happen in dynamic systems during pre-defined operational time" [6]. One of important kind of situation awareness is disasters awareness in disasters risk management [8, 9]. Correct disasters awareness is a first step to prevention and elimination of their consequences in context of expression "forewarned is forearmed". In its turn, disasters awareness is a phase of situational, or emergency, or crisis management in the case of disasters risk management.

2 System Architecture and Disaster Risk Management

Various systems, including organizational, describes their architecture. There are various definitions of system's architecture [10–12] and one of generalized definitions presented in the standard ISO/IEC/IEEE 42010:2011 "Systems and software engineering - Architecture description" [13]: architecture – fundamental concepts or properties of a system in its environment embodied in its elements, relationships, and in the principles of its design and evolution. Systems and enterprise architecture assembles different components for providing system aimful activity. Enterprise reference models includes components for providing:

- Staffing (who?);
- Motivation (why?);
- Localization (where?);
- Resource (what?);
- Timing (when?);
- Functioning (how?).

These components might be grouped as active and passive entities. Active entities perform processing and add value to passive entities. Because the essence of risk management is decision making for controlled domain then active entities are stakeholders of risk management and passive entities are information objects concerned with risk management area. In enterprise architecture of risk management, system staff (personnel) represents active entities and different resources are passive entities. According to reference architecture model, a staff is characterized by motivation, localization, timing and controlling of functioning (information processing). Resources are characterized by localization, timing, and involving to functioning (information processing) from another side. Thus, formal model of risk management process may be wrote as:

$$Y(t) = P(C(F(R(t)), t), \ F(R(t), t)) \tag{1}$$

where Y – result of system's functioning, P – function of processes management in system, C – function of information processing control in system, F – function of information processing, R – function of resource variation, t – time variable within domain of definition of function P (process lifetime period).

Risk management is the specific field of situational management. Risk management is a process based on the set of principles, realized by the appropriate framework. Relationships between the risk management principles, framework and processes are depicted in Fig. 1 [14].

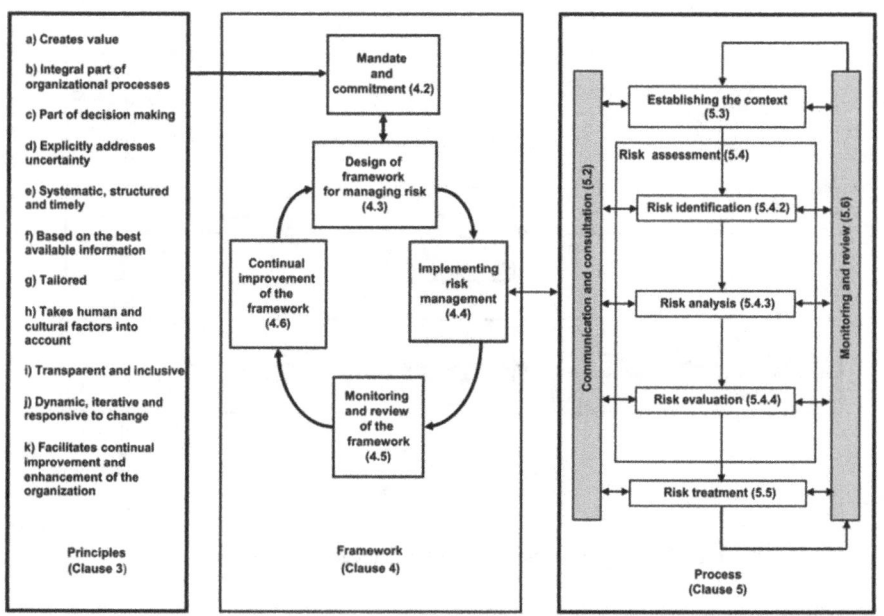

Fig. 1. Relationships between the risk management principles, framework and process [14].

Because situation management in general and disaster risk management (DRM) in particular concerned with unpredictable occasional events then appropriate regulatory system (DRM system) should be adapted to specifics of concrete disaster situation.

Such adaptation might be realized based on ad-hoc system architecture. General model of DRM as situation management is depicted in Fig. 2.

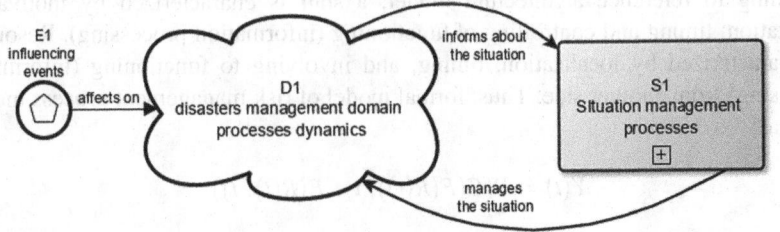

Fig. 2. General model of disaster management as situation management process.

Ad hoc architecture solutions might be designed for a specific problem or task, not generalizing solutions (only having stored for case based choice), without intending to be adapt them to other purposes. Thus, architectural views must reflect views concerted with situation context (semantics), stakeholders' positions and available required management means. Situation management process S1 (see Fig. 2) is a kind of project activity [4] that include subprocesses depicted in Fig. 3.

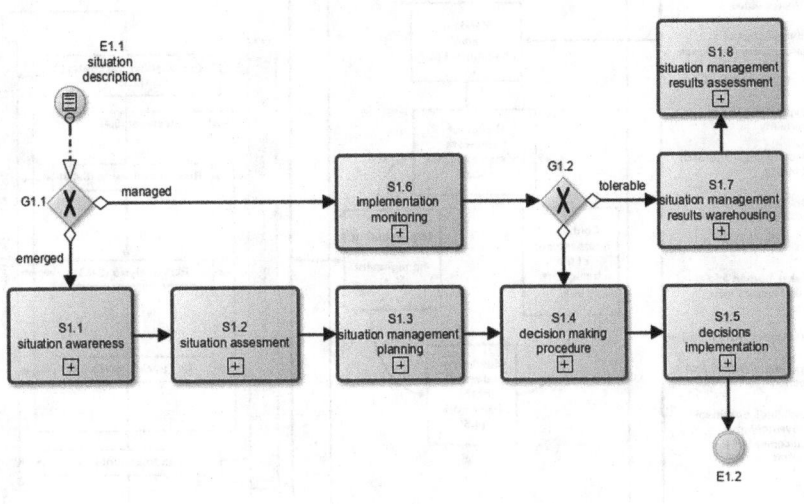

Fig. 3. Subprocesses of situation management process S1.

Pointed in Fig. 3 processes should be supported by system of situation management (DRM system) with appropriate type of ad-hoc architectural model. Because the main mission of DRM system is decision-making and their implementing then the main stakeholder is decision-approving person (DAP). DAP may be individual or collective. Other stakeholders are involved in process of risk management (see Eq. (1)) with appropriate roles to support subprocesses and use processing results as defined according to specifics of DRM domain. All stakeholders divided on two groups: personnel and experts. Personnel perform a supporting role and experts are participants of decision-making process.

3 Convergence in Ad-Hoc System Architecture

3.1 Model of Ad-Hoc System Architecture

Formal model of DRM system [15] is based on system's aspects presented by category model M_K, organizational model parameters M_O, architectural model M_A, process (functional) model M_F, logical model (including model of modalities) M_L:

$$W = \langle M_K; M_O; M_A; M_F; M_L \rangle. \tag{2}$$

Category model M_K is defined on the base of mission, objectives and tasks of DRM system functioning using composition of classification parameters groups. The first (general) group contains parameters of aim mission, subject domain, scale and tasks determinacy. Parameters of second group determine control aspects of DRM system functioning, in particular, subordination, staff, and methods of situational information processing, and time restrictions for decision-making. Third group parameters define constructive specifics of DRM system and contain deployment technique, universality, number and type of physical locations etc. Fourth group parameters define engineering and technological aspects of DRM system functioning with technical equipment list, situation modeling tools nomenclature, using technologies, security level, grade of automation of situational assessment etc. Parameters of DRM system organizational model M_O are defined by main coordination mechanism, organization core type (main part), general design parameters, situational factors (motivations). The architectural model M_A is defined by chosen architectural pattern (framework) for modeling of architecture for software intensive systems. Logical model M_L of DRM system based on modalities models that take into account the relevant modalities [16]. Modal logic and their extensions are used to formalize statements of weakly formalized systems, including natural languages. The logical model of modalities formed on the Kripke scale with the corresponding Kripke semantics [17].

Collaborative activities of staff can be viewed from the point of view agents-based approach and use the behavioral model of agents for this [18]. The behavior of staff agents is based on its knowledge and have some sense (situation semantics). Hence, the formalization of organizational support for staff agents' activity in situational semantics aspect is actual problem.

Resulting integrated behavioral model of service agent is presented as tuple:

$$A_b = \langle T, P, C, M, D, W \rangle \tag{3}$$

where T is a set of means of situation description; P is a set of means of communicative control in changeable communication environments; C is a set of means of coordination mechanism; M is a set of means of messaging between agents; D is a set of means of action description, W is a formal model of DRM system (see Eq. (2)) and defines the context of components T, P, C, M, D.

Typical workflow patterns (scheduled procedures) are supported by DRM system services [19]. Information processes in DRM system implemented based on the hierarchy of procedures of technological (routine), organizational (administrative) and subject area (profound, special) levels.

The meaning of the management processes in the DRM system is determined by the specific problems and tasks of risk management that need to be resolved. To ensure the effective operation of the DRM system, it is necessary to organize the appropriate environment of functioning. The main purpose of the DRM system is to provide organizational and technological services to participants in risk management processes to perform the functions assigned to them. Therefore, DRM systems can be considered as service management systems and must comply with the requirements of the relevant standards, in particular ISO/IEC 20000, ISO/IEC 17788, and ISO/IEC 17789. In particular, the ISO/IEC 17788 standard defines the lists of cloud services capabilities types and cloud services categories corresponding to these types of capabilities (see Table 1).

Table 1. Cloud service categories and cloud capabilities types.

Cloud service categories	Cloud capabilities types		
	Infrastructure	Platform	Application
Compute as a Service (CompaaS)	X		
Communications as a Service (CaaS)		X	X
Data Storage as a Service (DSaaS)	X	X	X
Infrastructure as a Service (IaaS)	X		
Network as a Service (NaaS)	X	X	X
Platform as a Service (PaaS)		X	
Software as a Service (SaaS)			X
Database as a Service (DBaaS)	X	X	X
Desktop as a Service (DTaaS)	X	X	X
Email as a Service (EMaaS)	X	X	X
Identity as a Service (IdaaS)	X		X
Management as a Service (MaaS)			X
Security as a Service (SecaaS)		X	X
Other Emerging Services	?	?	?

Implementation of the DRM system on the basis of the concept of service-oriented architecture (SOA) and cloud computing requires the creation of tools for configurations of DRM system in accordance with the conditions and requirements for their use. Since the DRM system is an organizational and technical complex, the result of the configuration of this one should be accorded with the architectural model of the organization and cover all levels of organizational and technical means that ensure its operation. Unlike the usual service management systems, DRM system should provide not separate information processing services, but technological services packages that are oriented to support the technological stages of risk management processes for a particular problem. Therefore, the tools for configuring the DRM system should support the creation of such technological packages.

The functioning of the DRM system takes place in the mode of multilateral cooperative activities of interested stakeholders and involves the convergence of scientific methods and technological means of various subject areas of activity related to the specific problems of risk management. Consequently, the configuration of service packages for DRM system should provide the possibility of convergence of the necessary scientific methods and technologies. Creation of technological packages can be based on knowledge of subject areas of risk management using the multi-agent approach. Convergence of methods and technologies within the technological package is carried out based on a formal description of the risk management problem, which includes the following elements of risk management:

- Characteristic of the problem;
- List of objectives criteria;
- Design model for solving the problem;
- Resources requirements;
- Resources constraints.

The description of the problem of risk management should be presented as a formal model of business processes of risk management taking into account certain resource requirements and constraints. Information about the requirements and constraints of the risk management environment is stored in the catalogues and reference books that characterize the relevant categories of services. Configuring the risk management environment for a particular problem is done using the system configuration tools based on the "Infrastructure as Code" (IaC) approach, in particular such as, Ansible, Puppet, CFEngine, and others.

3.2   Building of an Ad-Hoc Architecture

Ad-hoc architecture for realizing of formal processing model (see Eq. (1)) based on formal model of DRM system (see Eq. (2)) and formal behavioral model of DRM service agent (see Eq. (3)) might be presented using model based system engineering (MBSE) languages and tools, such as UML, SysML, Archimate, BPMN etc. Main aim of system architecture modelling and simulation is presenting relations and interactions between active entities called actors, and passive entities called architectural artifacts. Architecture models should include structural and dynamic aspects of the system.

Two types of project activities are coupled in ad-hoc DRM systems. The first one is project for building of DRM system to support the set of projects of second type for providing of situation risk management processes like depicted in Fig. 3. In essence, project activity for building of DRM system concerned with creating of technological platform for maintaining of situational risks management processes for specific groups of actor roles. Actors as intelligent agents are characterized by their capabilities based on beliefs, desires, intentions, obligations and restrictions as knowledge elements.

Technologies of risk management platform should met with requirements of each stage of processing according to assignment of separated processes of risk management taking into account actors' capabilities.

Convergence of intelligent agents' and technological platform capabilities provides functionality of DRM system in a whole.

3.3 Transformation of Information in DRM Systems

Situational management activity concerned with consolidation and processing of information of heterogeneous origin to receive semantic information. Hence, it is important to develop adequate means (principles, methods and tools) for information consolidation. Most common approach to information consolidation is based on information fusion methods.

According to Data Fusion Information Group (DFIG) Model [20] there are defined six levels of information fusion:

- Level 0 - Data Assessment;
- Level 1 - Object Assessment;
- Level 3 - Impact Assessment;
- Level 4 - Process Refinement;
- Level 5 - User Refinement;
- Level 6 - Mission Management.

To refinement of different levels, it is necessary to build sound hierarchy of notions concerned with basic notion of "information". This hierarchy called I-SDKW model [21] covers different cycles of thinking such as learning, intelligence, and decision cycles. Information is transformed through receiving, collecting, aggregating, filtering, representing, awaring, interpreting, estimating, using, enrichment, composing, and growing to higher-level stages. I-SDKW model is based on taxonomy of information that differs four categories of information: signal, data, knowledge and wisdom. Facilities of these categories by attributes, using and focus of processing are presented in Table 2.

Information transformation concerned with bidirectional transforming of different kinds of information in process of its use. Information perception begins from receiving a signal from environmental source, because the absence of signal means the absence of information ('it is impossible in a dark room to find a black cat that is not there'). Therefore, signal about some phenomena carries primary information about this phenomenon as symbol, or sign, or image, or dynamic process represented appropriate data structures. These data structures may be composed by meanings (context) in facts of TBox (terminological part of knowledge base) and ABox (assertions' part of knowledge base) [22] of some knowledge domain and the linked set of such facts are framed the knowledge base.

The problem is what and how observer(s) can know something about knowledge domain. The top-level fragment of I-SDKW ontology in OntoGraf view is depicted in Fig. 4. In this model, information appears and transforms in different manifestation. So information is manifested either signal, or structure, or theory (system), or

Table 2. Facilities of information categories [21].

Information categories	Category facility (feature)		
	Attributes	Usage	Focus
Signal	Source, medium, strength, time	Transmitting, receiving, communicating	Attributes
Data	Volume, type (structure)	Storing, warehousing	Structure
Knowledge	Semantic fullness	Understanding, interpreting, motivating	Logic model and expressiveness
Wisdom	Efficiency, effectiveness, usefulness, purposefulness	Decision making, reasonable behavior	Practical results, objectives achievement

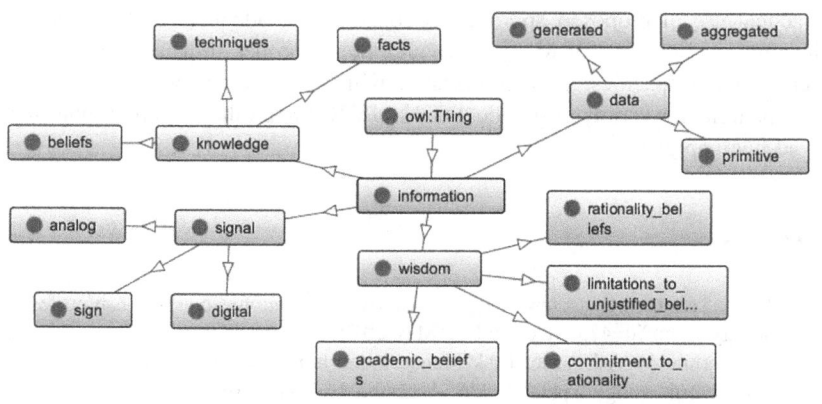

Fig. 4. Fragment of I-SDKW ontology in OntoGraf view [21].

recommendations, or best practices etc. However, knowledge is not enough for wise decision. Wisdom is that the decision should be conformed to context of situation.

I-SDKW ontology is the result of systematization of knowledge domain thesaurus. The information about problem domain is structured from signals (sequences, symbols, signs, and icons) to data structures, further to controlled vocabularies, further to taxonomies, further to thesaurus, further to ontologies. Therefore, we can to build perceptual hierarchy from signal to wisdom and effector hierarchy from wisdom to signal.

I-SDKW information transformation paradigm takes into account attributive properties of information and manner both of its representation and the use. It is especially actually for information processing during situational risk management when environmental situational information have different forms and assignments.

4 Conclusion and Further Research

Convergence and configuration of information technology in the DRM system based on formal models of business processes of risk management and artifacts catalogs of systems, allows adapting the DRM systems to solve various problems of risk management and provides sets of technological services depending on the context of the risk management.

Variety of DRM problems cause needs to adapt architecture of DRM system for specifics of problem domain. Such adaptation may be provided in the bounds of project activities of the building of ad-hoc architecture for DRM platform and its using to supporting of DRM processes in problem domain. Building of ad-hoc architecture is provided through coupling of active entities (actors) with passive entities (architecture artifacts) in accordance to formal model, described in architecture description language. Architectural model of DRM platform describes artifacts sets convergent composition. DRM processes on specific DRM platform are described by composition of dynamic artifacts of DRM processes fragments.

Practical use of proposed approach is concerned to adequate building of ad-hoc architectural models for DRM systems and theirs proper utilization according to problem domain specifics. Further research will be concerned with case study for creating patterns for variety of practical tasks of DRM and other situation management using ad-hoc approach.

References

1. UNDRR Terminology, Disaster. http://www.preventionweb.net/english/professional/terminology/v.php?id=475. Accessed 16 May 2019
2. UNDRR Terminology, Disaster Risk Management. http://www.preventionweb.net/english/professional/terminology/v.php?id=476. Accessed 16 May 2019
3. Situation. Merriam-Webster Dictionary. http://www.merriam-webster.com/dictionary/situation
4. Tatiana, V., Oleksii, E.K., Vladimir, K.: Organizational-information technology for providing and decisions making in situational management. In: Proceedings of the 14th International Conference on Advanced Trends in Radioelectronics, Telecommunications and Computer Engineering, TCSET 2018, 10 April 2018, vol. 2018-April, pp. 152–157. IEEE, Lviv-Slavske (2018). https://doi.org/10.1109/tcset.2018.8336176
5. Floridi, L.: Semantic Conceptions of Information. https://plato.stanford.edu/entries/information-semantic. Accessed 16 May 2019
6. Jakobson, G., Buford, J., Lewis, L.: Situation management: basic concepts and approaches. In: Popovich, V., Schrenk, M., Korolenko, K.V. (eds.) Information Fusion and Geographic Information Systems 2007. LNGC, pp. 18–33. Springer, Heidelberg (2007). https://doi.org/10.1007/978-3-540-37629-3_2
7. Naderpour, M., Lu, J., Zhang, G.: An intelligent situation awareness support system for safety-critical environments. Decis. Supp. Syst. **59**, 325–340 (2014)
8. Disaster Management: Types, Awareness and Schemes for Disaster Management. http://www.yourarticlelibrary.com/disasters/disaster-management/disaster-management-types-awareness-and-schemes-for-disaster-management/30169. Accessed 16 May 2019

9. Public awareness and public education for disaster risk reduction: a guide. http://www.ifrc.org/Global/Publications/disasters/reducing_risks/302200-Public-awareness-DDR-guide-EN.pdf. Accessed 16 May 2019

10. Zachman Glossary. https://www.zachman.com/ea-articles-reference/171-zachman-glossary. Accessed 16 May 2019

11. Federal Enterprise Architecture Framework (FEAF), version 2. https://obamawhitehouse.archives.gov/omb/e-gov/FEA. Accessed 16 May 2019

12. The TOGAF® Standard, Version 9.2. https://pubs.opengroup.org/architecture/togaf92-doc/arch/index.html. Accessed 16 May 2019

13. ISO/IEC/IEEE 42010:2011 Systems and software engineering – Architecture description. http://www.iso.org/iso/catalogue_detail.htm?csnumber=50508. Accessed 16 May 2019

14. ISO 31000:2009, Risk management – Principles and guidelines. https://www.iso.org/iso-31000-risk-management.html. Accessed 16 May 2019

15. Kovalenko, O.E.: The formalization of organizational support creation for systems of situational management. In: Proceedings of the 5th International Conference on Application of Information and Communication Technology and Statistics in Economy and Education, ICAICTSEE-2015, pp. 292–301, January 2015

16. Kovalenko, O.E.: Application of modal logic in decisions making on models of knowledge. Math. Comput. Model. Ser.: Tech. Sci. **6**, 106–112 (2012). (in Ukrainian)

17. Kripke, S.A.: Semantical analysis of modal logic I normal modal propositional calculi. Math. Logic Q. **9**(5–6), 67–96 (1963)

18. Kovalenko, O.E.: Models and means for service agents orchestration in situation management systems. Actual Probl. Econ. **154**(4), 462–467 (2014)

19. Kovalenko, O.: Construction of multilevel multiagent information systems based on knowledge. Inf. Technol. Secur. **4**(2), 146–154 (2016). (In Ukrainian)

20. Blasch, E.: One decade of the data fusion information group (DFIG) model. In: Next-Generation Analyst III, p. 94990L. International Society for Optics and Photonics (2015)

21. Kovalenko, O.: Information taxonomy and ontology for situational management. In: Proceedings of the 2018 IEEE 13th International Scientific and Technical Conference on Computer Sciences and Information Technologies, CSIT 2018, 8 November 2018, vol. 2, Article Number 8526723, pp. 94–97. IEEE, Lviv (2018). https://doi.org/10.1109/stc-csit.2018.8526723

22. Baader, F., Horrocks, I., Sattler, U.: Description logics. In: van Harmelen, F., Lifschitz, V., Porter, B. (eds.) Handbook of Knowledge Representation, pp. 135–179. Elsevier B.V., Amsterdam (2008). https://doi.org/10.1016/s1574-6526(07)03003-9

Conceptual Model of Debris Flow Information System

Valentina Nikolova[1], Plamena Zlateva[2(✉)], Boyko Berov[3],
Asparuh Kamburov[1], and Dimiter Velev[4]

[1] University of Mining and Geology "St. Ivan Rilski", Sofia, Bulgaria
[2] Institute of Robotics, Bulgarian Academy of Sciences, Sofia, Bulgaria
plamzlateva@abv.bg
[3] Geological Institute, Bulgarian Academy of Sciences, Sofia, Bulgaria
[4] University of National and Word Economy, Sofia, Bulgaria

Abstract. Debris flows are natural hazard triggered by intensive rainfall or snowmelt and represent rapid movement of water-saturated colluvial and pro-luvial earth masses. The propagation of this hazardous event could change ecosystems, increase the solid discharge in the rivers and dam siltation, and affect infrastructure and people. The compound character of debris flows requires collection and analysis of various information and for this purpose, the computer technology and geographic information systems provide great opportunity. The aim of the paper is to present a conceptual model of debris flow information system, which to be used for risk assessment and to support decision making. The study emphasizes to factors and prerequisites, debris flow data, analyses and visualization. A fuzzy logic model for integrated risk assessment of the debris flow due to the multiple natural factors (as rainfall duration, rainfall amount, slope, erosion etc.) is proposed. An example of geoinformation portal is presented.

Keywords: Debris flow · Information system · Fuzzy logic · Risk assessment

1 Introduction

In the internationally accepted classification proposed by Varnes [1] and developed by Cruden and Varnes [2] debris flows are a type of landslides that consist of a spatially continuous movements of a saturated mass of earth materials, such as debris and mud, mainly controlled by gravity and whose movement mechanics resemble that of a viscous liquid. There is a progression and a change from slides to flows according to water content, mobility and evolution of the movements. As a result of torrential rainfalls or rapid snowmelt in stripped of vegetation mountain slopes, composed mainly of eluvial and deluvial deposits, as well as cracked and rapidly eroding rocks, with landslides and collapses, a water-saturated mobile mud-stone mass is formed. It flows down the slope, drawing in extra bulk material. These masses fall into river beds and temporary streams, where they further destroy the banks and increase the amount of mud and stone material, forming a powerful flow [3]. It has to be taken into account

Y. Murayama et al. (Eds.): ITDRR 2019, IFIP AICT 575, pp. 146–158, 2020.
https://doi.org/10.1007/978-3-030-48939-7_13

that debris flows can return to slopes where they have already been and start in places they have never been before.

In regard to the above the debris flows are associated with the probability of negative impacts and are considered as limiting factors for people's lives and activities. Rising public awareness about natural hazards could improve the quality of life, save financial resources and even save lives. Development of computer technology and geographic information systems (GIS) allow effective analyses and visualization of the information and helps for better understanding of hazardous event.

Different types of information systems are described in the literature: knowledge information system, management information system (disaster management information system), decision support information system, hazard monitoring information system [4–7].

Disaster information systems use spatial information and disaster attribute information. The systems provide functions necessary for disaster management such as disaster zone management, geological analysis and automatized calculation of damage area, and made the efficient disaster management through the extraction of cadastral information and damage area more than certain scale by damage area [5]. Decision support systems provide data and tools for analyses and considering alternatives to help decision making. Hazard and risk assessment are important part of decision making process and are also closely related to monitoring of hazardous event. In case of compound events like as debris flow a big volume of data about factors and prerequisites, characteristics of the event and damage information should be acquired, sorted, analyzed and visualized in information system to ensure effective activities for risk mitigation and management. Building the information system have to take into account the properties of the hazardous natural phenomena and the purpose of which the system to be used.

Considering the properties of debris flows and their compound character, the aim of the current paper is to present a model of debris flow information system to be used for risk assessment and to support decision making.

2 Structure of the Information System

The information system is considered as an integration of computer hardware, software and data about the hazardous event, in the current case – debris flow. The spatial character of the debris flows allows development of the system in GIS environment. Four main modules determine the system: data acquisition/data entering; processing; analyses and visualization (Fig. 1). Hazard and risk assessment are results of the analyses and could be calculated on the base of the data and spatial analyses. Taking into account the complexity of the hazardous event and the importance of multi-criteria decision analysis as a tool to support decision makers this module is presented as a separate module in the system, allowing to choose the best alternative taking into account the results from risk assessment. The visualization is available at each stage of the system work. The data can be presented on maps and/or as a text and tables.

Data acquisition and processing are one of the most important part of the system. The data can be collected by field surveys (using UAVs, LiDAR, sediments sampling),

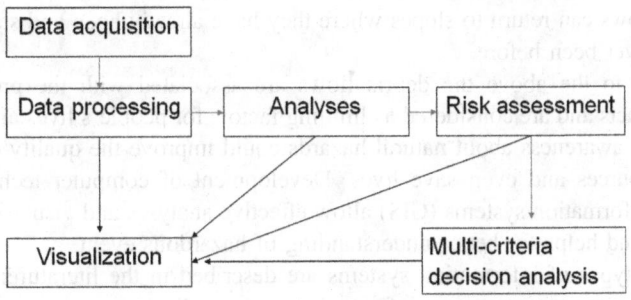

Fig. 1. Structure of the information system

automatic meteorological station (for precipitation and particularly for intensive rain) and literature and maps review. The data processing is mainly related to the consistency of the data, coordinate systems, projections and transformations, vector to raster conversion or vice versa etc. The module "Analyses" allows to make calculations about the debris flows properties, morphometric features of the basins, debris initiation area, transport and accumulation, to analyze the spatial distribution of the hazardous event and to evaluate the debris flow susceptibility and hazard. On the base of the analyses and taking into account the possibility the infrastructure and people to be affected risk assessment can be elaborated. The multi-criteria decision analysis is presented as a separate module of the system, taking into account the importance of the decision making and the need for quick response in case of risk and disaster. This analysis is not a decision making but it is a main tool to support decision making allowing to choose, sort and rank alternatives and solutions according to pre-defined criteria.

3 Main Characteristics of the Data Module

The data module includes the following main groups (Fig. 2): baseline data; factors and prerequisites (analysis that is resulted in debris flow susceptibility model); debris flow data; damage information and ecosystem information (used as indicators for calculating hazard and risk assessment).

Baseline data provides details of the regions and places where such events have been occurred for the compilation of the inventory maps. This map is a base for debris flow susceptibility and hazard assessment. Topographic data is of high importance for calculating and analyses of morphometric features of debris flows basins, which can be used as indicators for debris flow susceptibility evaluation. For example many publications consider the basin area, basin relief, relief ratio, Melton's index and slope as indicators for determining and analyses of debris flows initiation areas and propagation [8–14]. For the purpose of the analyses high resolution DEMs are needed.

Regarding the debris flows factors main triggering forces are intensive rainfall and rapid snowmelt. In this relation, the information system should contain data about daily precipitation, mean daily temperature and maximum daily temperature.

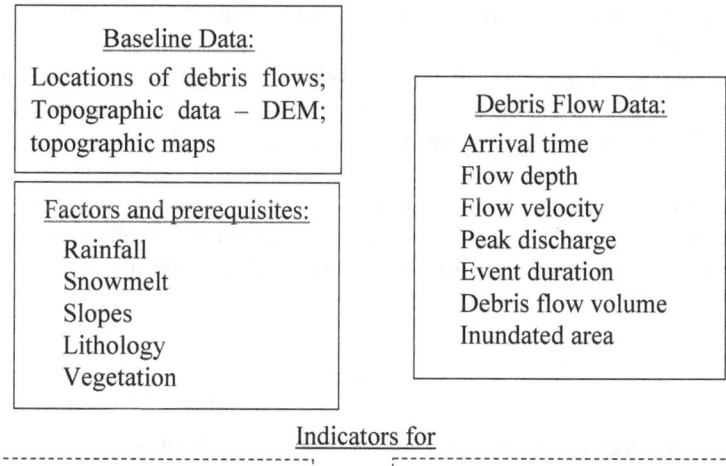

Fig. 2. Data module – main characteristics

Prerequisites for debris flows occurrence and propagation that have to be taken into account are slope, lithology, active faults and vegetation. Slope is the most significant topographic parameter in the debris flow initiation analysis [12]. Most of publications show that debris flow is initiated in an area steeper than 15° or 20° [11, 12, 15]. Existence of an unstable hillside in a steep slope is a prerequisite for landslides and debris flows. Having regard the results in the above publications and our investigations of debris flows areas in the Eastern Rhodopes (Bulgaria) we suggest the following classes of slope gradients (in degrees): 0–2; 2–5; 5–15; 15–30; 30–45 and >45, where slopes in a range 30–45° are most susceptible for debris flows initiation. Longitudinal gradient of riverbed, plane and longitudinal configurations of river course also have to be taken into account. The changes in the longitudinal profile of the slope or in the acceleration or deceleration of the flow can be presented by profile curvature of the topographic surface. Plan curvature indicates the changes in flow line divergence.

A data about lithological variations of the rocks, the presence of weathered rocks, sandy-clay sediments with inclusions of boulders and gravel, cover of altered soils should be entered in the information system for the purpose of debris flows suscepti-bility and hazard assessment. A special attention have to be given to unstable sediments and the following parameters: thickness of weathered soil layer in a hillside slope, thickness and amount of riverbed sediment, volumetric concentration and grain size distribution of the sediments, accumulated sediments due to slope failure.

Vegetation has a controlling role for debris flows occurrence. Usually forest areas are less prone to debris flows while bare soils and arable lands are considered as more prone to debris flows. The data about land use and land cover should be considered in the analysis of debris flow susceptibility and hazard. Fires and land cover changes also have to be taken into account. When a wildfire burns wooded mountain slopes, it increases the chance of debris flows for several years. Uncontrolled deforestation exposes slopes to rainfalls and erosion, and makes them vulnerable to rapid movement of slope materials.

Debris flows arrival time, flow depth, flow velocity, peak discharge, event duration, debris flow volume and inundated area are indicators used for hazard and risk assessment. The results of the assessment can be visualized as debris flow hazard maps and debris flow risk assessment.

Taking into account the possible impacts of debris flow on infrastructure and ecosystem, in the study it is suggested two separate subsets of "Data" module: damage information and eco-system information (Fig. 3) which provide information for risk assessment.

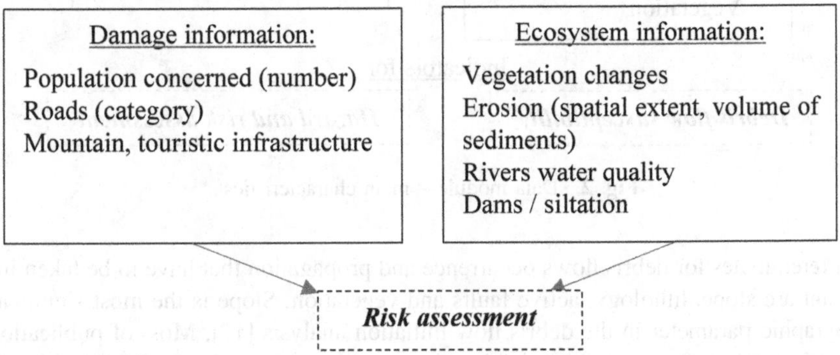

Fig. 3. Data module - indicators for risk assessment

4   Main Characteristics of the Analyses Module

The module "Analyses" of the system has to provide statistical and spatial analyses. Statistical analyses are needed to investigate the climate parameters and debris flows data like as frequency, peak discharge, flow velocity and debris volume.

The spatial character of the data concerned to debris flows allows application of spatial analyses like as spatial overlay, data reclassification, surface analyses etc. For example in result of spatial overlay of the data about factors and prerequisites for debris flows (Fig. 4) a susceptibility assessment is derived which allows to determine the debris flow prone areas. Of high importance in debris flow susceptibility assessment is assigning weights of different factors and prerequisites which to be applied in weighted overlay analysis. For this purpose Analytic Hierarchy Process can be done [16, 17].

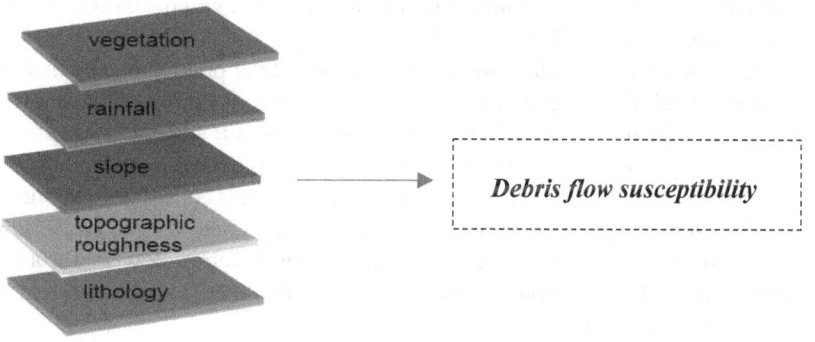

Fig. 4. Spatial overlay

5   Main Characteristics of the Risk Assessment Module

Risk assessment module is an important part of the proposed debris flow information system. Accepting that risk assessment is a function of hazard and following the concept of risk [18–20] the assessment can be considered in natural phenomena context (Fig. 5a) and in industrial context (Fig. 5b).

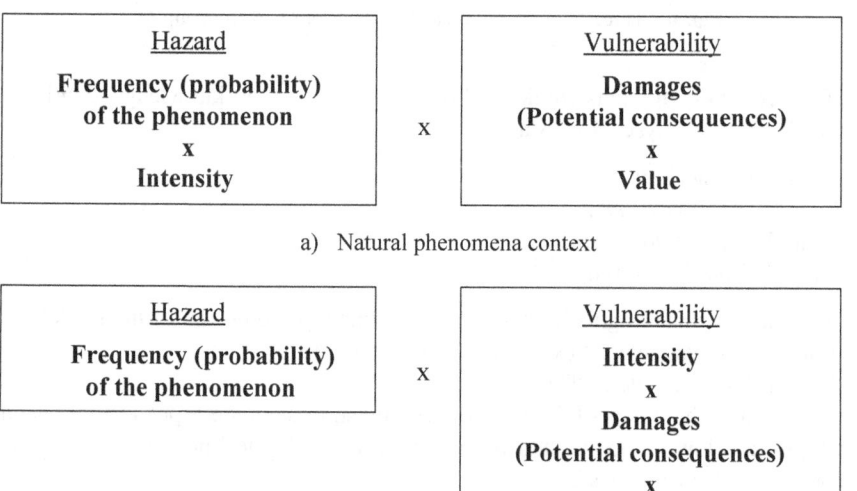

Fig. 5. Risk assessment

For the assessment of debris flow susceptibility, hazard and vulnerability a fuzzy logic can be applied. The risk assessment using fuzzy logic is particularly recommended in case of data limitation and unclear, gradual boundaries of the distribution of natural factors (indicators) [17].

In this study as a part of the risk assessment module is proposed to be included a fuzzy logic model for integrated risk assessment from the debris flow due to the multiple natural factors (as rainfall duration, rainfall amount, slope, erosion etc.). The idea is this fuzzy logic model to be designed as a hierarchical system with several inputs and one output. Each level of the hierarchical system is consisted from one fuzzy logical subsystem with several inputs. The fuzzy logic system output gives the integrated assessment of risk degree from the investigated debris flow in certain area regarding to the multiple natural factors. A scheme of the three-level hierarchical fuzzy system is presented on Fig. 6.

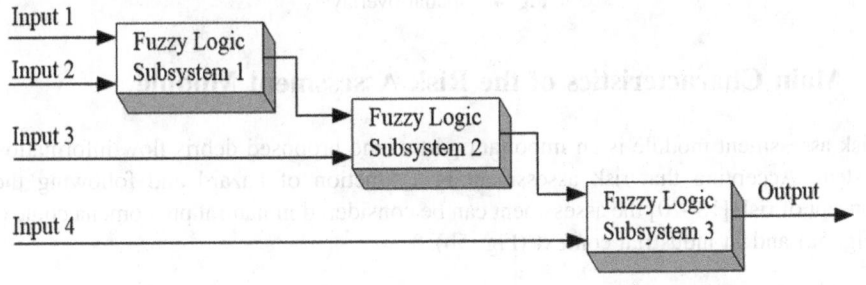

Fig. 6. Three-level hierarchical fuzzy system with four inputs

The fuzzy system inputs are defined on the basis of expert knowledge, debris flow data and current analyses, for example:

- Input 1 *"Flow depth"*;
- Input 2 *"Flow velocity"*;
- Input 3 *"Debris flow duration"*;
- Input 4 *"Inundated area"*.

Two intermediate linguistic variables are defined in the design of the model:
Intermediate variable 1 "Debris flow characteristics";
Intermediate variable 2 "Debris flow hazard".

In this case, the inputs of the first fuzzy logic subsystem are Input 1 "Flow depth" and Input 2 "Flow velocity", and the output variable is the Intermediate variable 1 "Debris flow characteristics".

The inputs of the second fuzzy logic subsystem are Intermediate variable 1 "Debris flow characteristics" and Input 3 "Debris flow duration", the output variable is the Intermediate variable 2 "Debris flow hazard".

The inputs of the third fuzzy logic subsystem are Intermediate variable 2 "Debris flow hazard" and Input 4 "Inundated area". The output of third fuzzy logic subsystem is output of the proposed fuzzy logic system – the integrated assessment of risk degree from the investigated debris flow in certain area regarding to the selected four factors. The higher value corresponds to the higher risk degree.

In the proposed fuzzy logic model, the all input linguistic variables, corresponding to the defined four inputs and two intermediate variables, are represented by five fuzzy membership functions, as follow: *"Very low* (VL)", *"Low* (L)", *"Moderate* (M)", *"High* (H)", and *"Very high* (VH)"*. The all input variables are assessed in the interval [0, 5] using trapezoidal membership functions (Fig. 7).

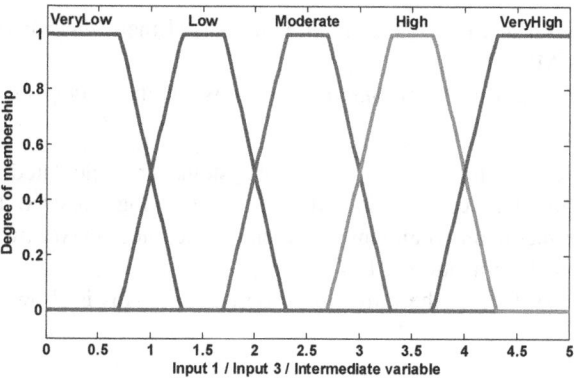

Fig. 7. Membership functions of the *Input* 1, *Input* 3 and *Intermediate variable*

The output of the fuzzy logic model (Integrated assessment of risk degree) is described by five fuzzy membership functions: *"Very low* (VL)", *"Low* (L)", *"Moderate* (M)", *"High* (H)", and *"Very high* (VH)"*. The output variables is assessed in the interval [0, 100] using trapezoidal membership functions (Fig. 8).

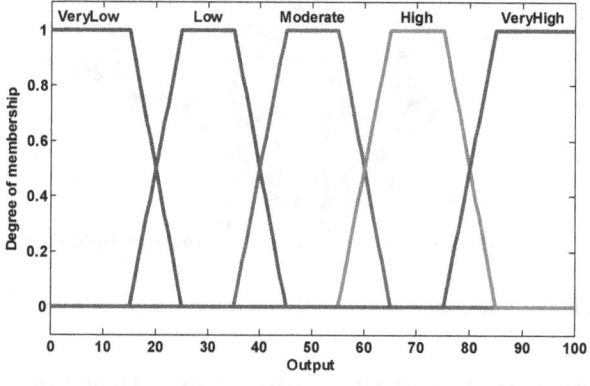

Fig. 8. Membership functions of the fuzzy logic system output

The inference rules in the three fuzzy logic subsystem are defined as "If - then" - clause. The number of rules in the knowledge base for each of the fuzzy logic sub-systems is 25. Some of the inference rules are defined as follow:

If *Flow depth* is VL and *Flow velocity* is H then *Debris flow characteristics* is M;
If *Flow depth* is L and *Flow velocity* is M then *Debris flow characteristics* is M;
If *Flow depth* is M and *Flow velocity* is VH then *Debris flow characteristics* is H;
If *Debris flow characteristics* is M and *Debris flow duration* is L then *Debris flow hazard* is M;
If *Debris flow characteristics* is M and *Debris flow duration* is VH then *Debris flow hazard* is H;
If *Debris flow hazard* is L and *Inundated area* is H then *Integrated assessment of risk degree* is M;
If *Debris flow hazard* is H and *Inundated area* is VH then *Integrated assessment of risk degree* is VH.

The outputs of the three fuzzy logic subsystems are calculated as an average weighted of all the inference rules, included in the fuzzy logic matrix. The three fuzzy logic models are based on Mamdani's inference machines, max/min operations and center of gravity defuzzification [21].

The inference surface of the third fuzzy logic subsystems is shown on Fig. 9.

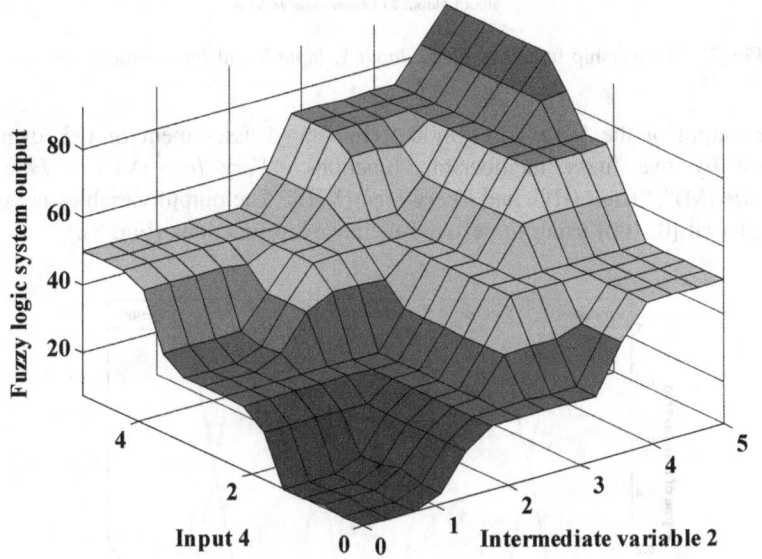

Fig. 9. Inference surfaces of the third fuzzy logic subsystem

6 Main Characteristics of the Multi-criteria Decision Analysis Module

The proposed information system needs to provide potential for multi-criteria decision analysis to support decision making. The Analytic Hierarchy Process is an easy-to-use multi-criteria decision-making method. This method is expressed in arranging the factors considered to be important for a decision in a hierarchic structure descending from an overall goal to criteria, sub-criteria, and finally alternatives at successive levels [19]. The main question that needs to be answered in case of occurrence of hazardous event is "where to take actions first?". For this purpose, specific indicators have to be considered. For example, in case of debris flow the following indicators have to be taken into account: importance of the affected roads, number of cars, affected people, connections to other roads, other infrastructure – buildings, dams, danger of flooding.

The multi-criteria decision analysis allows decision makers to take a motivated decision based on scientific and expert analysis of the data. In this regard the decision support information system contain three main components: data; scientific analyses, and risk assessment and decision-making analyses.

7   Presentation of a Geoinformation Portal

For optimal data management, mapping, visualization and sharing of the debris flow data and results of the analyses, a dedicated server-based enterprise GIS can be used. It is integrated through the entire organization so that all project users can manage, share, and use spatial data and related information to address a variety of needs, including data creation, modification, visualization, analysis, and dissemination. The GIS architecture of the project was developed using ArcGIS Enterprise 10.7.1 products and consists of the several software components (Fig. 10):

Fig. 10. Architecture of the geoinformation portal of University of Mining and Geology "St. Ivan Rilski" (Sofia, Bulgaria), [Source (with modifications): https://enterprise.arcgis.com/en/get-started/latest/windows/additional-server-deployment.htm]

- ArcGIS Server - a software feature that enables publishing of GIS data via web services and sharing across the organization and through an Internet connection. It also provides a client-server connection for geospatial data queries and analytical operations. Server management is available to authorized users at https://maps.mgu.bg:6443/arcgis/manager;
- ArcGIS Web Adapter (available at https://maps.mgu.bg/arcgis) is registered to the server and provides access to its resources to anyone with an Internet connection.

- ArcGIS Portal - a corporate cloud (Software-as-a-Service) service for easy access to data publishing, web mapping, sharing, and performing of analytical tasks. The portal access is organized in hierarchical model with different task-specific roles to the users. Administrative access to the server and portal is only allowed for the project GIS administrator. The ArcGIS server is federated to the Portal, thus the publishing services are managed entirely by the latter component. The Portal's home page is publicly available at https://maps.mgu.bg/arcgis/home/.
- ArcGIS Data Store - an application for easy configuration of databases for storage and operation of hosted GIS layers, created through the hosting server from ArcGIS Portal. Two databases (relational and cached) are registered in the GIS server.
- ArcGIS Desktop – a standalone GIS platform for managing databases, mapping, performing analytical tasks, with the help of which hosted GIS layers are created in the Portal.
- Web App Builder - an HTML/JavaScript web application development platform integrated into the GIS Portal. It is used to create mapping web applications. The project's web app is available at: https://maps.mgu.bg/arcgis/apps/View/index.html?appid=3836f023c6b34beeb0bd2422e1a777a6 (Fig. 11).

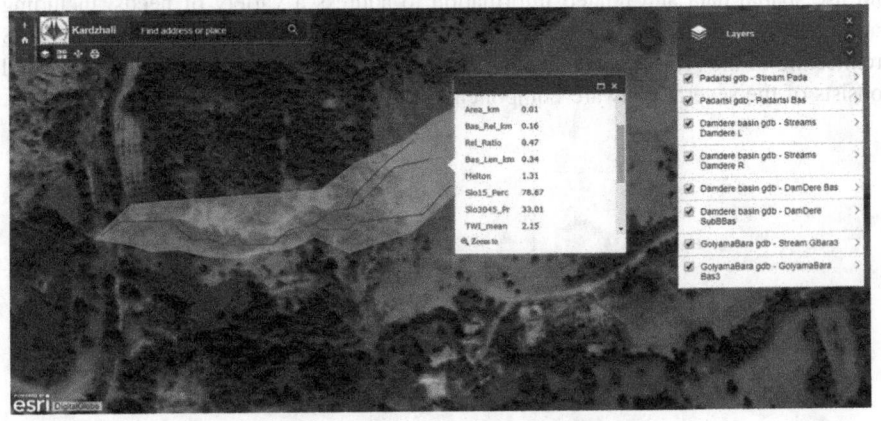

Fig. 11. The main interface of the web mapping application

A gully induced debris flow basin is presented on the Fig. 11. The basin is depicted as a polygon layer and morphometric parameters and debris flow data are entered in the polygon attribute table.

The machine which runs the software components has the following technical parameters: Microsoft Windows 10 Enterprise (with web server component enabled - IIS); Intel (R) Core (TM) i5-6600 CPU @ 3.30 GHz, 3301 MHz, 4 cores; 32 GB RAM; graphics card - NVIDIA GeForce GTX 1060 6 GB. The machine is named MIGGEOSERVER, and is part of the internal LAN of UMG "St. Ivan Rilski" (192.168.2.108 at mgu.bg), with external IP 78.90.247.26 and DNS maps.mgu.bg.

The implementation of the geoinformation portal for the needs of the debris flow study and monitoring proved successful and enabled seamless data management and public sharing of the results.

8 Conclusion

The presented model of debris flow information system can be used in debris flow monitoring and to support decision making in case of occurrence of this hazardous event. The quantity and quality of the initial data are the most important elements of the system, of which the results depend on. The possibility of development and using geoinformation portal allow better communication of the information, analyses and data management, and increases the opportunity for taking a motivated decision. The public access to the portal has a great contribution to rising awareness about the debris flows, increasing the preparedness and mitigating the hazard.

Acknowledgments. This work has been carried out in the framework of the National Science Program "Environmental Protection and Reduction of Risks of Adverse Events and Natural Disasters", approved by the Resolution of the Council of Ministers № 577/17.08.2018 and supported by the Ministry of Education and Science (MES) of Bulgaria (Agreement № Д01-322/18.12.2019).

References

1. Varnes, D.J.: Slop movement types and processes. In: Schuster, R.L., Krizekq, R.J. (eds.) Special Report 176: Landslides: Analysis and Control. TRB, National Research Council, Washington, D.C., pp. 12–33 (1978)
2. Cruden, D.M., Varnes, D.J.: Landslide types and processes. In: Turner, A.K., Schuster, R.L. (eds.) Landslides. Investigation and Mitigation, Special Report 247, Transport Research Board, National Research Council, Washington D.C., pp. 31–75 (1996)
3. Iliev-Bruchev, I. (ed.): Geological hazard in Bulgaria. In: Sofia (ed.) Explanatory Text to a Map in M 1: 500 000. Bulgarian Academy of Sciences, 143 p. (1994)
4. Dorasamy, M., Raman, M.: Information systems to support disaster planning and response: problem diagnosis and research gap analysis. In: Proceedings of the 8th International Conference ISCRAM 2011, Lisbon, Portugal (2011)
5. Yun, H.-C., Kim, J.-B., Jung, K.-Y., Kim, M.-G.: Application of disaster information system for disaster management. In: Kim, T.-H., Ramos, C., Kim, H.-k., Kiumi, A., Mohammed, S., Ślęzak, D. (eds.) ASEA 2012. CCIS, vol. 340, pp. 401–408. Springer, Heidelberg (2012). https://doi.org/10.1007/978-3-642-35267-6_53
6. Krumay, B., Brandtweiner, R.: The role of information systems to support disaster management. WIT Trans. Built Environ. 301–313, (2015). https://doi.org/10.2495/dman150271. ISSN 1743-3509
7. Beydoun, G., Dascalu, S., Dominey-Howes. D., Sheehan. A.: Disaster management and information systems: insights to emerging challenges. Inf. Syst. Front. **20**, 649–652 (2018). https://doi.org/10.1007/s10796-018-9871-6
8. Jackson, L.E., Kostaschuck, R.A., MacDonald, G.M.: Identification of debris flow hazard on alluvial fan in the Canadian Rocky Mountains. Geol. Soc. Am. Rev. Eng. **7**, 115–124 (1987)

9. Bovis, M.J., Jakob, M.: The role of debris supply conditions in predicting debris flow activity. Earth Surf. Process. Land. **24**, 1039–1054 (1999)
10. Wilford, D.J., Sakals, M.E., Innes, J.L., Sidle, R.C., Bergerud, W.A.: Recognition of debris flow, debris flood and flood hazard through watershed morphometrics. Landslides **1**, 61–66 (2004). https://doi.org/10.1007/s10346-003-0002-0
11. Zhou, W., Tang, Ch., Van Asch, Th.W.J., Chang, M.: A rapid method to identify the potential of debris flow development induced by rainfall in the catchments of the Wenchuan earthquake area. Landslides **13**, 1243–1259 (2016). https://doi.org/10.1007/s10346-015-0631-0
12. Kang, S., Lee, S.-R., Vasu, N.N., Park, J-Y., Lee, D-H.: Development of an initiation criterion for debris flows based on local topographic properties and applicability assessment at a regional scale. Eng. Geol. **230**, 64–76 (2017). http://dx.doi.org/10.1016/j.enggeo.2017.09.017
13. Baltakova, A., Nikolova, V., Kenderova, R., Hristova, N.: Analysis of debris flows by application of GIS and remote sensing: case study of western foothills of Pirin Mountain (Bulgaria). In: DEBRIS FLOWS: Disasters, Risk, Forecast, Protection. Proceedings of the 5th International Conference, Tbilisi, Georgia, 1–5 October 2018, pp. 22–32 (2018)
14. Dotseva, Z., Gerdjikov, I., Vangelov, D.: Modern debris flow activity in southern slopes of Rila Mountain, with an example from the area of Cherna Mesta village. In: National Conference with international participation "GeoSciences 2019". Review of the Bulgarian Geological Society, vol. 80, part 3, pp. 227–229 (2019)
15. Takahashi, T.: Estimation of potential debris flows and their hazardous zones: soft countermeasures for a disaster. J. Nat. Disaster Sci. **3**(1), 57–89 (1981)
16. Saaty, R.: The analytic hierarchy process – what it is and how it is used. Math. Model. **9**(3–5), 161–176 (1987)
17. Nikolova, V., Zlateva, P.: Geoinformation approach for complex analysis of multiple natural hazard. Int. Arch. Photogramm. Remote Sens. Spatial Inf. Sci. **XLII-3/W4**, 375–381 (2018). https://doi.org/10.5194/isprs-archives-XLII-3-W4-375-2018
18. Tacnet, J.-M.: Prise en compte de l'incertitude dans l'expertise des risques naturels en montagne par analyse multicritères et fusion d'information. Thèse de doctorat en sciences et génie de l'environnement, Ecole Nationale Supérieure des Mines, Saint-Etienne, France (2009)
19. Tacnet, J.-M. (coord.): Decision support guidelines methods, procedures and tools developed in PARAmount (WP 7), Version 1.0 (2012)
20. Mortureux, Y.: Techniques de l'Ingénieur - Traité 'L'entreprise industrielle', chapter La sûreté de fonctionnement: méthodes pour maîtriser les risques - Ref. AG 4670, pp. 1–17 (2001)
21. Bede, B.: Mathematics of Fuzzy Sets and Fuzzy Logic. Studies in Fuzziness and Soft Computing, vol. 295, Springer, Heidelberg (2013). https://doi.org/10.1007/978-3-642-35221-8

Towards an Indoor Navigation Application for Emergency Evacuations and Persons with Visual Impairments – Experiences from First Responders and End Users

G. Anthony Giannoumis^(⊠), Terje Gjøsæter, and Cristina Paupini

Oslo Metropolitan University, Oslo, Norway
gagian@oslomet.no

Abstract. As natural and human disaster are increasingly affecting people's lives around the globe in a growing and variegated way, the need to be prepared for a variety of conditions is imperative. Notwithstanding the relevance of ICT in assisting in preparedness and the importance of addressing the diversity of the population have been recognized, there are still gaps in understanding *How* to properly apply these principles in emergency management. This study explores how indoor navigation technology can contribute to faster, better and safer evacuations by providing useful information to emergency personnel and affected public at the scene of the evacuation. For this purpose, the ongoing INSIDE project aims to take an existing mobile app that provides universally designed indoor-navigation at Oslo Metropolitan University, the *OsloMet application*, and re-design it to support first responders with situational awareness assistance as well as to assist the public in evacuating efficiently. Contextually, a survey has been conducted among emergency services' representatives, in order to identify what information and functionality could be valuable for their work during emergency evacuations.

Keywords: Universal design · Accessibility · Disability · Emergency situations

1 Introduction

Natural as well as man-made disasters are affecting people's lives around the world in a very disruptive manner. The increasingly felt effects of climate change and human conflicts are contributing to the necessity of being prepared for a variety of emergency situations. There is much research on how ICT can assist in preparedness, mitigation and rescue operations during emergencies, and there is also an increasing awareness of the need of taking into account the diversity of the population [1], as well as the need for ensuring that the relevant ICT tools are accessible by all [2]. UNDRR's Sendai Framework for Disaster Risk Reduction (SFDRR) of 2015 in particular addresses people with disabilities in disaster risk reduction and the need for universal design [3]. However, there are still gaps between these goals and the current reality that need to be bridged:

© IFIP International Federation for Information Processing 2020
Published by Springer Nature Switzerland AG 2020
Y. Murayama et al. (Eds.): ITDRR 2019, IFIP AICT 575, pp. 159–167, 2020.
https://doi.org/10.1007/978-3-030-48939-7_14

- Understanding *what/who* vs. understanding *how*:
  - It is well known that we need to pay attention to diversity in disaster situations e.g. during evacuation and make sure that in particular people with disabilities and the elderly are taken care of, but it may be less obvious how to do this in practice [2].
- *Motivation* vs. *implementation*:
  - Even if the requirements are clear, the implementation may fail to consider all aspects the situation and the diversity among users; e.g. to properly cover the needs of people with disabilities [4] and those affected by situational disabilities in disaster situations [5].

Universally designed ICT-assisted indoor navigation is a promising approach to the problem of evacuating a building with a diverse group of people, including employees that may know the building well, but also first-time visitors and people with visual impairments [6]. The ongoing INSIDE project aims to take an existing mobile app that provides universally designed indoor-navigation at Oslo Metropolitan University, the *OsloMet application*, and re-design it to support first responders with situational awareness assistance as well as to assist the public in evacuating efficiently [7]. The original OsloMet application is based on a network of low-energy Bluetooth (BLE) beacons paired with a mobile app to provide a way-finding solution for everyone, including persons with visual disabilities. The approach of using BLE beacons for indoor wayfinding has been successfully tested in laboratory and controlled experimental settings [8]. The application is iOS-based and uses the VoiceOver functionality of the operating system to provide voice control.

The main objective of this study is to investigate how indoor navigation technology can contribute to faster, better and safer evacuations by providing useful information to the emergency personnel and the affected public at the scene of the evacuation.

The rest of the article is organized as follows: This introduction is followed by a literature review in Sect. 2, while Sect. 3 provides an overview of the methods used in this study. Section 4 presents and analyzes results, and finally discussion followed by conclusions and future work are covered in Sects. 5 and 6.

2   Literature Review

2.1   Human Rights and Emergency Situations

The protection of human rights has without doubt improved since the promulgation of the Declaration of Human Rights in 1948 and on a national and international level governments have made numerous steps forward. However, an acceptable standard of conduct by States during internal conflict is far from achieved [9]. Research suggests that public emergencies pose a heightened threat of serious and systematic human rights abuse when States employ extraordinary powers to address threats to public order [10]. To reduce this risk, the United Nation adopted the International Covenant on Civil and Political Rights (ICCPR) in 1966, which requires the States to notify the international community hastily when a suspension of their human rights obligations is required due to national crises (art. 41). The derogation of human rights obligations is possible thanks to two criteria expressed by the ICCPR: the presence of a public emergency threatening the life of the State, and the necessity to adopt emergency measures due to the exigencies of the situation [9]. Nonetheless, states of emergency have been declared by governments around the world to face a vast assortment of crises, including political unrest, general civil unrest, criminal or terrorist violence, labor strikes, economic emergencies, the collapse of public institutions, the spread of infectious diseases, and natural disasters (U.N. Treaty Collection Database). These initiatives are actually in contrast with the "Lawless" criteria for declaring a state of emergency, which affirms that the threat must be present or imminent, exceptional, and a "threat to the organized life of the community". As a consequence, even the threat posed by terrorist groups such as Al Qaeda seldom justify a declaration of emergency [11]. To overcome the ambiguity of these parameters, the academic world has suggested four non-derogable human rights: 1) the right to life; 2) prohibition of torture; 3) prohibition of slavery; 4) prohibition of retroactive penalties for crimes [9]. The said four points are to be added to the three non-derogable human rights already highlighted by the ICCPR: the prohibition of imprisonment for breach of contract, the right to recognition as a person before the law and the right to freedom of thought, conscience and religion. Not considering the theoretical aspect, there is no evidence of a universal acceptance of any of these [9]. It is also unclear whether and to what extent obligations for accessibility constitute a non-derogable right for persons with disabilities.

2.2   Universal Design

According to the U.S. Census Bureau, disadvantaged populations include persons with disabilities, elderly, indigent and illiterate, and cover more than 50% of the U.S. population. In view of the above, it is clear that keeping on using the term "special needs" does a disservice to the groups included in the definition and reduces the chances of planning interventions for specific needs and, consequently, providing an efficient, inclusive response [12]. It is also important to notice that disasters, terrorism and other emergency situations tend to instantly increase the number of people with disabilities and functional limitations, temporarily or permanently, both as a physical or psychological consequence of the traumatic event and due to the environment's conditions [13].

Eliminating the use of a "special needs" category could improve disaster preparation and emergency response processes, procedures and systems introducing the consideration of humanity as a totality of different individualities into the fabric and culture of emergency management and disaster planning. If disability and other socially disadvantaged groups keep being considered as unique or special isolated entities the system's existing inefficiencies and inefficacies will continue [12]. To achieve this necessary upgrade the universal design perspective needs to be adopted, in order to address the needs of a variegated population that deserves consideration.

3 Methods and Research Design

The data collection has been conducted in two parts. First, a quantitative research study was conducted amongst emergency service personnel in order to understand their needs and interest for implementing an indoor navigation application in their work with evacuations. Second, a framework for user testing was developed with an aim of determining improvement areas in the indoor navigation application.

The survey consists of a combination of open-ended and closed questions: Open-ended questions were used to address specific concerns that demanded qualitative feedback, whereas closed questions were used to collect quantitative data for statistical purposes. The main target group for the survey was emergency response personnel from the Norwegian fire-and-rescue department, police and paramedics. Some factors that differentiates them from the rest of the respondents are:

1. their location when the emergency occurs (outside of the evacuation site). Emergency response personnel cover large areas and move in to assist where they are needed. This implies less local knowledge about the specific buildings they are called out to and a longer response time than personnel stationed on-site.
2. Higher level of responsibility. This group carries the main responsibility for the evacuation and public safety once arrived at the scene.

Based on these factors, one can assume an indoor navigation solution could be very valuable for this group. Nevertheless, the personnel working on-site with evacuations cannot be omitted since most evacuations take place before the emergency response personnel arrive at the scene. One major group within this segment is security officers. Other relevant groups are personnel that work with emergency preparedness, Environment Health Safety, as floor or chief wardens. Great care was taken in choosing whom the survey was distributed to since the survey responses were anonymous, which would make any link between the response and a specific person impossible to determine. Thereby, the answers were provided only by the qualified personnel. Each response was also thoroughly checked during the translation - and data analysis - process to verify whether had occurred any invalid or duplicated responses. Three of the responses were removed before data analysis, two of which derived from the pre-test of the survey from persons that had never taken part in an evacuation before, which made them not entitled to answer. Personal identifiable information about the personnel the project team corresponded with directly has also been anonymized due to confidentiality rights. The correspondence was conducted via e-mail and personal Facebook messages between the personnel and the project group.

A survey has been conducted with emergency services' representatives with the intention to identify what information and functionality could be valuable for their work during emergency evacuations. Personnel from the fire-and-rescue services, paramedics, police and security offices took part in the questionnaire. The questions were formulated to provide crucial information considering their roles, experiences and outlooks on emergency situations procedures. The amount of the obtained survey responses was equal to one hundred and twenty-two (122).

The survey consisted of three parts. The objective of the first part was to collect necessary data about the respondents' background and their experience with emergency evacuations. The second segment aimed to obtain information considering those situations they had assisted in. Finally, the third part intended to investigate the utility of the OsloMet application's implemented and planned features.

Lastly, a framework for user testing was developed with an aim to determine possible improvement areas in the OsloMet application. For this purpose, the users were asked to fill in two surveys and fulfill the requirements adding to the user test. The first questionnaire was a System Usability Scale (SUS) followed by a user test of the application, where the participants had to find a location in the building. Notes and comments were made by both users and conductors.

4   Results and Analysis

In the first part of the analysis, the results from the survey with emergency service personnel will be presented. Then the second part of the analysis will present the results of the indoor navigation usability tests.

4.1   Results from Emergency Service Survey

The emergency service personnel came from a variety of backgrounds. Nearly half of the respondents came from fire-and-rescue service providers. Other respondents included police officers (28%), paramedics (13%), security officers (7%) and others (7%). 78% of respondents had a leadership role in their organization, and the remaining had non-leadership roles. All respondents had assisted in emergency evacuations with 53% having assisted in 15 or more evacuations, 7% in 10 to 14, 17% in five to nine, and 23% in less than four. The most common types of emergency evacuation with which the respondents were involved included fire (n = 113), followed by terrorism and life-threatening violence (n = 31), gas leakage (n = 52), natural disaster (n = 31). Less common were accidents (n = 5), other emergency situations (n = 9).

Respondents also provided useful results on their experiences during emergency evacuations. During emergencies, their primary source of information came from callers and call centers (33%). In addition, respondents also cited their leaders (16%), people on the scene (16%), radio communication (13%), local guides (12%) and their own experiences or training (10%) as their primary source of information. However, these results differ based on whether the respondent had a leadership or non-leadership role in their organization. For respondents in a leadership role, they primarily turned to callers and call centers (41%), local guides (33%), other leaders (23%), radio communication (14%), people on the scene (14%), and their own experience or training (9%). The differing results suggest that persons in leadership positions in emergency situations rely to a greater extent on callers and call centers, other leaders, and local guides than persons in non-leadership positions. The results also suggest minor differences between leaders and non-leaders when it comes to primarily receiving information from people on the scene, radio communication, and personal experience and training (Table 1).

Table 1. Primary sources of information during an emergency evacuation.

Information source	Overall	Leaders
Callers and call centers	33%	41%
Leaders	16%	23%
People on the scene	16%	14%
Radio communication	13%	14%
Local guides	12%	33%
Personal experience and training	10%	9%

The respondents were also asked about the kinds of devices that they use during emergency evacuations. The majority of the respondents used a radio (n = 106), with a smaller minority using a smartphone (n = 37), tablet (n = 25), other device (n = 16), or computer (n = 15). Only one respondent reported using pen and paper.

Finally, the respondents were asked a set of questions that focused on the functional requirements of an indoor navigation emergency evacuation application. The majority of the respondents (n = 89) considered an application that provided an overview of the users located inside the building as very useful (the best of 5 ratings). Similarly, the majority of the respondents (n = 84) considered an alarm for users with injuries as very useful. An even larger majority (n = 88) considered an alarm for users in need of evacuation assistance as very useful. A smaller majority (n = 77) rated sensor data from motion detectors, gas alarms, and temperature as very useful. An even smaller majority (n = 64) believed that an automatic alarm from immobilized users or a message service to contact users who triggered an alarm would be very useful. A larger majority of respondents (n = 72) consider an indoor navigation system as very useful.

4.2 Results from Usability Testing of Indoor Navigation System

The results from the usability tests of the indoor navigation system showed that respondents generally considered the system unusable (see Fig. 1). This finding contrasts with existing studies of similar indoor navigation systems, which showed high levels of usability among persons with visual impairments [1]. Unlike prior research, this article targeted persons without disabilities. The respondents varied in age from 19 to 43 years old, with an average age of 24. All respondents identified as either women (n = 18) or men (n = 10). Nearly all respondents (n = 22) reported having problems with using the system. These problems may explain the lower levels of reported usability. The system usability score, based on the SUS, ranged from 40 to 60 with an average of 50 (n = 28). Research shows that usability scores above 68 are considered usable [2]. The difference in average scores between men (50, n = 10) and women (51, n = 18) and users that spoke Norwegian (52, n = 10) and those that did not (50, n = 18) were negligible. The only area where respondents reported slightly different average system usability scores were between users who experienced problems during the test (51, n = 22) and those that did not (48, n = 6). This discrepancy contradicts the expectation that users who experienced problems using the system would report lower average usability scores. However, due to the low number of respondents (n = 6) of the users who did not experience a problem, the results are inconclusive.

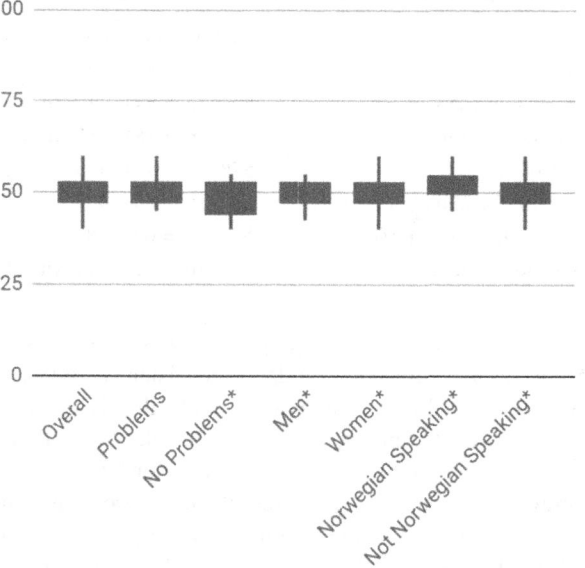

Fig. 1. Boxplot diagrams showing the average SUS scores overall and broken down by the category of users. *SUS has been validated for samples n > 20, asterisk indicates where n < 20

Research using the SUS typically uses short qualitative responses as a means to explain and calibrate the scores. Due to an error in the data collection procedure, this information was not systematically recorded. However, the respondents did provide some comments regarding the problems that they experienced. Respondents who did not speak Norwegian commented that the app was only available in Norwegian and used commands spoken only in Norwegian. As a result, they commented that they could not use some of the app's functionalities. Norwegian speakers commented on spelling mistakes. The respondents also commented that the blue dot, which identifies where the user is located, moved occasionally when the user was standing still and did not change floors automatically during navigation.

5   Discussion

There are a couple of methodological weaknesses in the data collection that have to be mentioned. First, the results in Table 2 were based on a five-item Likert scale. The Likert scale ranged from 1 "Not useful at all" to 5 "Very useful". Typically Likert scales are balanced in the sense that items 1 and 5 and items 2 and 4 reflect similarly positioned responses – e.g., 1 "Very Unuseful" and 5 "Very Useful", with 2 "Unuseful" and 4 "Useful". However, due to the skewed distribution of the data showing a majority of respondents considering the functional requirements as "Very Useful", it is unlikely that the unbalanced Likert scale has biased the results.

Table 2. Functional requirements of an emergency evacuation application.

Requirement	Very useful	Useful or not useful
Overview of users inside building	73% (n = 89)	27% (n = 33)
Alarm from injured users	69% (n = 84)	31% (n = 38)
Alarm from users needing assistance	72% (n = 88)	28% (n = 34)
Building sensor data	57% (n = 70)	43% (n = 52)
Automatic alarm for immobilized users	52% (n = 64)	48% (n = 58)
Message service for users triggering alarm	52% (n = 64)	48% (n = 58)
Indoor navigation system	59% (n = 72)	41% (n = 50)

Concerning the user evaluation of the app, there was a weakness in the SUS data collection procedure as the researchers did not consistently collect short qualitative responses to explain and calibrate the scores. While this is the generally accepted practice in using the SUS instrument, the data nonetheless provide a useful point of reference to consider the usability of indoor navigation systems, particularly as it contrasts with previous research on the usability of indoor navigation systems for persons with visual impairments. While the qualitative responses would provide a more detailed explanation of the scores, the results nonetheless have merit on their own.

Despite these weaknesses, the results are valuable in pointing out weaknesses and bugs as well as missing features in the current implementation of the OsloMet application, and for providing insights on which features to prioritize for the next version, from the first responders' point of view.

6   Conclusions and Next Steps

It is clear that the current implementation of the OsloMet app has several weaknesses and shortcomings when it comes to usability, as uncovered by the user testing, but most of these issues are bugs rather than inherent problems and can be fixed with relative ease. In addition, the input from first responders also points to a potential for significant usefulness. During the survey the respondents highlighted a few important implementation on the OsloMet app that would improve the efficiency of the rescue operations, such as an overview of the users located inside the building and alarms for users with injuries and in need of evacuation assistance. Sensor data from motion detectors, gas alarms and temperature was also considered useful information to be added to the app in order to give rescuers a more complete look to the emergency. A smaller majority of the respondent finally individuated an important upgrade in the implementation of an automatic alarm from immobilized users and a message service to contact alarm-triggering users. It is also notable that a vast majority of the respondents indicated an indoor navigation system as very useful during emergency situation, confirming the direction to follow in order to improve the emergency management. The most important next step in our project is now to implement the revised app based on the input gathered in this study, followed by extensive field-testing with users, security officers and first responders during evacuation training exercises for validating its usefulness in practice.

Acknowledgements. The research leading to this article was funded by the Norwegian Association of the Blind and Partially Sighted (Blindeforbundet). In addition, the authors would like to express their sincere gratitude to Keren Sømåen, Jolan Franssen, Małgorzata Orpel, and Nathan Rodier who have contributed to the collection of the data presented in this article.

References

1. Bennett, D., Phillips, B.D., Davis, E.: The future of accessibility in disaster conditions: how wireless technologies will transform the life cycle of emergency management. Futures **87**, 122–132 (2017)
2. Gjøsæter, T., Radianti, J., Chen, W.: Universal design of ICT for emergency management. In: Antona, M., Stephanidis, C. (eds.) UAHCI 2018. LNCS, vol. 10907, pp. 63–74. Springer, Cham (2018). https://doi.org/10.1007/978-3-319-92049-8_5
3. Stough, L.M., Kang, D.: The Sendai framework for disaster risk reduction and persons with disabilities. Int. J. Disaster Risk Sci. **6**(2), 140–149 (2015). https://doi.org/10.1007/s13753-015-0051-8
4. Radianti, J., Gjøsæter, T., Chen, W.: Universal design of information sharing tools for disaster risk reduction. In: Murayama, Y., Velev, D., Zlateva, P. (eds.) ITDRR 2017. IAICT, vol. 516, pp. 81–95. Springer, Cham (2019). https://doi.org/10.1007/978-3-030-18293-9_8
5. Gjøsæter, T., Radianti, J., Chen, W.: Understanding situational disabilities and situational awareness in disasters. In: Franco, Z., González, J.J., Canós, J.H. (eds.) 16th International Conference on Information Systems for Crisis Response and Management (ISCRAM 2019) (2019)
6. Fagernes, S., Grønli, T.-M.: Navigation for visually impaired using haptic feedback. In: Kurosu, M. (ed.) HCI 2018. LNCS, vol. 10902, pp. 347–356. Springer, Cham (2018). https://doi.org/10.1007/978-3-319-91244-8_28
7. Anthony Giannoumis, G., Gjøsæter, T., Radianti, J., Paupini, C.: Universally designed beacon-assisted indoor navigation for emergency evacuations. In: Murayama, Y., Velev, D., Zlateva, P. (eds.) ITDRR 2018. IAICT, vol. 550, pp. 120–129. Springer, Cham (2019). https://doi.org/10.1007/978-3-030-32169-7_9
8. Giannoumis, G.A., Ferati, M., Pandya, U., Krivonos, D., Pey, T.: Usability of indoor network navigation solutions for persons with visual impairments. In: Langdon, P., Lazar, J., Heylighen, A., Dong, H. (eds.) CWUAAT 2018, pp. 135–145. Springer, Cham (2018). https://doi.org/10.1007/978-3-319-75028-6_12
9. Fitzpatrick, J.: Human Rights in Crisis: The International System for Protecting Rights During States of Emergency, vol. 19. University of Pennsylvania Press, Philadelphia (1994)
10. Oraá, J.: Human Rights in States of Emergency in International Law. Oxford University Press, Oxford (1992)
11. Criddle, E.J., Fox-Decent, E.: Human rights, emergencies, and the rule of law. Hum. Rights Q. **34**(1) (2010)
12. Kailes, J.I., Enders, A.: Moving beyond "special needs" a function-based framework for emergency management and planning. J. Disabil. Policy Stud. **17**(4), 230–237 (2007)
13. Nick, G.A., et al.: Emergency preparedness for vulnerable populations: people with special health-care needs. Public Health Rep. **124**(2), 338 (2009)

Cyber Crisis Management Roles –
A Municipality Responsibility Case Study

Grethe Østby[⊠] and Basel Katt

Norwegian University of Science and Technology, Gjøvik, Norway
{grethe.ostby, basel.katt}@ntnu.no

Abstract. In this paper we propose a role model that can be applied in societal cyber crisis management to build safety and standard procedures during cyber security crisis. We define societal cyber crisis as the cyber crisis which affect the society in which disaster is or might be the consequence. The process to create our model started by analyzing regulations and responsibilities in Norwegian municipalities, and we used steps of a design science research (DSR) research approach to create our suggested artifact. A combination of conventional crisis management and cyber crisis management is proposed to identify the interrelationships among diverse stakeholders when managing the preparation for and reaction to a cyber crisis incident. We present a cyber incident handling role model (CIHRM) which is usable for visualizing cyber crisis in a diversity of organizations. After our model has been reviewed by the cyber security research community, we plan to implement the model when analyzing crisis management in various organizations to prepare for instructions, training and exercises at our training environment - The Norwegian Cyber Range.

Keywords: Cyber crisis · Cyber management · Management roles · Crisis management · Societal cyber crisis

1 Introduction

Bruer research has shown that the current competence levels on digitalization process among leaders in public sector in Norway has led computer security activities to be isolated from strategic planning daily operation [1]. Consequently, upper management leaders is focused on efficiency, rather than society readiness and emergency preparedness [2]. This is also supported by the Norwegian Auditor General's administration study nb 1, 2018 about digitalization in governmental sector, which concluded that the digitalization among departments and directorates is going too slow [3]. Cyber security and safety are not mentioned in any part of the report, only personal information in the matter of how to transfer these data from one department to another, and consequently the managers are forced to focus on the digitalization.

However, NOU 2015: 13 Digital vulnerability – safe society (Lysne committee), is describing how the civil protection system also should include the handling of cyber-incidents, both system failures and malicious attacks [4]. At the same time the Lysne committee also observed that there is lack of a cyber-security arena within the sector of the municipalities. They described that many municipalities have an increased need of

© IFIP International Federation for Information Processing 2020
Published by Springer Nature Switzerland AG 2020
Y. Murayama et al. (Eds.): ITDRR 2019, IFIP AICT 575, pp. 168–181, 2020.
https://doi.org/10.1007/978-3-030-48939-7_15

counselling and education to make good risk- and resilience analyses, and to establish control-systems to handle cyber-incidents. In addition, a municipality CERT is recommended in the study of municipalities common need of competence-center to deal with handling cyber-security incidents made by NorSIS 2017 [5].

In general, between an individual and an organization, there are teams, and more specifically, crisis management groups. Groups of people and teams from different worlds, with very different cultural responses to risk and emergency, having often very distinct prejudices about the threats to be dealt with and the goals to be met, and whose individual and corporate interests lend themselves poorly to broader cooperation. And they are all expected to work together under pressure [6].

In Norwegian (and other countries) traditional emergency-organizations, as for example the military forces, the police forces, the civil defense forces and others, roles have been defined to avoid dependency on individuals and to have a long-time rollover in these roles. Norwegian governmental regulations and guidance on municipalities' responsibilities is still suggesting tasks to be managed, and crises to be led by the municipality management. For several years, roles in such crisis responsibilities have been suggested in a number of municipality crisis management courses run by the Norwegian Civil defense national competence center, which those municipalities have adopted and have used with success during crisis.

The Norwegian municipality guidance suggests establishing a crisis staff to support the crisis management, but it does not define the roles of the staff. A lot of tasks are outlined, but they are not regulated in roles to deal with them [7]. Thus, it is easy to understand why decision makers responsible for crisis management want ways to respond to these challenges. It is important to recruit competent individuals, but it is also crucial to build teams and organizations that compensate for moments of individual weakness [6]. In this paper, we try to tackle these issues by studying two comparable crises with different causes. These crises could be analyzed within organizational tiers and thereby model roles and tasks to handle a variety of crisis, specifically societal cyber crisis. We use the municipality crisis management responsibility as a case to combine this responsibility with cyber crisis which affects municipality society. We aim to combine traditional incident command system roles with the organization–governed networks responsibilities.

Based on the analyzed crises, we suggest a model to best implement roles in management teams of societal cyber crisis on how to handle the crisis. We define societal cyber crisis as cyber crisis which affect the society in such a context of which disaster is or might be the consequence. We discuss the cyber incident management in all phases of the crisis on strategic, tactical and operational tiers in organizations to support other/overall crisis management decisions. Cyber-incidents require vast knowledge on all tires, and there will be a need of bringing in diverse experts in management-teams on the different tires, such as experts from SOCs, CERTs and other real-life stakeholders. These vast tasks require excellent capabilities to manage such teams and will be one of the most important ranges of roles to frame for managing societal cyber crisis.

The paper is structured as follows: After the introduction in Sect. 1, in Sect. 2 the background and relevant literature is presented. In Sect. 3, our research approach is discussed together with the use of municipalities crisis management responsibilities. In

Sect. 4, we present the municipality management roles, and discuss how to bring in cyber crisis roles. In Sect. 5 we exemplify the outcome of our model and outline our prospects for further research.

2 Background and Relevant Literature

In the literature on social–ecological systems, the term 'resilience' is used to describe the ability of a system to absorb or withstand changes inflicted onto the system from the outside [8]. Walker et al. [8] define the resilience of a system as: the capacity of a system to absorb disturbance and reorganize while undergoing change to still retain essentially the same function, structure, identity, and feedbacks. Resilience research is also interested in studying what kind of interactions can occur in complex interdependent infrastructures, but not with the aim to only identify the most critical relations. Rather, the aim is that operators and middle managers learn about complex system behavior to enable them to perform real-time resilience, or "operating at the edge of failure without falling off" [9]. Risk analysis, business continuity management and crisis management training are often performed within the context of a single organization or sector and are seldom addressing the holistic analysis of multiple infrastructures [9].

The process of disaster management is commonly visualized in several phases. The disaster management cycle illustrates the ongoing process by which governments, businesses and civil society plan for and reduce the impact of disasters, react during and immediately following a disaster, and take steps to recover after a disaster has occurred. The significance of this concept is its ability to promote a holistic approach to disaster management as well as to demonstrate the relationship between disasters and development. The pre-disaster activities are done before the hazard interacts with the vulnerable community to cause a disaster, usually referred to as mitigation and preparedness, which includes major activities such as preparedness through response, from prevention, mitigation and readiness, through relief, recovery and rehabilitation [10].

Disaster management is dealing with the immediate aftermath of the disaster, including short-term relief and response. This relates to activities such as evacuation, search and rescue and medical care. Post-disaster is the period of recovery until community returns to a normal condition. The concept of sustainable development is frequently associated with long-term recovery, which strongly aligns to the multiple-state definition of resilience, whereby a community should maximize the capacity to adapt and focus on long-term growth to a state of reduced vulnerability [11].

The NIST Framework for Improving Critical Infrastructure Cybersecurity, commonly referred to as the NIST Cybersecurity Framework, provides organizations with a structure for assessing and improving their ability to prevent, detect and respond to cyber incidents. Version 1.0 was published by the US National Institute of Standards and Technology (NIST) in 2014 and was aimed at operators of critical infrastructure. The framework guides cybersecurity activities and considers cybersecurity as a part of an organization's risk management processes. In this paper we present a model for the response and recovery phase as suggested in Fig. 1.

Fig. 1. NIST cyber security framework [12]

From a cyber security incident perspective Kulikova et al. [13] suggests four steps in crisis management comparable to NIST's framework, and FEMA suggests four stage activity cycle of mitigation, preparedness, response and recovery [14]. These approaches are comparable to NIST, and response and recovery are important in all suggestions.

As mentioned before, there should be roles pre-defined to cope with the response and recovery. When an emergency is unfolding, the people and systems involved in watching it unfold must determine what has already happened, what is currently happening, and what is likely to happen in the future; then, they make recommendations for reaction based on their situational awareness [15]. To be able to understand the situation, the responsible staff role should be able to visualize the incident.

As van der Aalst pointed out, event data is the major source of information [16]. Therefore, all these available events are numerous and the data and information they contain is more or less reliable, comes from varied sources, in various types and formats, and are time-dated. Incident Command Systems (ICS) is used to coordinate multiple response organizations under a temporary central authority with a hierarchical structure [17]. It is better understood as a highly centralized mode of network governance, designed to coordinate interdependent responders under urgent conditions. The contrast between a network governance and hierarchical view of the ICS is illustrated in Fig. 2. The left-hand side of the figure represents the dominant view of the ICS [18]. In this figure, a hierarchy allows the incident commander to direct the crisis functions of logistics, operations, planning, and finance/administration. But if we consider the ICS in terms of its members, we see it as a network, albeit a highly centralized one (on the right-hand side). The incident commander is at the center of the network, surrounded by organizations that have ongoing inter-crisis dyadic relationships, as illustrated by the right-hand side of Fig. 2.

When it comes to roles, the National Institute of Standards and Technology (NIST) has ranged three different tiers in the framework of risk management, which can help organize roles in these tiers. These tiers are strategic, tactical and operational [19] (Fig. 3).

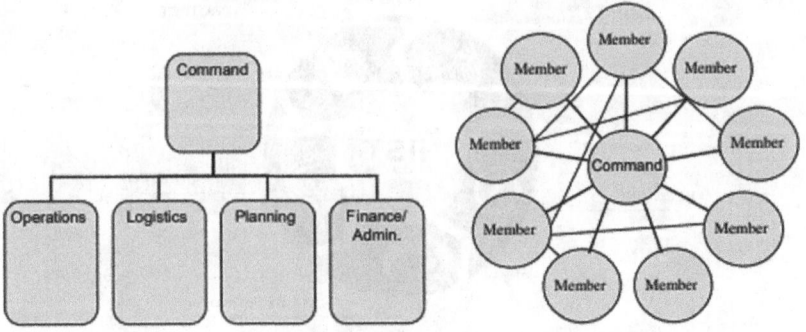

Fig. 2. Traditional incident command system and organization–governed networks [17]

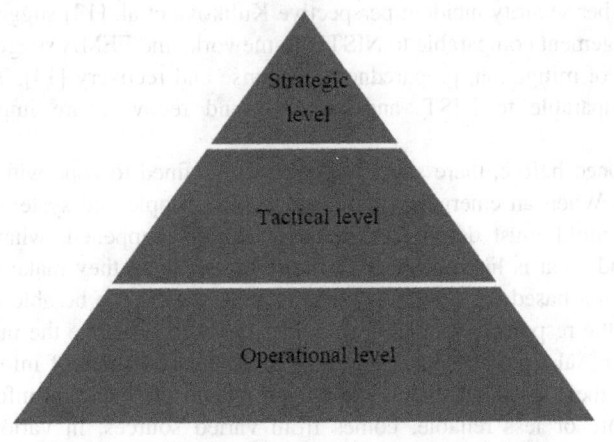

Fig. 3. Tiers in framework of risk management (NIST)

Every tier is led by managers, and different crises require different management roles on each layer. This can be transferred into diverse organizations on national, sectorial and local public responsibilities.

Boeke investigates how different models of public–private partnerships shape cyber crisis management in four European countries: the Netherlands, Denmark, Estonia, and the Czech Republic. Using Provan and Kenis's modes of network governance, an initial taxonomy of cyber governance structures, he presents two suggestions: First, national CERT/CSIRT teams are to be embedded inside or outside the intelligence community. Second, if cyber capacity can be centralized in one unit or spread across different sectors [20].

In this paper, we use the municipality crisis management responsibility as a case to discuss cyber crisis which affects municipality society to argue for a solution which combine Boeke's suggestions. We aim to combine traditional incident command system roles with the organization–governed networks responsibilities as outlined in this section.

3   Research Approach

In this paper, we approach the cyber security challenges using what can be referred to as a naive inductivist approach. The naïve inductivist approach starts by first observing a phenomenon and then generalizing the phenomenon which leads to theories that can be falsified or validated [21]. This approach will use the methodology out-lined by design science research in information systems (DSRIS) [22]. This methodology uses artifact design and construction (learning through building) to generate new knowledge and insights into a class of problems.

DSRIS requires three general activities: (1) construction of an artifact where construction is informed either by practice-based insight or theory, (2) the gathering of data on the functional performance of the artifact (i.e., evaluation), and (3) reflection on the construction process and on the implications the gathered data (from activity (2)) have for the artifact informing insight(s) or theory(s) [22].

How to work on these steps was presented in a thesis written by Karokola [23]. He visualized this approach as outlined in Fig. 4. As we are approaching our work in a naive inductivist approach, we modified the logical formalism in the model from abduction to induction.

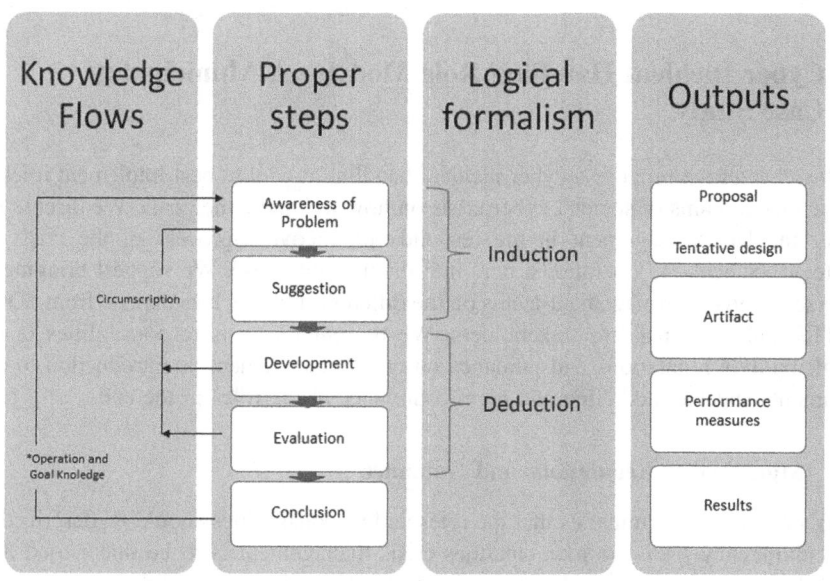

Fig. 4. Design research methodology - modified

To propose an artifact in an inductive approach we started up by analyzing municipalities responsibilities when handling crisis in general and cyber-incidents in special (first step in the 2nd column). For the next step we suggest a model to deal with the problem in crisis management when handling cyber incidents (second step in the 2nd column). The goal of the paper is to propose a tentative design (first step in the 4th

column), in which we want to present and test when executing cyber training and exercises in our training environment.

Apply the Case of Municipalities Crises Management Responsibilities
The Norwegian law concerning the municipality's emergency duty, civilian preparedness and the Civil defense organization outlines the municipality's responsibility to analyze and make emergency preparation based on risk and resilience in their geographical designated area [24].

The municipalities should outline prepared societal emergency work that will [25]:

- Protect the population and contribute to uphold critical infrastructure.
- Give an overview of knowledge and awareness of societal critical challenges and what effect these challenges would have on the society and communities.
- Reduce risk and vulnerability through preventive work.
- Ensure good emergency preparedness and crisis contingency.
- Attend to ensure collaboration and coordination with internal and external societal emergency partners in the municipality.

In this idea-paper, we start by presenting as-is crisis-management roles that are defined and evolved based on the guidelines and try to combine this with roles needed in a cyber crisis.

4   Cyber Incident Handling Role Model – A Municipality Case Study

In this chapter we propose a cyber incident handling model to best implement roles in management teams of societal cyber crisis on how to handle the crisis. We discuss the cyber incident management in the respond and recovery process of the crisis on strategic, tactical and operational tiers in a municipality case. We suggest bringing in diverse experts in management-teams on the different tires, such as experts from SOCs, CIRTS and other real-life stakeholders. We present the as-is responsibilities in the municipality's regulations and guidance on crisis management as introduction to our arguments and the modelling and give a summary of the roles in the end.

4.1   Municipality Regulations and Guidance

DSB's guidance recommends that the roles and responsibilities should be described in the contingency plan, the municipalities crisis management is to be understood as a critical societal function, and is supposed to be maintained throughout any event, no matter of time, both in peace, security political crises and in armed conflicts. The guidance also suggests that the municipalities crisis management can be expanded by supporting personnel and subject responsibilities, dependent on the crisis nature and extent.

Our experience in this matter is that it takes too much effort not to start out with the necessary experts to begin with, and that it is better to call out subject responsibilities which will adapt to the incident, and then dismiss staff as the crisis is going into pre-crisis phase. We suggest key personnel to be on predefined roles-lists, to quickly do replacement in the specific subject role.

The guidance suggests that the municipality should consider the need of safety-clearance of key personnel in the crisis management. To be able to consider who needs this clearance, roles must be defined, and what personnel can fill the roles. This also supports our suggested role-modelling.

The guidance suggests the crisis management to be prepared on the following:

- Quickly decide efforts within the municipality's responsibilities, i.e. public information establishes evacuation center and psycho-social support teams.
- Be the public "face" and ensure good communication with the population, internal employees and media.
- Attend to coordinate local handling of the crisis through internal and external societal security organizations.
- Provide recourses to handle crises based on contractual agreements.
- In special cases – discuss priorities and diffusion of limited recourses in collaboration with other societal critical organizations, and neighboring municipalities.
- Communicate needs of resources to the county or/and other regional security organizations.
- Surveillance of the situation, and dialogue with other emergency organizations affected by the crisis.
- Develop and communicate gathered understanding of the situation based on information from the responsible department in the municipality.
- Inform the political parties on a regular timeline
- Inform county on collaboration channel
- Make sure substitute/deputy personnel is in place in case of regular members absence.

The guidance suggests establishing a crisis staff to support the crisis management, but it does not define the roles of the staff. As you can see a lot of tasks is outlined, but they are not regulated in roles to deal with them. We suggest the diversity of crisis responsibilities roles should be defined on strategic level, tactical level and operational level.

4.2   Different Crises, Comparable Roles

Typically, the strategic level consists of the municipality's management, the tactical levels consists of the managers running the different local municipality elderly homes, schools, kindergartens, water-supply departments etc., while the operational level consists of staff and employees on the ground, like doctors, nurses', teachers and engineers. When the incident is an elderly home on fire, the roles in the organization based on regular crisis, and crisis management regulated in contingency plans. When the incident is an elderly care-taker system out of order, the need of ICT-expert teams is necessary, and regular crisis management roles does not cover experts needed. There is a need to include these roles, as regular municipality crisis management might not have the competence to handle those crises. However, the crisis still must be handled manually by the regular crisis management. This means that a cyber crisis will need additional management and will thereby be more challenging to handle. Our discussion is visualized in Fig. 5.

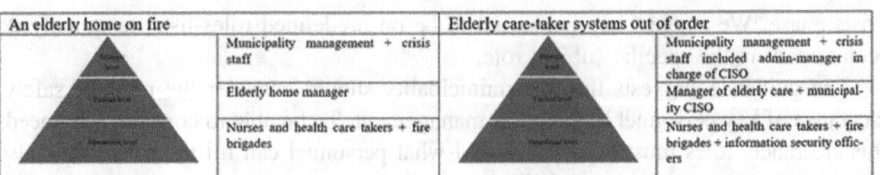

An elderly home on fire		Elderly care-taker systems out of order	
	Municipality management + crisis staff		Municipality management + crisis staff included admin-manager in charge of CISO
	Elderly home manager		Manager of elderly care + municipality CISO
	Nurses and health care takers + fire brigades		Nurses and health care takers + fire brigades + information security officers

Fig. 5. Regular crises vs. cyber security crises

As suggested in the guidance it is the municipality management with their responsibilities which should take the roles as crisis management. In a crisis as suggested – fire at the elderly home, some managers will be more affected than others, and it is of course the health and elderly manager that will follow up on the employees, elderlies and their situation. The chief municipal executive will take the role as the crisis manager and will make sure that other members of the crisis management less influenced by the incident contribute with necessary supply and logistics. The major will follow up on media information, meet the elderlies and their next of kin. To get necessary support on media tasks, the major typically get support from a press coordinator. In such a crisis both the police contact, a fire brigade officer and the chief municipal medical officer will be a part of the crisis management to bring situational awareness into the group. They will get updates from forces alarm centrals and the forces alarm centrals get update from operative teams at the elderly home.

Crisis management and/or staff management is set up as a team working together in a safe environment to ensure the contingency of the management throughout the crisis. The regulations require a plan to move the crisis management if necessary [26]. The crisis management is therefore in need of the right information about the situation to make the right decisions. On the other hand, the information needs outside the crisis management is also not just pushing boundaries to the regular organization but are vast and mixed as visualized in Fig. 6.

These information needs require extra focus and handling during crises, and we have chosen to define information roles as requested in the regulations, as separate roles in the crisis management [26]. These roles are also specifically outlined in Fig. 7, on both strategic, tactical and operational levels.

On the tactical level the health and elderly manager team will support the elderly home manager with regulations from the contingency plans, more specific evacuation and necessary health support from next door municipalities etc. On operational level the elderly home manager will follow up on drilled tasks in such an incident.

As mentioned before, information in such crises is vital, and the tactical information team will monitor information in the crisis management systems, in newspapers and social media. They will also publish information both external in social media, and internal to the employees in the municipality. And of most importance: support and gather information back and forth to the 1st line service desk personnel. 1st line service

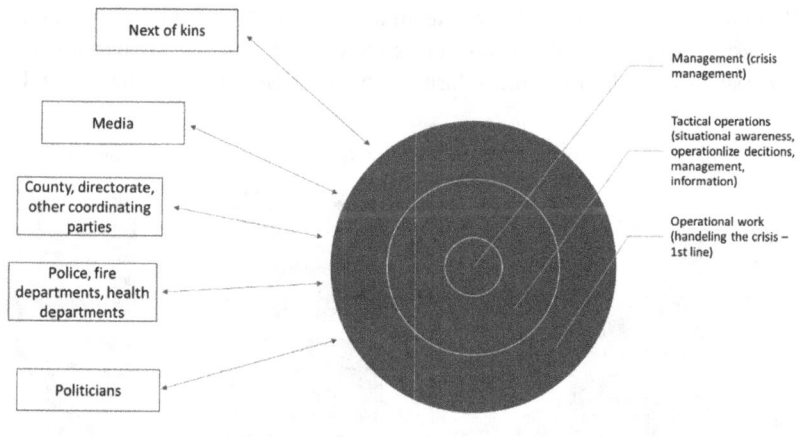

Fig. 6. Needs of crisis information

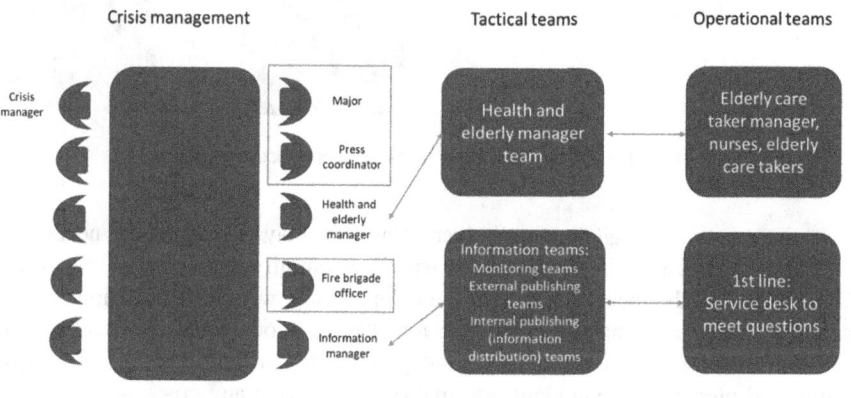

Fig. 7. Incident handling roles in conventional crises management

desk personnel are commonly strengthened with more personnel in such crises. This regulated way of handling crisis is presented in Fig. 7.

As previously stated regarding our other suggested crises: an elderly care-taker system out of order, that will require additional tasks. We have discussed which other roles could have incorporated these tasks, but as the principle of nearness and likeness is the foundation of crisis management, we suggest new roles to support the crisis.

First, we suggest that the municipality ICT-manager should be a part of the crisis management. In such a case the timeline to provide redundant systems or get the system back up and running is crucial information to the crisis management decisions. Next a tactical ICT management team should coordinate information between the management and the operational teams and get the responsibility to communicate with municipality CERT and organizations like National security authorities if necessary. Third, at operational level, investigation and recovery operations like suggested by NIST cyber security framework (Fig. 1) should take place.

Additionally, the operational cyber team should collaborate with police investigators and system users. The other tasks during the crisis remain the same as in any other crisis. Our suggested additional roles during cyber incident crisis is visualized in Fig. 8.

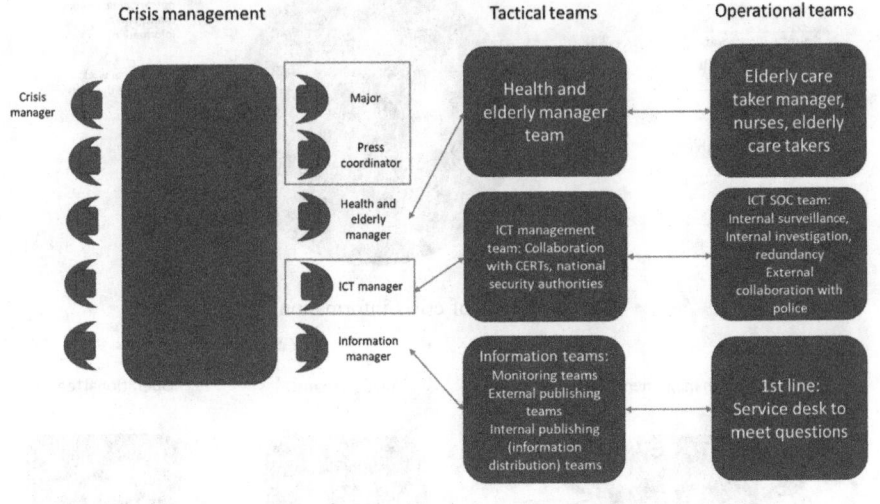

Fig. 8. Incident handling roles in cyber security crisis

As the mentioned digitalization is increasing, one may also argue the necessity of this type of organization in any societal crisis. To exemplify this, we argue the need of ICT personnel in the mentioned fire at the elderly home were an evacuation will take place, but also in conventional crises like forest fires, floods, hurricanes and others.

All information flow in such crisis is today digitalized, and to follow up information security and prepare for redundant information flow during any crisis, we suggest the ICT-roles as an essential part of the crisis management on a regular basis, regulated in contingency plans.

4.3   Summary

Using well known crises to visualize and implement cyber crises in municipality crises management appear useful in understanding and defining roles as it gives us a good indication about relevant tasks and information sharing on both strategic, tactical and operational level.

An overview of municipality crisis management roles when cyber crisis occur is presented in Table 1.

Table 1. Tasks and roles in societal cyber crises: an overview

	Management roles	Internal team tasks	External team tasks
Strategic	Chief municipal executive Municipality management Major Press coordinator Information manager ICT-manager	Chief municipal executive leading the crisis Municipality management = crisis management handling crisis in departments Major and press coordinator meet media, elderlies and next of kin Information manager coordinates all information ICT-manager: Managing ICT-crisis	Might be coordinated by county governor and directorate
Tactical	Department manager team Information teams ICT management team	Health and elderly manager team: Follow up on the employees, elderlies and their situation Information teams: Monitoring teams External publishing teams Internal publishing (information distribution) teams ICT management team: Collaboration with CERTs, national security authorities	Other municipalities CERT NSM
Operational	Operational manager and employees ICT SOC Team Municipality service desk	Elderly care-taker manager, nurses, elderly care takers: ICT SOC team: Internal surveillance, Internal investigation, redundancy External collaboration with police 1st line: Service desk to meet public questions	Police investigators

5 Conclusion and Future Research

The cyber incident handling roles model (CIHRM) presented in Fig. 8 is usable to visualize both regular crisis and cyber crisis. We propose to name this crisis handling visualizing model a cyber incident handling role model (CIHMR).

Visualizing crisis tasks and roles enables us to introduce more holistic and near-to-life elements needed to be factored in handling crisis. We need to verify and validate the findings suggestions we have made, and to enhance and improve the cyber incident management roles in more detail. To validate the framework, we plan to test suggested roles model when setting up exercises in our training environment, the Norwegian

Cyber Range (NCR). NCR will be an arena where testing, training, and exercise are tools to expose people, businesses, and units to realistic events and situations in a realistic but safe environment. The arena ensures efficient transfer of knowledge and building of real-world competence, that links together the strategic, operational, tactical and technical levels of decision making, by simulating the impacts of cyber security events on the levels of society, digital value chains and cyber infrastructure without harming the entities involved and their critical infrastructure.

In this paper we propose roles by using only one specific example of cyber crisis. In future work we will test if these roles are transferable to other societal emergency cyber crises. We intend to use the cyber incident handling role model (CIHRM) presented in Fig. 8 to visualize cyber crisis in various aspects of cyber crisis.

To ensure the best possible effect in the NCR, current suggested roles and tasks will be facilitated as most accurate comprehension of exercises fitted the different roles. Additionally, there will be need of preparedness learning based on real life incidents. We plan the preparedness learning as instruction for adults using action research by instructors with reflection throughout lectures.

When analyzing the outlined definitions of roles, we found that there is no clear definition of cyber crisis management roles. We based the suggested roles on NIST management tiers and will also need to consider NATO management tiers. Moreover, as mentioned before, there are examples of real-life incidents roles which might be analyzed to compare best practices. We consider this as an area, which can be developed better in combining role-definitions and scenarios and have a long-time work in progress in this matter.

References

1. Bruer, A.: Ny undersøkelse: Stort etterslep på mellomlederes IT-kompetanse i offentlig sector. digi. no, 09 August 2017
2. Baugerød Stokke, O.P.: Advarer it-sjefer mot effektivitet. Computerworld, 23 March 2009
3. Office of the Auditor General of Norway, admin report nb. 1 (2018)
4. NOU 13 Lysne commitee: Digital vulnerability – safe society (2015)
5. NorSIS: The study of municipalities common need of competence-center to deal with handling ICT-security incidents (2017)
6. Lagadec, P.: Preventing Chaos in a Crisis Strategies for Prevention, Control and Damage Limitation (1993). Preface: tools for thinking about, preventing, and managing crisis ix
7. DSB: Municipality Guidance, Emergency Duty (2017)
8. Walker, B., Holling, C.S., Carpenter, S.R., Kinzig, A.: Resilience, adaptability and transformability in social–ecological systems. Ecol. Soc. 9(2), 1–9 (2004)
9. De Bruijne, M., Van Eeten, M.: Systems that should have failed: critical infrastructure protection in an institutionally fragmented environment. J. Contingencies Crisis Manag. 15 (1), 18–29 (2007)
10. De Guzman, E.M.: Towards total disaster risk management approach (2002)
11. Haigh, R., Amaratunga, D.: An integrative review of the built environment discipline's role in the development of society's resilience to disasters. Int. J. Disaster Resil. Built Environ. 1 (1), 11–24 (2010)

12. Anderson, E.: How to comly with the 5 functions of the NIST cybersecurity framework. Forecoun (2017). https://www.secmatters.com/blog/how-to-comply-with-the-5-functions-of-the-nist-cybersecurity-framework
13. Kulikova, O., Heil, R., Van Den Berg, J., Pieters, W.: Cyber Crisis Management: a decision-support framework for disclosing security incident information. In: Proceedings of the 2012 ASE International Conference on Cyber Security, CyberSecurity 2012, pp. 103–112 (2013)
14. FEMA: The Federal Emergency Management Agency Publication 1 (2016)
15. Pfleeger, S.L., Caputo, D.D.: Leveraging behavioral science to mitigate cyber security risk. Comput. Secur. **31**(4), 597–611 (2012)
16. van der Aalst, W.M.P.: Data scientist: the engineer of the future. In: Mertins, K., Bénaben, F., Poler, R., Bourrières, J.-P. (eds.) Enterprise Interoperability VI. PIC, vol. 7, pp. 13–26. Springer, Cham (2014). https://doi.org/10.1007/978-3-319-04948-9_2
17. Moynihan, D.P.: The network governance of crisis response: case studies of incident command systems. J. Public Adm. Res. Theory **19**(4), 895–915 (2009)
18. FEMA: National incident management system (2017)
19. Locke, G., Gallagher, P.D.: Managing Information Security Risk Organization, Mission, and Information System View Joint Task Force Transformation Initiative, pp. 800–839. NIST Special Publication (2011)
20. Boeke, S.: National cyber crisis management: different European approaches. Governance **31**(3), 449–464 (2018)
21. Kowalski, S.: IT insecurity: a multi-disciplinary inquiry. Stockholm University (1994)
22. Kuechler, W., Vaishnavi, V.: A framework for theory development in design science research: multiple perspectives (2012)
23. Karokola, G.R.: A framework for Securing e-Government Services: the case of Tanzania. Stockholm University (2012)
24. Justis-og beredskapsdepartementet: Lov om kommunal beredskapsplikt, sivile beskyttelses-tiltak og Sivilforsvaret (sivilbeskyttelsesloven). Norwegian Government (2010)
25. DSB: Guidance to holistic risk and vulnerability assessment in the municipality. DSB (2019)
26. Norwegian government, FOR-2011-08-22-894. Norwegian Government (2011)

Mathematical Model of Management of the Integral Risk of Emergency Situation on the Example of Fires

S. Kravtsiv[1(✉)], O. Sobol[1], V. Komyak[1], O. Danilin[1], and O. Al'boschiy[2]

[1] National University of Civil Defence of Ukraine, Kharkiv, Ukraine
kravtsiv1992@gmail.com
[2] National Academy of Interior Forces of Ukraine, Kharkiv, Ukraine

Abstract. At present, there is a process of reforming the State Service of Ukraine for Emergency Situations, the purpose of which is to ensure an adequate level of safety of the vital activity of the population, its protection against extreme situations, fires and other dangerous events.

Keywords: Emergency situation · Mathematical model · Risk management

1 Introduction

1.1 Problem Setting

In accordance with DSTU 3891: 2013 [1], the risk of an emergency is the likelihood that in the event of the emergence and development of arousal factors of an emergency, there may be an emergency situation determined by the relevant qualifications. According to the Emergency Risk Management Concept [2], Ukraine needs to implement the conceptual framework for managing the risks of emergencies. Risk management is an early prediction of risk, the identification of the damaging factors of the sources of emergencies that affect (may be affected), taking measures to reduce these impacts taking into account these influences taking into account the effectiveness of the implementation of measures.

At present, there is a process of reforming the State Service of Ukraine for Emergencies [3], the purpose of which is to ensure an adequate level of safety of the vital activity of the population, its protection against emergency situations, fires and other dangerous events. The result of the reforms should be to ensure an adequate level of safety of life of the population, protection of economic entities and territories from the threat of emergencies, the creation of an effective modern European emergency and emergency prevention system, improvement of the system for responding to fires, emergencies and other dangerous events, reduction of losses of national economy and population in the event of fires, emergencies, dangerous hydrometeorological tech phenomena, creating optimal management unified state system of civil protection and improve its functioning. In this case, an important role is assigned to the application of a risk-oriented approach to justify measures in the field of civil protection. At the same

Y. Murayama et al. (Eds.): ITDRR 2019, IFIP AICT 575, pp. 182–195, 2020.
https://doi.org/10.1007/978-3-030-48939-7_16

time, there is an actual scientific and practical problem, which consists in the development of the theoretical foundations of man-made, in particular fire risk. Since in modern literature there is practically no scientific research, in which the levers that influence the level of a particular risk would be clearly determined, and models of risk management were built.

One of the tasks, the solution of which will contribute to the solution of this problem, is the construction of a mathematical model and methods for controlling integral fire risk, which will allow the justification of measures regarding the valuation of resources of the subsystem of response to emergency situations (fires).

1.2 Recent Research and Publications Analysis

The paper [4] analyzed the main integral fire risks in Ukraine and showed that the risk value for a person to die from a fire significantly exceeds normative values. An analysis of the principles of risk valuation is presented in [5] and indicates the ranges of values. In the article [6] calculations of fire risks for the Kharkiv region were carried out. Modeling problems are also considered in the works [7–9].

1.3 Paper Objective

In this paper, it is necessary to develop a mathematical model for managing the integral risk of an emergency situation on the example of fires and to investigate its features in order to further normalize the resources of the operational and rescue units, which will minimize the consequences of emergencies and reduce the integral risk to economically justified levels.

2 Presentation of the Main Research Material

The study of the dynamics of emergencies and the state of technogenic safety in Ukraine has shown that in general, the number of emergencies tends to decrease, in particular, in 2016, the lowest number of emerging industrial emergencies during the period of observations for 1997–2016 was recorded. But for the objective assessment of the level of technogenic safety in our country, it is necessary to analyze the integral risks of emergencies and dangerous events of anthropogenic nature and draw conclusions about the acceptability of the levels of these risks.

According to the National Classifier of the DK 019: 2010 "Classifier of Emergencies" [10] in Ukraine over the past 10 years, the following emergencies have been recorded as man-made:

- emergencies due to fires, explosions;
- emergencies due to traffic accidents and accidents (except for fires and explosions);
- emergencies due to accidents on life support systems;
- emergencies due to the sudden destruction of buildings and structures;
- emergencies due to accidents in power systems;

- emergencies due to the presence of harmful (contaminating) and radioactive substances in the environment above the maximum permissible concentration;
- emergencies as a result of accidents with the release (hazard of dumping) of hazardous chemicals;
- emergencies due to accidents in oil and gas industrial complex systems.

On the basis of the analytical review of the state of man-made and natural safety in Ukraine during 2011–2016 [11–16], the share of each type of man-made emergency over the past 6 years was identified (see Fig. 1). It should be noted that the highest share is due to fires, explosions (57%) and emergencies due to accidents and accidents in transport (except for fires and explosions) (24%).

According to [17], the main integral risks of emergencies (e.g. dangerous events) are:

- the risk for a person to deal with an emergency (dangerous events) (its dangerous factors) per unit time, R_1:

$$R_1 = \frac{N_{events}}{Q_{people} \cdot T};\qquad(1)$$

where N_{events} – the number of emergencies (dangerous events) recorded in the region for the period T; Q_{people} – the number of people living in the region;

- risk R_2 for a person to die at an emergency (a dangerous event) (to become her victim):

$$R_2 = \frac{M_{victims}}{N_{events}};\qquad(2)$$

where $M_{victims}$ – the number of deaths due to fires in the region during the period T;

- the risk R_3 for a person to die from an emergency (dangerous events) per unit time:

$$R_3 = R_1 \cdot R_2 = \frac{M_{victims}}{Q_{people} \cdot T}\qquad(3)$$

In order to assess the negative effects of each type of emergencies of technogenic character, the integral risks of these emergencies were calculated in accordance with the expression (3). The graphic interpretation of integral risks is shown in Fig. 2, with the highest levels corresponding to the integral risk of emergencies due to fires and explosions, $2{,}95.10^{-6}$ 1/year, and the integral risk of emergencies due to accidents and vehicle accidents (except for fires and explosions) $1{,}98.10^{-6}$ 1/year. The levels of integral risks of other types of emergencies are less than one order (several orders of magnitude) of the above-mentioned risks.

It should be noted that the analysis of only integral risks of emergencies of technogenic character for the estimation of the level of technogenic safety in the territory of Ukraine is not sufficiently informative as it does not take into account hazardous events that are not classified.

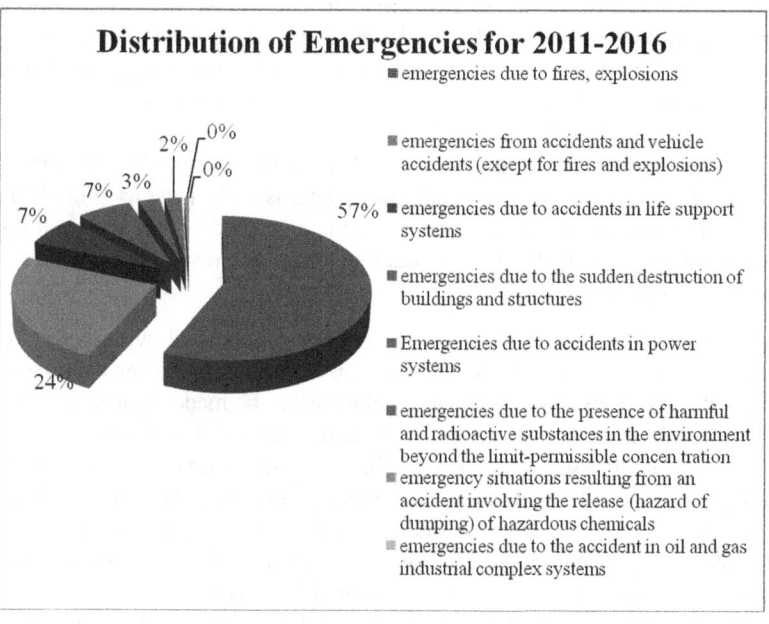

Fig. 1. Diagram of the distribution of emergencies of technogenic character by species during 2011–2016.

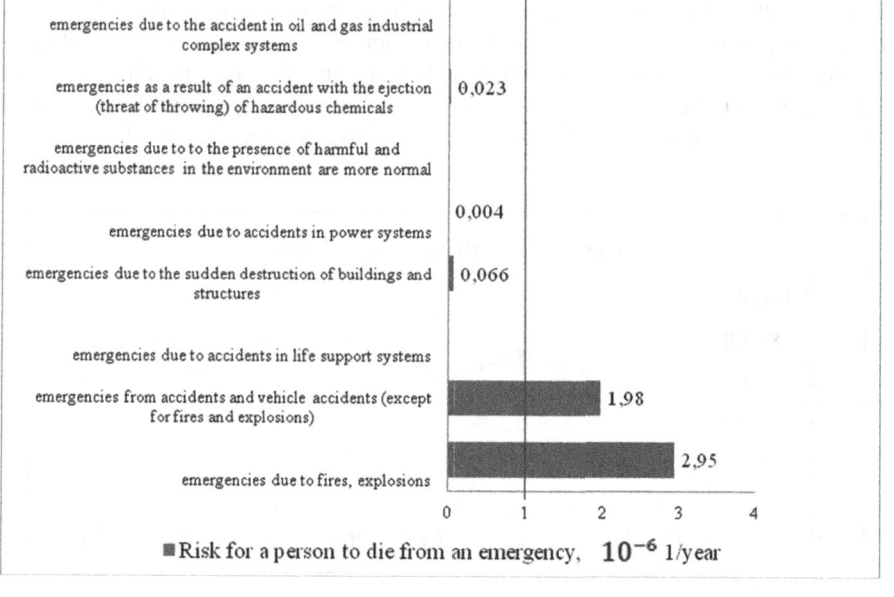

Fig. 2. Levels of integral risks of various types of emergencies of technogenic character.

The study of such dangerous events as fires and explosions and road accidents allowed to reveal the following:

1) the average value of the number of fires and explosions in 2011–2016 is 69338 (Fig. 3), with the average number of deaths due to these dangerous events is 2363 persons. For the same period, the average number of emergencies related to fires and explosions is 49, and the average number of deaths resulting from these emergencies is 127 people [11–16];

2) the average number of accidents during 2011–2016 is 16,9991, and the average number of deaths due to these dangerous events is 4423 persons (Fig. 4). For the same period, the average number of emergencies related to accidents and disasters in transport is 21, and the average number of deaths resulting from these emergencies is 85 people [11–16].

It is obvious that the number of emergencies associated with both fires and explosions and accidents and vehicle disasters is several times lower than the number of relevant dangerous events. A similar conclusion can be made regarding the death of people as a result of the above-mentioned emergencies and dangerous events. That is, in order to objectively assess the level of technogenic safety on the territory of Ukraine, it should be investigated, in addition to emergency situations, as well as various types of dangerous events of technogenic character and their consequences. In this regard, consider the more detailed dynamics of the number of fires and explosions, road accidents, as well as their consequences during 2011–2016.

Figures 3 and 4 show the dynamics of the number of fires and explosions and the dynamics of traffic accidents during 2011–2016, respectively. From the graphs, it is clear that the dynamics of the number of fires and explosions tends to increase, and the regression line is decreasing for the traffic accidents. Nevertheless, if we compare the average number of events for the period under study, we see that the average number of fires and explosions is 69338, and the average number of accidents – 169991, which is 2.45 times more than the number of fires and explosions. Calculate the human risks of perishing from these dangerous events. For this it is necessary to consider statistical data [11–16] on the number of deaths from each type of hazardous event.

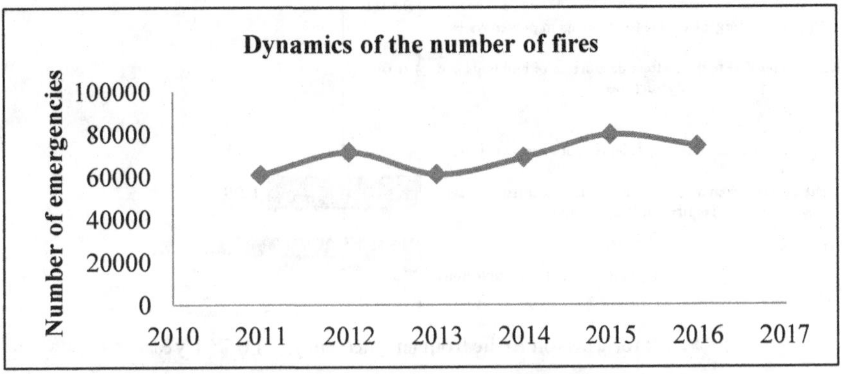

Fig. 3. Dynamics of the number of fires and explosions during 2011–2016.

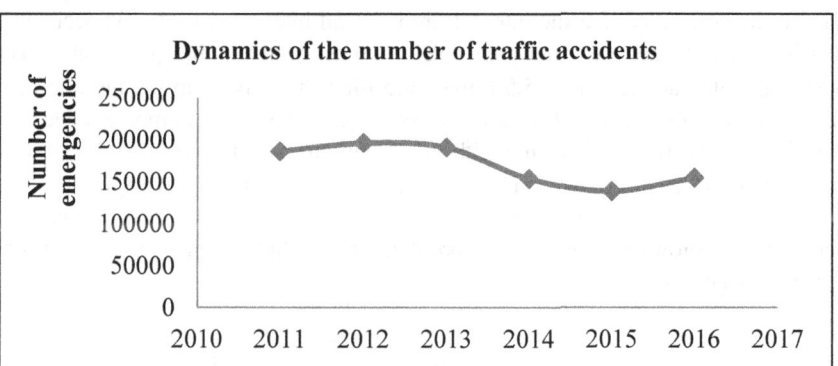

Fig. 4. Dynamics of the number of traffic accidents during 2011–2016.

Figure 5 shows the dynamics of integral risk, which characterizes the consequences of fires and explosions. From the figure, there is a tendency to reduce the risk, but nevertheless, the value of the identified risk is still high enough and more than 5 times exceed acceptable limits [2].

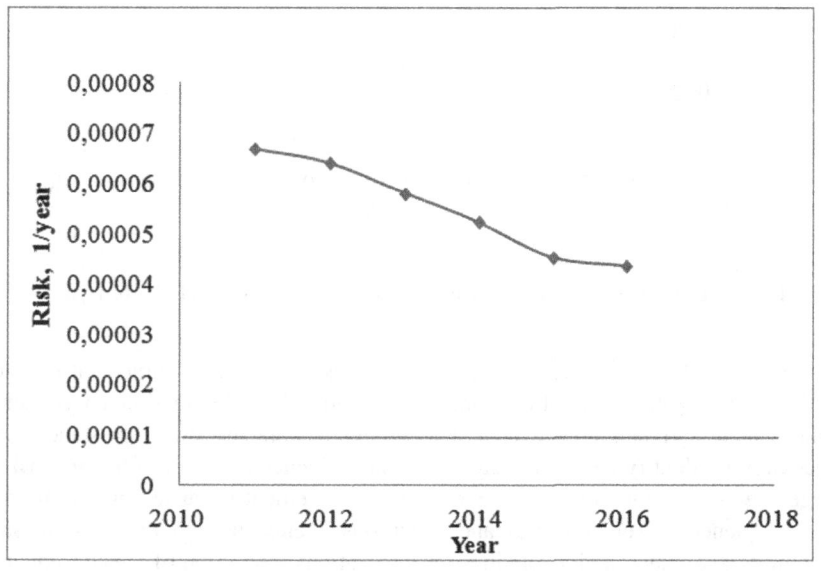

Fig. 5. Dynamics of integral risk of road accidents during 2011–2016, 1/year.

Figure 6 shows the dynamics of integral risk R_3, which characterizes the consequences of road accidents. The level of integral risk R_3 for traffic accidents as well as the number of traffic accidents is reduced, but the risk of road deaths exceeds the norm by more than 10 times. Having analyzed Fig. 4 and 6, we see that the number of traffic accidents and integral risk R_3 is directly related.

It can be concluded that the integral fire risk and integral risk of road accidents in 2011–2016 tend to decrease, but their level exceeds the maximum permissible. Thus, the level of integral fire risk is 5.5 times exceeding the maximum permissible (10^{-5}, 1/year), and the integral risk of road accidents – 10.3 times. If we compare the levels of the above integral risks in Ukraine with the maximum permissible level of risk in the developed countries of the world ($1 \cdot 10^{-6}$, 1/year), the integral fire risk value exceeds this level by 55 times and the integral risk of road accidents is 100 times. That is, the given situation shows the presence of problems in the field of providing technogenic safety in our country.

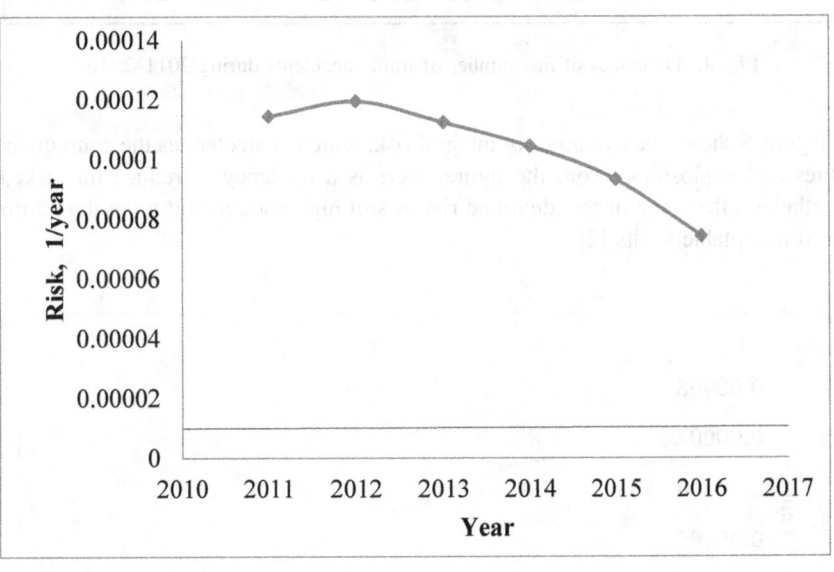

Fig. 6. Dynamics of integral risk of road accidents during 2011–2016, 1/year.

To increase the level of technogenic safety, it is necessary to implement measures aimed at reducing the levels of relevant risks, i.e. to reduce the possible consequences of emergencies and dangerous events of technogenic character. But at the same time, it is necessary to identify the main factors that can influence the level of integral risks of emergencies and dangerous events. Since risk management is carried out to minimize the consequences of emergencies and hazardous events through the distribution of rescue units that play a major role in rescue operations (reduction of the consequences of emergencies and hazardous events), the factors of influence on integral risks should characterize the process of data retrieval subdivisions. It should also be noted that the task of minimizing the consequences of emergencies and dangerous events is the task of multi-criteria optimization, and the integral risks of emergencies and dangerous events of technogenic character are considered as criteria. The task of multicriteria optimization, as a rule, can be reduced to the task of one-criterion optimization using the following methods:

1. the definition of the main criterion (target function), and for other criteria - the formation of restrictions;
2. representation of the objective function as a convolution of partial criteria.

In this paper we will focus on the first method, since the integral risks of emergencies and dangerous events of technogenic character differ by more than an order of magnitude.

To determine the main criterion of the task of minimizing the consequences of emergencies and dangerous events, consider the distribution of the departures of the operational and rescue units, which is shown in Fig. 7.

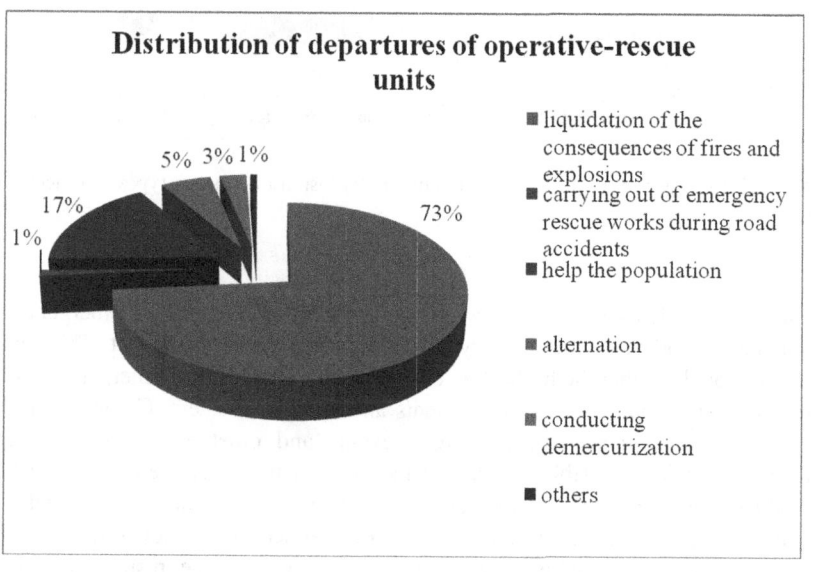

Fig. 7. Distribution of departures of operational and rescue units in Ukraine during 2011–2016.

It is obvious that 73% of the trips are to be used to eliminate the consequences of fires and explosions, 17% to help the population (for example, in the event of unfavorable domestic or non-standard situations), 5% for duty, 3% for demercuration, 1% for road accidents and other departures.

It should be noted that the bulk of fires and explosions occur in the residential sector, approximately 72% of the total number of events. Figure 8 shows the risks for a person to die as a result of a fire and an explosion on various types of objects.

It is obvious that the risk for a person to die due to a fire and explosion in the residential sector is 5.27 times higher than the maximum permissible level.

The analysis of the distribution of departures of operational and rescue units allows to assert that as the main criterion in solving the problem of minimization of the consequences of emergencies, it is expedient to consider the integral fire risk, and other integral risks of emergencies and hazardous events should be taken into account in the constraints.

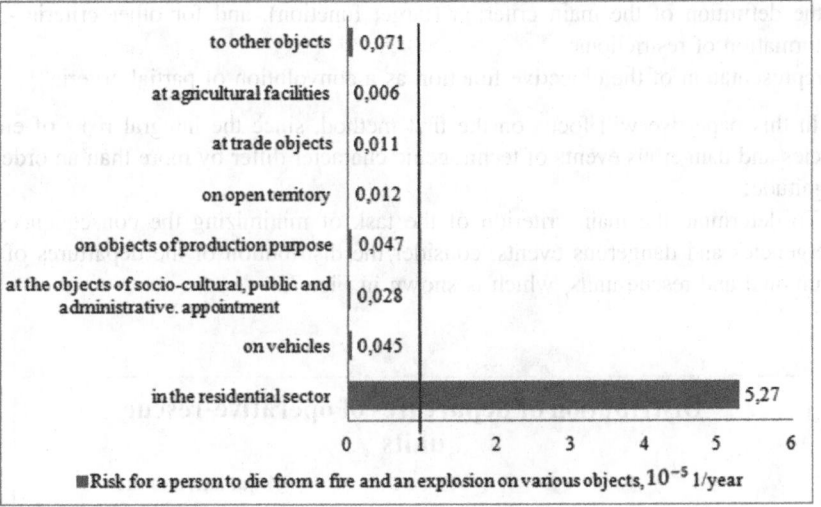

Fig. 8. Risk for a person to die from a fire and an explosion on various types of objects, 10^{-5} 1/year.

Thus, the analysis of risks characterizing the consequences of emergencies of technogenic character on the territory of Ukraine has been carried out. This made it possible to conclude that the highest levels have integrated risks of emergencies related to fires and explosions, as well as accidents and vehicle disasters. Comparison of the quantity and consequences of dangerous events and emergencies of technogenic character has made it possible to state the fact that for the objective assessment of the level of technogenic safety on the territory of Ukraine, it is necessary to take into account the specified dangerous events. It was determined that the levels of integral fire risk and integral risk of road accidents in the territory of Ukraine, respectively, are 5.5 and 10.3 times exceeding the maximum permissible level, which indicates the presence of problems in the field of technogenic safety in our country. To increase the level of technogenic safety, it is necessary to implement measures aimed at reducing the level of appropriate risks, that is, to reduce the possible consequences of emergencies and dangerous events of technogenic character. Since the task of minimizing the consequences of emergencies relates to the tasks of multicriteria optimization, in order to reduce it to the task of one-criterion optimization, the choice of the main criterion (integral fire risk) was justified, and other integral risks of emergencies and dangerous events should be taken into account in the constraints.

It was assumed that the risk R_3 depends on factors such as: N_{fire} – the number of fires recorded in the region; M_{3a2} – the number of deaths due to fires in the region; τ_{arrive} – the time of the fire and rescue units' follow-up to the place of emergencies (fires); τ_{loc} – localization time of the fire; τ_{liq} – time of fire liquidation.

A correlation matrix (Table 1) was constructed to determine the causal relationships between the investigated factors, which makes it possible to determine the relationship between the integral fire risk and the revealed factors. It is obvious that the coefficients 0.936, 0.895 and 0.779 show a close relationship between the level of integral fire risk and factors τ_{arrive}, τ_{loc} and τ_{liq}. Thus, one of the levers of the impact on the integral fire risk R_3 is the time of the fire and rescue units' follow-up to the place of emergencies (fires) and the time of localization of the fire, which depend on the location and resources of the fire and rescue units.

Table 1. Correlation matrix of the main factors.

	R_3	N_{fire}	$M_{victims}$	τ_{arrive}	τ_{loc}	τ_{liq}
R_3	1,000	−0,832	1,000	0,836	0,895	0,779
N_{fire}	−0,832	1,000	−0,832	−0,528	−0,697	−0,419
$M_{victims}$	1,000	−0,832	1,000	0,836	0,895	0,779
τ_{arrive}	0,836	−0,528	0,836	1,000	0,795	0,934
τ_{loc}	0,895	−0,697	0,895	0,789	1,000	0,714
τ_{liq}	0,779	−0,419	0,779	0,934	0,714	1,000

As a result of the correlation-regression analysis, the dependence of the integral fire risk R_3 on the significant parameters was obtained:

$$R_3 = \left(0,203\overline{\tau}_{loc} + 0,117\overline{\tau}_{liq} - 0,17 \cdot 10^{-4}N_{fire} + \varepsilon\right) \cdot 10^{-5} \qquad (4)$$

Standard error of estimation thus makes $0,13701 \cdot 10^{-5}$. Since the average value of the dependent variable is equal $5,27 \cdot 10^{-5}$, the error is only 2.6%, which is satisfactory.

It should be noted that in expression (4) the variable N_{fire} has a negative coefficient. This is due to the fact that, according to available statistical information, with an increase in the number of dangerous events (fires and explosions), there is a tendency to reduce the number of deaths, as evidenced by the Fig. 9.

Thus, the following problem arises. Let the area S_0 in the form of a polygon in a global coordinate system be given. The area S_0 has prohibited objects L_ξ, $\xi = 1, \ldots, L$ in which it is inadmissible to place fire and rescue units. It is necessary to minimize the risk for a person to perish from a fire per unit time in the region S_0 by determining the additional number of fire and rescue units P_i, $i = 1, \ldots, N$ (these areas are polygons with variable metric characteristics), with the following restrictions:

- the minimum cross-sectional area for the operation of fire and rescue units;
- affiliation of areas of operation of the fire and rescue subdivisions of the region S_0;
- minimum area of intersection of areas of operation of fire and rescue units with areas of prohibition L_ξ, $\xi = 1, \ldots, L$;
- the presence of high-risk objects and potentially hazardous objects S_d, $d = 1, \ldots, D$ and the areas M_d of intersection of areas of operation of fire and rescue units providing emergency response (fire) to the high-risk objects or potentially hazardous objects according to the call number;

- time of arrival of fire and rescue units to the most remote point of departure P_i, $i = 1, \ldots, N$, must not exceed the given T^*;
- placement of fire and rescue units is carried out taking into account the existing P_q, $q = 1, \ldots, N_q$;
- placement of fire and rescue units is carried out taking into account of the limited resources.

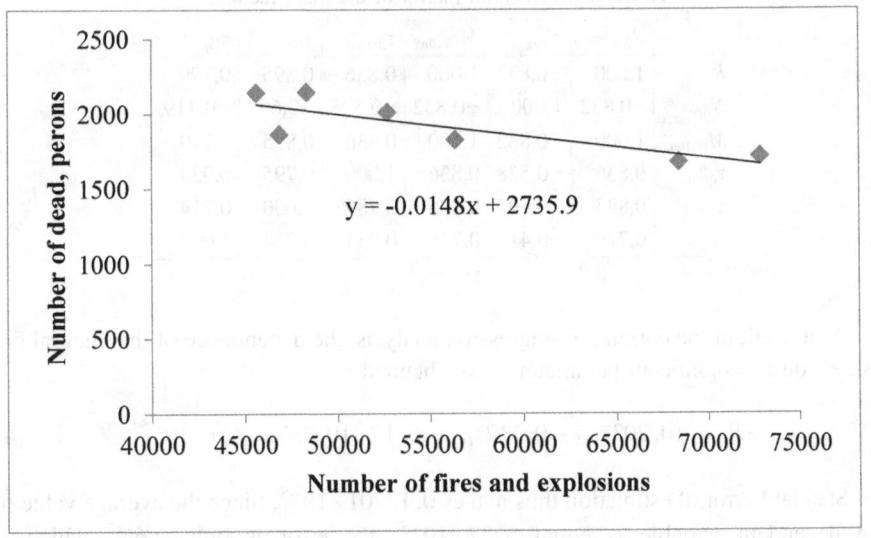

Fig. 9. Dependence of the number of deaths from the number of fires and explosions.

It should be noted that this task is relevant and complies with the Strategy of Reform of the State Service of Ukraine for Emergencies [3].

The mathematical model of risk management for a person to perish from a fire per unit time has the following form:

$$\min_{u \in W} R_3 \left(N_{fire}, \ M_{victims}, \ \tau_{arrive}, \ \tau_{loc}, \ \tau_{liq}, \ u \right); \ u = \{m_i; v_i\}; \ i = 1, \ldots, N; \qquad (5)$$

where W:

$$\omega\left(m_i, m_j, v_i, v_j\right) \rightarrow \min; \qquad (6)$$

$$i = 1, \ldots, N; \ j = i + 1, \ldots, N;$$

$$\omega(m_i, m_{cS_0}, v_i, v_{cS_0}) \rightarrow \min; \qquad (7)$$

$$i = 1, \ldots, N; \ S_0 \bigcup cS_0 = R^2;$$

$$\omega(m_i, m_\xi, v_i, v_\xi) \rightarrow \min; \tag{8}$$

$$i = 1, \ldots, N; \ \xi = 1, \ldots, L;$$

$$S_d \in \bigcap_{k=1}^{M_d} P'_k; \ d = 1, \ldots, D; \ P'_k \in \{P_i\}; \ i = 1, \ldots, N; \tag{9}$$

$$\tau_{arrive}(P_i) \leq T^*; \ i = 1, \ldots, N; \tag{10}$$

$$\omega(m_i, m_q, v_i, v_q) \rightarrow \min; \tag{11}$$

$$i = 1, \ldots, N; \ q = 1, \ldots, N_q;$$

$$Q_{res}(N) \leq Q^*_{res}. \tag{12}$$

In the model (5)÷(12), the expression (5) is the target function of the task, while m_i – the metric characteristics of the objects P_i, $i = 1, \ldots, N$ (for example, the coordinates of the vertices of the polygons in the local coordinate system), v_i – the parameters of the location of objects P_i (the position of the local system coordinate i of an object in the global coordinate system); expression (6) – a condition for the minimum cross-section of objects P_i and P_j; expression (7) is the condition for the minimum crossing of objects P_i with the addition of the region S_0 to the Euclidean space; expression R^2; (8) – a condition for the minimum interconnection of objects P_i with areas of prohibition L_ξ, $\xi = 1, \ldots, L$; expression (9) – the condition of the membership of objects P_i, which represent points in S_0, the area of intersection of objects P'_k belonging to the set of objects P_i; expression (10) – a condition regarding the admissible time of arrival of fire and rescue units to the place of call; expression (11) – the condition of minimum interconnection of objects P_i and P_q; expression (12) – the condition that the resources for the additional introduction of fire and rescue units do not exceed the allocated Q^*_{res}.

It should be noted that the constraints of the model (6)÷(8), (11) are represented by the co-coating function introduced by Yu. Stoyana and S. Yakovleva [6].

Under fire and rescue units we will understand the units of not only state fire protection, but also local and voluntary. Thus, a risk-based approach to determining of the parameters of the emergency response subsystem (fires) at the regional level is used.

Let's consider the features of the model (5)÷(12):

- the task of managing the risk for a person to perish from a fire per unit time refers to tasks of nonlinear programming;
- the domain of admissible solutions is determined, in the general case, by a system of nonlinear equality and inequalities and is limited and inconsistent;
- the total number of sets of equality and inequalities through which the formalization of the limitations of the task is equal $C_N^2 + N(L + N_q + 2) + D + 1$;
- this task can be solved without taking into account the restriction (12);

- if the existing fire-rescue units are not taken into account, then the model does not take into account the limitations (10).

Thus, a mathematical model for risk management for a person to perish from a fire per unit of time will further develop a well-founded method for solving the problem $(5) \div (12)$.

3 Conclusions

The work analyzes the emergencies of technogenic character and identifies the risks of various types of emergencies. It is determined that the level of integral fire risk is 5.5 times exceeding the maximum permissible (10^{-5}, 1/year). The correlation matrix for the investigated parameters is calculated and close relationships between the fire risk and the time of travel to the place of call, localization and liquidation of the emergency (fire) are established. The mathematical model of risk management for a person to die from a fire for a unit of time has been developed and its features have been investigated. Further research will be aimed at developing a method, algorithmic and software solution to the task.

References

1. DSTU 3891:2013 Bezpeka u nadzvychainykh sytuatsiiakh. Terminy ta vyznachennia osnovnykh poniat. 34 s (2014). (in Ukraine)
2. Pro skhvalennia Kontseptsii upravlinnia ryzykamy vynyknennia nadzvychainykh sytuatsii tekhnohennoho ta pryrodnoho kharakteru. http://zakon.rada.gov.ua/laws/show/37-2014-p. (in Ukraine)
3. Pro skhvalennia Stratehii reformuvannia systemy Derzhavnoi sluzhby Ukrainy z nadzvy-chainykh sytuatsii. (2017). http://zakon2.rada.gov.ua/laws/show/61-2017-%D1%80. (in Ukraine)
4. Kravtsiv, S.Ya., Sobol, O.M., Maksimov, A.V.: The analysis of integral risks of the territory of Ukraine. In: Problems of Emergency Situations, vol. 23. pp. 53–60. NUCDU, Kharkiv (2016). http://nuczu.edu.ua/sciencearchive/ProblemsOfEmergencies/vol23/Kravtsiv.pdf
5. Kravtsiv, S.Ya., Sobol, O.M.: Analiz zakordonnoho dosvidu derzhavnoho rehuliuvannia rivnia pryiniatnoho ryzyku. Visnyk Natsionalnoho universytetu tsyvilnoho zakhystu Ukrainy. Seriia: Derzhavne upravlinnia, №. 2, pp. 297–302 (2016) http://nuczu.edu.ua/sciencearchive/PublicAdministration/vol5/Visnyk_NUCZU_41_2016_2(5).pdf. (in Ukraine)
6. Kravtsiv, S.Ya., Sobol, O.M.: Analiz integralnogo pozhezhnogo ryzyku na terytoriyi rajoniv Xarkivskoyi oblasti. Collection of scientific works of KNUAF, vol. 4. №. 49, pp. 177–179. KNUAF, Kharkiv (2016). http://repositsc.nuczu.edu.ua/bitstream/123456789/2037/1/Visnyk_NUCZU_41_2016_2%285%29.pdf. (in Ukraine)
7. Komyak, Va., Komyak, Vl., Danilin, A.: A study of ellipse packing in the high-dimensionality problems. East.-Eur. J. Enterp. Technol. 1/4(85), 17–23 (2017)
8. Komyak, V., et al.: Computer simulation of the partitioning by mutually orthogonal lines. In: IEEE 15th International Conference on the Experience of Designing and Application of CAD Systems (CADSM), Polyana, pp. 16–19 (2019) https://ieeexplore.ieee.org/document/8779343

9. Yakovlev, S., Kartashov, O., Komyak, V., Shekhovtsov, S., Sobol, O., Yakovleva, I.: Modeling and simulation of coverage problem in geometric design systems. In: IEEE 15th International Conference on the Experience of Designing and Application of CAD Systems (CADSM), Polyana, pp. 20–23 (2019) https://ieeexplore.ieee.org/document/8779303

10. DK 019:2010 Natsionalnyi klasyfikator Ukrainy «Klasyfikator nadzvychainykh sytuatsii» (2010). http://kharkivoda.gov.ua/content/documents/6/546/Attaches/20110211klassifikator.pdf. (in Ukrain)

11. Natsionalna dopovid Pro stan tekhnohennoi ta pryrodnoi bezpeky v Ukraini u 2011 rotsi. Rozdil 3. Zahrozy tekhnohennoho kharakteru ta zakhody shchodo minimizatsii yikh nehatyvnykh naslidkiv. http://undicz.dsns.gov.ua/files/Національна%20доповідь/2011/3_2011.pdf. (in Ukraine)

12. Natsionalna dopovid Pro stan tekhnohennoi ta pryrodnoi bezpeky v Ukrani u 2012 rotsi. Rozdil 3. Zahrozy tekhnohennoho kharakteru ta zakhody shchodo minimizatsii yikh nehatyvnykh naslidkiv. http://undicz.dsns.gov.ua/files/Національна%20доповідь/2012/3_2012.pdf. (in Ukraine)

13. Natsionalna dopovid Pro stan tekhnohennoi ta pryrodnoi bezpeky v Ukrani u 2013 rotsi. Rozdil 2. Zahrozy tekhnohennoho kharakteru ta zakhody shchodo minimizatsii yikh nehatyvnykh naslidkiv. http://undicz.dsns.gov.ua/files/Національна%20доповідь/2013/2_2013.pdf. (in Ukraine)

14. Natsionalna dopovid Pro stan tekhnohennoi ta pryrodnoi bezpeky v Ukrani u 2014. Hlava 1 Stan tekhnohennoi bezpeky. http://undicz.dsns.gov.ua/files/Національна%20доповідь/2014/1_2014.pdf. (in Ukraine)

15. Analitychnyi ohliad stanu tekhnohennoi ta pryrodnoi bezpeky v Ukraini za 2015 rik. Hlava 1. Stan tekhnohennoi bezpeky. http://undicz.dsns.gov.ua/files/Аналітичний%20огляд/Glava_1.pdf. (in Ukraine)

16. Analitychnyi ohliad stanu tekhnohennoi ta pryrodnoi bezpeky v Ukraini za 2016 rik. Hlava 1. Stan tekhnohennoi ta pryrodnoi bezpeky. http://undicz.dsns.gov.ua/files/Національна%20доповідь/2016/3. (in Ukraine)

17. Brushlinskii, N.N., et al.: Osnovy teorii pozharnykh riskov i ee prilozheniia: monografiia. Moskva: Akademiia GPS MChS Rossii, 192 s (2012). (in Russian)

3D Simulation to Validate Autonomous Intervention Systems Architecture for Disaster Management

Tullio Tanzi[✉] and Matteo Bertolino

LTCI, Télécom Paris, Institut Polytechnique de Paris, Paris, France
tullio.tanzi@telecom-paris.fr

Abstract. The use of autonomous robots either on the ground (i.e., Rover) or flying (i.e., Drone) constitutes a major progress in the support of a crisis. To work properly and to reach the desired level of autonomy, they have to be correctly configured though. Indeed, errors on robot configuration can lead to imprecise or erroneous data and, consequently, erroneous decisions can result from them. Before the beginning of the mission, it is important also to achieve a strong level of confidence about the usage of the sensors (for example, LIDARs) with respect to the context of the mission. Many aspects of these validations cannot be performed during the mission, for example verifying the behaviour of a rover following a strong collision with an external actor (such as debris) that can potentially damage or break some components. Moreover, during a real mission it is not always possible making huge modifications in the system configuration. In this respect, simulating the behaviour of the system in a virtual environment, similar to the real physical world, can constitute a good validation approach before the mission. These simulations allow to validate the behaviour and the configuration of the system as well as the most appropriate equipment of it.

Keywords: Autonomous system · Simulation · Models · Disaster

1 Introduction

The usage of autonomous systems for rescue operations constitutes a great improvement in the conditions of intervention on a site after a disaster-type event. However, in order to be truly effective, these systems shall be perfectly in-line with the objectives of the mission as well as the conditions in which they have to evolve. This means that they must be configured for each mission assigned to them, customizing them from a physical point of view (hardware) and in terms of embedded intelligence (software).

This raises a series of important questions: how to check the adequacy between the architecture of the system (in a broad sense) and the mission? How to do this check before operating on site?

Our objective is to avoid discovering an inadequacy between the autonomous system and the mission during the mission itself. Our work therefore focuses on this verification in order to adapt this configuration before the on-site departure of the equipment.

© IFIP International Federation for Information Processing 2020
Published by Springer Nature Switzerland AG 2020
Y. Murayama et al. (Eds.): ITDRR 2019, IFIP AICT 575, pp. 196–211, 2020.
https://doi.org/10.1007/978-3-030-48939-7_17

1.1 Disaster Management

With the growing improving and reliability of technologies, we can rely on information technology (IT) to elaborate and refine a disaster recovery management strategy. A disaster recovery management strategy is intended to be the set of plans, processes and techniques to be implemented, with the final goal to saving lives as well as finding survivors or let the life restarts back to normal in the shortest possible time [1]. After a disaster, the impacted area could have suffered huge mutations due to terrain's alterations or presence of debris, for example. Some information can be obtained only after an in-place reconnaissance and not easily. The communication with the local inhabitants may be hindered by physical constraints or by the fact that people abandoned the area after the catastrophe. Even a local inspection presents strong limitations. For example, the poor visibility range can result in erroneous decisions based on incomplete or erroneous data. However, completeness and correctness information are necessary for the decision-making process that precedes the emergency intervention [2].

1.2 Benefits from Robot Usage

In this respect, the usage of Autonomous Systems (A.S.) such as rovers or drones can assist the recovering operations for many tasks. For example, A.S. can be used for Rapid-Mapping or to scan the affected area for finding survivors, among others. Figure 1 contains the 3D CAD view of our ArcTurius Rover [2], an A.S. for post-catastrophe humanitarian mission. It has been designed and developed by LabSoc, a research group on complex digital electronic systems from LTCI laboratory of Télécom Paris.

Fig. 1. ArcTurius Rover: autonomous system for post-catastrophe humanitarian mission (3D CAD view).

ArcTurius Rover has to work for several days in total autonomy, underground (subsoil and basement given by building ruins), searching for the presence of survivors.

Its design implies many challenges. Specifically, the environment of the mission prevents the rover by communicating with the operational centre by using radio-navigation means. Moreover, the length of the mission in terms of time introduces the problem of energy consumption. Thus, the design and the configuration have to be strongly considered in order to achieve the desired behaviour while considering the power management. In the context of this article, ArcTurius is our reference in the study of the rover behaviour within a virtual environment. Towards 3D-based simulations, our goal is to validate the design and the configuration (specific to a particular mission) of ArcTurius in order to enhance the effectiveness of A.S. usage after a catastrophe. Our laboratory works in the design of techniques that facilitate the recovery process in an environmentally critical context. In this regard, we propose a new approach, based on 3D simulations of the real world that speeds-up the definition of a recovery management strategy. Our research work aims to get a role immediately after a disaster happens, while the rescue teams are approaching the place of the crisis. It targets two main objectives:

1. Finding the best design and the best configuration of the A.S. for the target mission. To work properly and to reach the desired level of autonomy, A.S. have to be correctly designed and configured. Indeed, errors on robot configuration can lead to imprecise or erroneous data and, consequently, erroneous decisions can result from them. Before the beginning of the mission, it is important to achieve a strong level of confidence about the usage of the sensors [2–4] (for example, LIDARs) with respect to the surrounding world. For instance, we can evaluate the positioning of a LIDAR in order to minimise the impact of external noise, or whether the terrain's discontinuity perturbs data acquisition [5].
2. Acquiring a better knowledge of an area that the rescue teams do not know or do not know more because of environmental alterations. While the recovery teams are reaching the crisis area, A.S. can autonomously operate performing the above mentioned tasks. Their result will help the definition of a strategy, even complex, or they can help modifying run-time an existing plan [2, 6].

The configuration of an A.S. depends by some key points that include: i) the configuration of the devastated area and ii) the main objectives of the Search and Rescue (SaR) mission such as damage assessment, people search and location, etc. The choice of the right equipment such as the set of sensors to be mounted as well as the best physical placement is a non-trivial task. A bad choice in this step may make the A. S. not reliable as expected.

2 Simulation

We propose a 3D-simulation, which the direction of the rescue team can perform before their arrival. Briefly, an initial map of the real world is taken, for example through satellites' data, then it is injected onto a graphical engine. We define through a model-driven engineering approach the physics of the terrain and the physics of the actors that populate the world. Environmental conditions are taken into account too. We need to model the design and the geometry of the A.S. under examination and to provide a description of its behaviour. In this respect, the modelling of sensors and actuators, part of the A.S. and that interact with the external world, plays a main role. Through a physical engine, we are allowed to rapidly testing algorithms, designing robots and simulating their behaviour in realistic scenarios. The 3D vision enhances and speeds-up the comprehension of the designers.

Figure 2 shows an overview of the proposed simulation system. It is composed by several computational blocks that communicate through the exchange of high-level messages. The main components are:

1. Graphical engine that includes the rendering of textures, lights, shadows, etc.
2. Physical engine that allows realistic physics simulation and that is able to interact with the graphical engine with computer animation API
3. A comprehensive description (architecture, physics and behaviour) of the A.S. under examination. Sensors and actuators are included in this component of the system
4. An engine able to generate realistic terrain data
5. An engine that created realistic environment actors and conditions close to the real conditions due to a catastrophe.

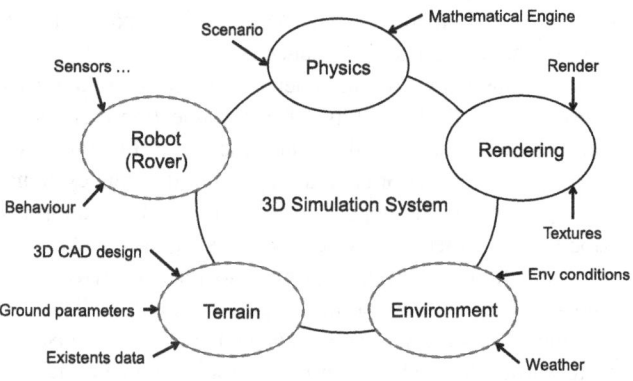

Fig. 2. 3D simulation system general architecture

The system in Fig. 2 is based on an existing system named Gazebo Simulator [7]. Gazebo is a well know 3D robot simulator that allows to rapidly testing robots in a physically realistic scenario. The input of the system is a precise modelling of the A.S. as well as the surrounding environment where the physical properties of each element are described. Starting from these models, Gazebo is able to perform reliable physical simulations and to represent them in a realistic rendering. Unfortunately, with respect to disaster management, the only Gazebo supports well only the blocks responsible for the physics and the rendering (blocks characterized by a black continuous line in Fig. 2), whereas features miss to obtain fast and realistic simulations in a disaster environment. Moreover, we need a way to establish the communication between all the components of the system. To do that, we built our system on Robot Operating System (ROS), deepened in Sect. 3.

2.1 Robot Modelling

In order to correctly reproduce the behaviour and the interaction of an A.S. in a surrounding world, we have to provide to the simulation system the following inputs: i) architecture, ii) physical properties, iii) behaviour and iv) sensors and actuators.

The architecture of an A.S. is intended to be the shape and the geometry of each component that is part of the A.S and the connections between them. In this respect, there are two possibilities that are characterized by different level of granularity. The first approach is object-oriented and it models the geometry of A.S. components through simplified shapes (box, cylinder, etc.) to whom are associated static and dynamic characteristics. Alternately, the A.S. architecture can be expressed in a more refined way through 3D designs. In this respect, the CAD models in Fig. 1 can be a possibility. In both cases, the input of the system is a XML-like file in which the description and the origin of each component is made explicit. Providing the architecture of each mechanical component is not enough though. Indeed, physical properties of them have to be defined as well as the characteristics of their interconnections. With physical properties we intend, for example, the characteristics features of rigid bodies: mass, inertia, the respect of kinematics laws, any kind of friction, coefficients that describe the reaction to an impact, etc. More physics parameters are provided, more the reliability of the simulation is enhanced.

Modelling the junctions between components enhance the reliability of the model too, for a dual reason. First of all, the type of interconnection permits to describe the physical movement of the system. In this regard, there is a difference between a fixed connection with no degrees of freedom and a hinge joint that rotates along the axis and has a limited range specified by the upper and lower limits. For example, the latter can be used to describe the movement of a wheel with respect to the chassis to which it is attached. Secondly, junctions description permits to play a key-role in the physical integrity of the system, because they permit to perform more realistic safety analysis. Supposing to run the A.S. in a extreme environment that, because to its intrinsic danger, can lead to partial damages to the rover architecture. In such conditions, we have to be sure to make the correct design choices in order to enhance the A.S. survivability. In this respect, parameters such as the maximum effort and the maximum velocity that a junction can endure are important. Indeed, if an A.S. is subject to an huge strength in correspondence to a contact point, we have to be sure to avoid a fragmentation of A.S. components.

According to the object-oriented paradigm, we modelled ArcTurius rover with a chain of 3 boxes, interconnected by a custom junction that allows flexibility to each body to the chain. Wheels are cylinders, connected to each body through a revolute joint. Part of the future work include the ArcTurius representation starting to 3D-CAD model, keeping unchanged the physical properties associated to each component and junction.

A possible goal of the system is checking and analysing the behaviour of the A.S. during its interaction with the surrounding world. Because of that, an important part of A.S. representation is its behaviour. Through ROS, the system accepts as an input a program that has the role to move the A.S. during the simulation. In the context of rover ArcTurius, the simplest version of such program moves the virtual rover within a virtual environment applying a force to the junctions that connect the wheels with the chassis of the rover. The movement decisions can be based on the data acquired during the simulation. Even though sensors are logically part of an A.S., they have a different nature. For this reasons, we treat them in Sect. 2.2.

2.2 Sensors and Noise

Sensor output can be captured during the simulation and analysed through third-part programs. Even for sensors an architectural description has to be provided, in the same manner as rigid bodies used to model A.S. architecture. Indeed, they are physical components. However, because of they interact with the external environment only by acquiring data, the description of physical properties of their design has a secondary role with respect to A.S. modelling. Thus, the behaviour of sensors plays a key-role for a realistic representation of the system. Except for few features (such as the acquiring frequency), each sensor has quite unique set of features that have to be taken into account separately.

Table 1. Modelling choices for Hokuyo LIDAR in ArcTurius

Parameter	Value
Range measurement	$[-\pi/3, \pi/3]$ [radians]
Update rate	20 [Hz]
Accuracy	± 30 [mm] *(distance < 10 m)*
Measurement resolution	1 [mm]
Angular resolution	0.25 [degrees]
# rays per cycle	640
Noise	Gaussian: $\mu = 0.0$, $\sigma = 0.01$

We decided to use a LIDAR on ArcTurius rover, and we represented its behaviour on the system. With respect to sensor modelling, the parameters taken into account have been taken directly from the datasheet of a real LIDAR, in this case an Hokuyo UTM-30LX Scanning Laser Rangefinder [8]. The choice has been motived by the fact that this kind of product intrinsically supports the ROS paradigm [9]. As a matter of fact, a ROS package, ready to be integrate in real simulations, already exists and it is supported and maintained [10]. Starting from its maximum and minimum specifications [8], we customized Hokuyo LIDAR model according to ArcTurius design. Indeed, we work with a low data-rate in order to keep the consumptions moderated, increasing the time of the mission. Moreover, an excessive data-rate can lead to a larger number of corrupted data. Table 1 shows our modelling choices for some parameters of Hokuyo LIDAR.

About the latter, sensors are noisy components and we have to consider the noise to enhance the realism of the simulation. Currently, it is possible to model the inferences who affect them through a Gaussian distribution with a moment parameterization (i.e., providing mean and standard deviation of the distribution) [11]. In this case, assuming to work within 10-distance meters, it is possible to simulate an accuracy of 30 mm assuming that the 99.7% of the measurement is correct. This is achieved modelling the noise with a Gaussian distribution whose mean is 0 and standard deviation is 0.01.

Data coming from a virtual sensor, whatever it is, can be used with a double goal. Firstly, they can be used by the virtual A.S. for any purpose. For example, the program responsible for navigation associated to A.S. behaviour can take decisions starting from data produced by sensors. As already mentioned, ROS handles this data exchange. However, the deepening of all the algorithms that rely on sensor data is not part of this paper. Regardless of the usage that A.S. modules make of data produced by virtual sensors, engineers in charge to find the best configuration of an A.S. upon a disaster can rely to a 3D sensor date representation that enhance the comprehension of the simulation. Thus, the second stated goal is facilitating the understanding of the telemetry results checking how the A.S. is seeing at each simulation step. This can lead to a faster decision making, reducing the effort in the interpretation of telemetry results whenever possible. In this respect, Figs. 3 and 4 shows the capturing of laser data through RViz [12], a 3D visualization tool for ROS. Its usage will be deepened as well in Sect. 3.

Fig. 3. Example of Sensor (LIDAR) model - Global view

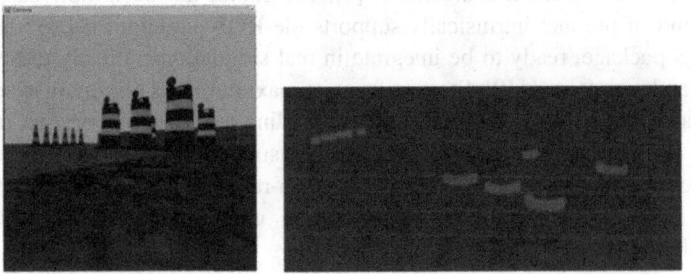

Fig. 4. Bottom, left: video view, right: 3D scene reconstruction with RViz.

2.3   Terrain Generation and Modelling

In SaR missions ground characteristics take a crucial role. Indeed, a correct representation of the ground permits to answer to many questions about the configuration of the A.S. during the simulation phase. Our simulation system is intended to speed-up the configuration of A.S. that support rescue teams during a mission. In this respect, rescue teams are mainly composed by rescuers and fire-fighters with limited engineering competences. The goal of this part is to avoid huge modification in A.S. configuration and mechanics once their arrival in catastrophe place. First of all, this would constitute a waste of time. Moreover, the environmental conditions do not always allow an easy intervention. A proper modelling of the terrain plays a key role in the preliminary evaluation of some issues related to the interaction of A.S. with the surrounding world.

For example, taking as a reference ArcTurius rover, we can evaluate if the depression of the terrain involve in a roll-over of it, or whether wheels of a different size are more appropriated for the mission, for example. Performing these kinds of simulations in advance permits rescuers to save time and to avoid a task for which they have limited competences.

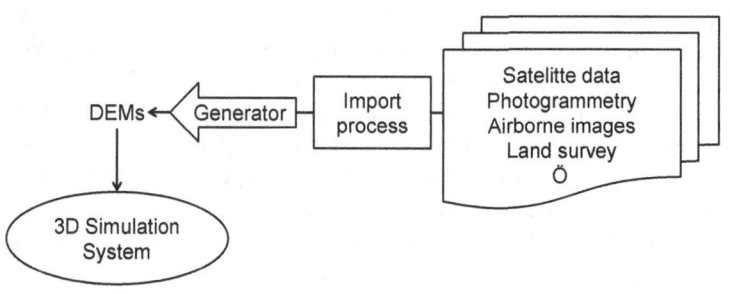

Fig. 5. Terrain input process to simulation system

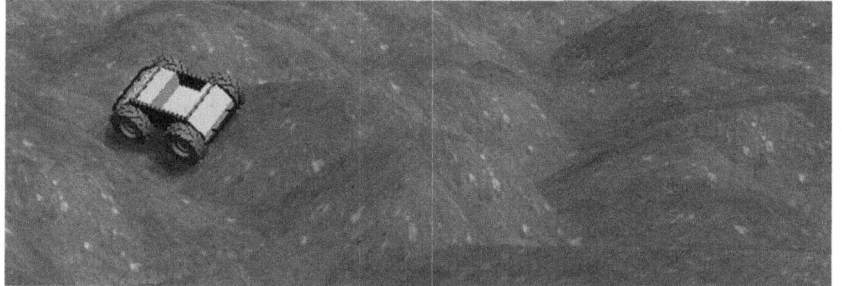

Fig. 6. South-west of Haiti imported in Gazebo-3D

Figure 5 shows the process to integrate realistic terrains in the simulation system. The starting point are real images obtained by different and real sources such as LIDAR, radar, cameras, photogrammetry, InSAR, land surveying and their combinations. There are processed to generate Digital Elevation Models (DEMs) that constitute the real input of the system [13]. DEMs show surface elevation data, sampled at regularly-spaced horizontal intervals. If the terrain elevation is represented as a grid of elevations (raster), DEM can be seen as a grey-scale height-map. In height-maps, elevation data are represented by associated the colour of a grey-scale pixel with an elevation. Specifically, a white pixel corresponds to the point of maximum elevation, whereas a black pixel represents a point characterized by the minimum depression for the considered ground. Figure 6 shows the result upon the application of the schema in Fig. 5 that we used in the context of our project. The terrain represents an area in the south-west of Haiti and it has been generated by merging data coming from ASTER [14], USGS NED [15] and SRTM30+ [16]. ASTER is a well-known survey of elevation of Earth, characterized by a high coverage and resolution (about 30 m). SRTM30+ provides coarse data (900 m of resolution) and they are used to the general contours of the land. USGS NED provides precise elevation data (up to 10 m of resolution) for zones close to United States geography.

Terrains generated from DEMs files do not usually contain external components that can be useful for simulation purposes, such as rocks, rubble, fails, etc. However, they can be integrated in the ground, according to the extended process present in Fig. 7. A possibility is to use a Drone that runs a low altitude to map them in a precise way. However, they can be generated and integrated in a realistic way. We can use mathematical functions, common in remote sensing applications, in order to estimate the roughness of the terrain. After, the physical properties of obstacles (such as density, bounciness, etc.) have to be defined, at least providing a range of values for each parameter. Finally, Monte Carlo method can be used to generate random distribution of these actors distributed over the terrain. To physically see the obstacles populating the world, a 3D description of them has to be provided too. Figure 5 schematically resumes the steps for the generation of terrains based on DEM models.

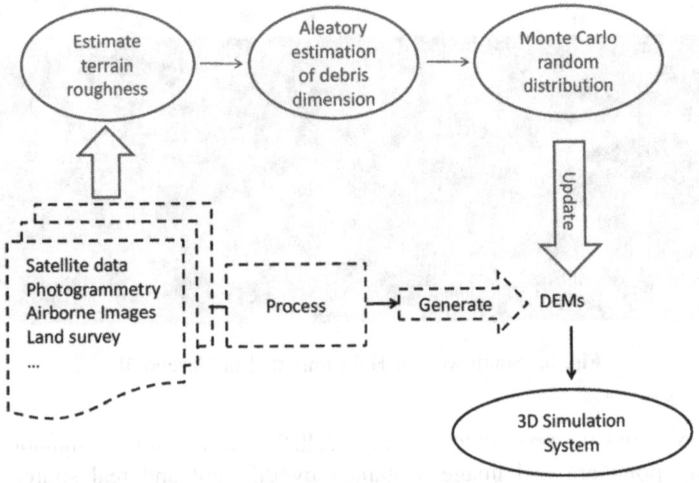

Fig. 7. Enhanced input integration process (DEM based example).

2.4 Environment Parameterization

Environmental conditions can dramatically change the results given by a simulation and they have to be modelled in the more realistic way possible. For example, a simulation that involves the usage of A.S. equipped with LIDARs can suffer from the light in particular times of the day. By properly modelling the light, it is possible to derive a different positioning of LIDARs with respect to the chassis of the rover depending by the time of the day. For example, lights can be described specifying position, orientation, attenuation factors and direction, among others. Many other perturbations can derive by the different state of the environment, and each of them would require a strong analysis performed by a physician and they are not deepened here. For example, the study of how weather conditions, such as rain, snow or wind, temperature, magnetic field, other forces act in the system or in the rest of the environment (e.g., the terrain). In this respect, lots of work has to be performed, both from a physical and a computer science point of view. In our view, this is a key-point for the simulation of A.S. in the domain of disaster management

Indeed, through simulation it is possible to evaluate the behaviour of an A.S. in a post-disaster area, also considering external environment conditions that can limit the domain of validity of the simulation. A huge realism is obtained at cost of a precise physical modelling, which is usually done by people expert in the domain.

3 Graphical Engine, Physical Engine and Communications

To assure the communication between the different parts of the simulation system we chose Robot Operating System (ROS) [17]. ROS is commonly used by the scientific community and despite its name, rather than a classical Operating System, it is more a framework that contains libraries, code, modules, configuration files, third-part software in support to robotics development. Its main goal it is to provide a standard communication interface to the different, heterogeneous elements that compose a robotics system. The latter are seen as "Nodes". Nodes can produce data, consume data or both. The exchange of data happens following a standard syntax, even though nodes can have a very different nature each other. In particular, the exchange of data may happen in a continuous way (e.g., sensors nodes that send their value to a 3D-visualizer node) or they can occur one-off (e.g., a master node that express a request and wait for a reply to a slave node). In the first case, the nodes exchange data through ROS messages sent over ROS topics, with a reference paradigm similar to the Publisher/Subscriber. In the second case ROS messages are sent over artefacts named ROS services, with a reference model Client/Server. In our respect, ROS is used to connect all the elements intrinsic to the simulation (such as rover, environmental actors, sensors, etc.) and the data analysis tools that we use for the evaluation of the measurements. However, ROS is more than a meta operating system that provides a standard connection way. As already mentioned, it includes many other modules that can be useful to robot simulation. In this article, we especially focused on two of them: RViz and Gazebo-3D.

RViz: RViz [12] is a 3D visualization environment for ROS. The decision-making for A.S. configuration can be difficult without exactly knowing what the A.S. is seeing.

Data obtained from telemetry can be difficult to be interpreted, not only in 3D but also in 2D. Indeed, these data often are a set of coordinates with information associated. Instead, visualising the world with rover eyes in 3D coordinates allows an easier debug of engineers in charge to configure an A.S. before a mission. Naturally, the telemetry continues to have a key-role during the operating mission of the A.S. There are two ways to inject simulation data into RViz:

1. It understands data from cameras, lasers, point-clouds, coordination frames, etc. sent through ROS topics
2. It is able to receive customized visual markers obtained by sending primitive shapes such as coloured cubes, arrows, etc.

A combination of two methods is accepted too. In fact, it is the most common method among algorithms in ROS navigation package [18].

Gazebo-3D: Many graphical engines are available in the domain. For several reasons, only hinted in this paper, we chose Gazebo-3D [7]. Gazebo-3D is a graphic engine that includes a physical engine such as ODE [19]. It is able to perform 3D physical simulations while displacing a rover within a surrounding virtual world. Moreover, it can be used to rapidly evaluate different kinds of algorithm, to design robots and to simulate their behaviour in realistic scenarios. For that, it is necessary to realise realistic models of A.S., sensors, actuators, environment conditions and external actors. Models are expressed with a XML-like syntax following SDF specifications [20]. They have to describe the physical properties (e.g., shape, collision domain, kinematics, friction, etc.) of the different actors that compose the simulation. It is possible to address a behaviour through the usage of plugins. For example, sensors shall transmit their measurements to a third-part analyser. Moreover, rover shall be able to move in a external environment and to interact with it, eventually basing its decisions on the values taken by the sensors. Gazebo-3D was chosen because of the experience of our laboratory on it and because it merges the graphical and the physical engine while maintaining a strong level of customization. Indeed, starting from the capabilities offered by Gazebo-3D, it is possible to define custom components able to interact with the simulator. The customization can occur both at graphical and behavioural level. Even though its expressiveness is very powerful, it is not useful whether not supported by a strong modelling of system features as well as an appropriate behaviour description of the various components through the usage of plugins. The latter can use Gazebo API to interact with the engines and can be developed in a custom way to describe the behaviour of rovers/drones, sensors, external agents, etc. Simulation data can be transferred from a virtual environment in Gazebo-3D to analysers through ROS.

4 Expected Results

The purpose of the system is exploiting the results of the 3D simulation in order to identify possible situations in which an A.S. may underperform (or not working at all) and to take countermeasures before the mission. This can enhance the utility of A.S. and reduce the errors during a mission. Beyond the adequacy assessment, the other expected results are the mission success expectancy and the A.S. survival probability after the mission.

The research of an optimal configuration is realized following the cyclic pattern *research, simulations, modification*. That means that there is always a set of simulations that verifies the configuration after an integration of a component. If the simulation results show that the configuration is not optimal after the integration, it is possible that the component is not suitable to achieve the proposed goal. Thus, variation in the component architecture or behaviour can be tested and that lead to invent characteristics of the instrument you need even before knowing them.

5 Illustration of the Concept

The vast domain of this approach allows the representation of several and different case studies. For example, a 3D simulation can be performed to evaluate the positioning of a sensor, in order to find the position that minimises the number of useless samples taken during the mission. Another possibility, deepened in this section, is the evaluation of the mechanical configuration of the A.S. (a simple representation of ArcTurius rover, in this example) with respect to a terrain characterized by an non-negligible roughness level. In this set of simulations, we integrated in the simulation system the landing site of Apollo 15 (Apennine Mountains region) [21], whose elevation models has been provided by NASA organization. It has been selected because the represented area is characterized by an irregular ground, suitable for an adequacy analysis of mechanical equipment (e.g., wheels, chassis, etc.). Figure 8 shows a 3D-reconstruction of the terrain.

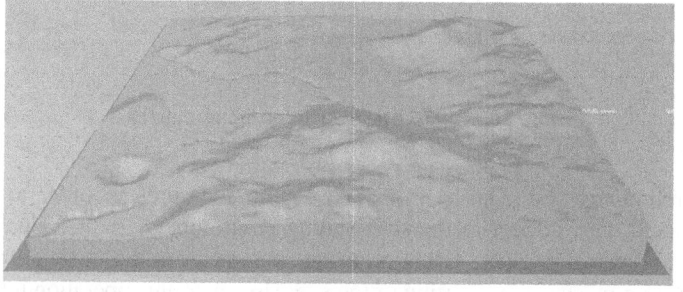

Fig. 8. 3D reconstruction of Apollo 15 landing site

In the simple representation of ArcTurius rover used for this simulation, the rover has been modelled with 3 boxes connected each other by a rigid junction, whereas wheels are represented using solid cylinders. Sizes and weights have been chosen according to original ArcTurius design [2]. In this set of simulations, we would like to verify whether ArcTurius rover is able to easily cross an irregular terrain such as the one that characterize Apollo region. If not, the results of the simulation can lead us to easily understand where is necessary to act.

Figure 9 shows the results of the first simulation. The simple representation of ArcTurius rover runs over the terrain in a straight line, but he fails to overcome a depression in the terrain. This is confirmed by the contacts points showed in Fig. 10. Indeed, the chassis of the rover touches the ground (red circle in Fig. 10) whereas a wheel is raised from the ground (the absence of contact points in the green square in Fig. 10).

Fig. 9. Starving after a depression

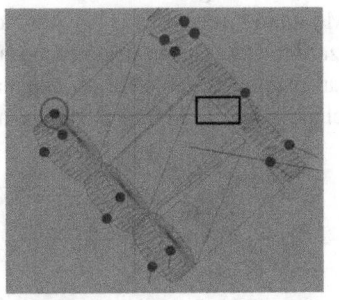

Fig. 10. Contact points (Color figure online)

This preliminary result leads us to take countermeasures in order to make the system adapted with respect to the surrounding environment. A first idea can be to enhance the power of engines, acting on torque parameter in the models. In fact, that leads the system in a success crossing of the site. However, this operation involves in a larger power consumption with the consequent reduction of the rover autonomy as well as the time mission.

For this reason, we wonder whether an architectural change can lead to a success, keeping the power consumption unchanged. We though to replace the wheels with other characterized by a bigger size and height. This lead to an architectural problem: the lack of free space implies to switch to an architecture characterized by 3 connected bodies and 4 wheels instead of 6, as depicted in Fig. 11. Also in this time, the autonomous system succeeded in the crossing of the area.

The research of a new configuration can involve several other critical issues that have to be taken into account before running the real rover in a post-disaster environment. With respect to the last illustration, the fact to have a standalone body can cause a balancing problem. Indeed, the body in the middle of the chassis has to be balanced in order to avoid awkward behaviours while crossing a non-straight terrain. In the last simulation, we injected a component in the body in order to cause a parasitic sway of the system. This is showed in Fig. 12, where we can notice the centres of mass of wheels (right and left side) and of the central body after the integration of a component, located in correspondence of the green box. In the bottom of the image, we can notice the contact points of the body to the ground, behaviour that shall be avoided in a real context.

Fig. 11. Architectural variation

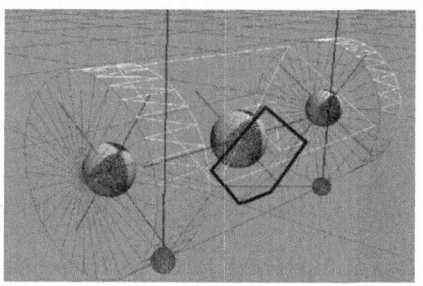

Fig. 12. Integration of a new component – Balancing problem (Color figure online)

Before the integration a new component in the system (such as sensors, batteries, etc.) we expect to perform this and many other kind of analysis. In this respect, the immediate visual returning given by the 3D system can enhance the understanding of engineers in charge to configure an autonomous system in order to make it adapted before a mission.

6 Discussion and Conclusion

The use of autonomous engines either on the ground (Rover) or flying (Drone) is without any doubt an improvement. They are able to attain unattainable and dangerous locations. Moreover, they are less sensitive to both environmental conditions such as meteorology and stressful situations for human beings. However, in order to achieve this autonomy several difficulties have to be resolved. In the first hours after a disaster, during the rescue team deployment, our 3D-based simulation system allows a real gain in terms of timing. In conclusion, from the proposed approach we can expect to:

- Increase the knowledge of the devastated area
- Validate the A.S. behaviour (moving, data acquisition, etc.)
- Validate the adaptation of the payload sensors configuration for this (these) mission (s)

This is a first work towards the proposal of a new approach than can support the support rescue missions that expect a contribution of A.S. Today we are able to generate terrain data based on satellites and DEM model, to customize them and to import them in the simulation environment. Moreover, we can correctly model rigid bodies and their physical properties, such as the mechanical parts that compose a rover with their interconnection points (junctions). We are able to associate a behaviour to the rover, to model the most common sensors (such as camera, LIDARs, odometers) and display their results. On the other hand, more work has to be done in the context of environment conditions. Part of the future work will include the reaction of the terrain (intended as the modification of its physical parameters) to a natural event such as rain on snow. This work will open the door to many others scenarios in the context of simulation in support to disaster risk reduction [22–24].

References

1. Mukhopadhay, B., Bhattacherjee, B.: Use of information technology in emergency and disaster management. Am. J. Environ. Prot. **4**, 101–104 (2015). https://doi.org/10.11648/j.ajep.20150402.15
2. Tanzi, T.J., Isnard, J.: Autonomous system for data collection: location and mapping issues in post-disaster environment. Comptes Rendus Physique (2019). https://doi.org/10.1016/j.crhy.2019.03.001
3. Chandra, M., Tanzi, T.J.: Drone-borne GPR design: propagation issues. In: Journées scientifiques de l'URSI-France (JS'17) (2017)
4. Servigne, S., Gripay, Y., Pinarer, O., Samuel, J., Ozgovde A., Jay, J.: Heterogeneous sensor data exploration and sustainable declarative monitoring architecture: application to smart building. In: First International Conference on Smart Data and Smart Cities, 30th UDMS, 9 September 2016, Split, Croatie, pp. 97–104 (2016). https://doi.org/10.5194/isprs-annals-iv-4-w1-97-2016
5. Tanzi, T.J., Roudier, Y., Apvrille, L.: Towards a new architecture for autonomous data collection. ISPRS Geospatial Week 2015: Workshop on civil Unmanned Aerial Vehicles for geospatial data acquisition, La Grande Motte (Montpellier), France, 1–2 October 2015

6. Stormont, D., Allan, V.: Managing risk in disaster scenarios with autonomous robots. J. Syst. Cybern. Inform. **7**, 66–71 (2009)
7. Koenig, N., Howard, A.: Design and use paradigms for Gazebo, an open-source multi-robot simulator. In 2004 IEEE/RSJ International Conference on Intelligent Robots and Systems (IROS) (IEEE Cat.No.04CH37566), Sendai, vol. 3, pp. 2149–2154 (2004). https://doi.org/10.1109/iros.2004.1389727
8. Hokuyo UTM-30LX Scanning Laser Rangefinder. https://www.hokuyo-aut.jp/search/single.php?serial=169
9. ROS Components UTM-30LX. https://www.roscomponents.com/en/lidar-laser-scanner/87-utm-30lx.html
10. Package Summary hokuyo node. http://wiki.ros.org/hokuyo_node
11. Burgard, W., Fox, D., Thrun, S.: Probabilistic Robotics. The MIT Press, Cambridge (2005)
12. Kam, H.R., Lee, S.-H., Park, T., Kim, C.-H.: RViz: a toolkit for real domain data visualization. Telecommun. Syst. **60**, 1–9 (2015). https://doi.org/10.1007/s11235-015-0034-5
13. Digital Elevation Models. https://en.wikipedia.org/wiki/Digital_elevation_model
14. ASTER - Global Digital Elevation Map. https://asterweb.jpl.nasa.gov/gdem.asp
15. USGS DEM - National Elevation Dataset (NED). https://en.wikipedia.org/wiki/USGS_DEM
16. SRTM30+ - Shuttle Radar Topology Mission. https://www2.jpl.nasa.gov/srtm/
17. Quigley, M., et al.: ROS: an open-source robot operating system. In: ICRA Workshop on Open Source Software, vol. 3 (2009)
18. ROS navigation package. http://wiki.ros.org/navigation
19. Drumwright, E., Hsu, J., Koenig, N., Shell, D.: Extending open dynamics engine for robotics simulation. In: Ando, N., Balakirsky, S., Hemker, T., Reggiani, M., von Stryk, O. (eds.) SIMPAR 2010. LNCS (LNAI), vol. 6472, pp. 38–50. Springer, Heidelberg (2010). https://doi.org/10.1007/978-3-642-17319-6_7
20. SDF data format. http://sdformat.org/
21. Apollo 15 landing site. https://nasa3d.arc.nasa.gov/detail/Apollo15-Landing
22. Apvrille, L., Tanzi, T.J., Roudier, Y., Dugelay. J.-L.: Drone "humanitaire": état de l'art et réflexions. Revue Française de Photogrammétrie et de Télédétection, N 213-04-26, pp. 63–71 (2017)
23. Tanzi, T.J., Chandra, M., Isnard, J., Camara, D., Sebastien, O., Harivelo. F.: Towards drone-borne disaster management: future application scenarios **III-8**, 181–189 (2016). https://doi.org/10.5194/isprs-annals-iii-8-181-2016
24. Chandra, M., Tanzi, T.J.: Wave propagation and radar system. Aspects for designing a "drone borne" GPR for humanitarian application. In: IEEE Conference on Antenna Measurements & Applications (CAMA), Antibes, France (2014)

Classification of Social Media Messages Posted at the Time of Disaster

Kemachart Kemavuthanon[1]([⊠]) and Osamu Uchida[2]([⊠])

[1] Graduate School of Science and Technology, Tokai University,
Hiratsuka-shi, Kanagawa, Japan
kemachart.kem@mfu.ac.th

[2] Department of Human and Information Science, Tokai University,
Hiratsuka-shi, Kanagawa, Japan
o-uchida@tokai.ac.jp

Abstract. Nowadays, social media is one of the essential sharing of information and proliferation tools because it spreads text messages, news, pictures, or videos in real-time. During the disaster, Japanese people use social media to exchange real-time information for their social interaction. Twitter is the most popular tool that has been used for disaster response in Japan. Even though many disaster systems have been created and used for disaster mitigation in Japan, most of them are assumed to be used by the Japanese in the Japanese language. From this problem, this study focuses on the way to create a disaster response system and community service to help, collect, and extract information on social media to help disaster mitigation becomes more important. This paper aims to investigate the tweets by focusing on noun keywords during the Osaka North Earthquake on 18 June 2018 with a data set of more than 9,000,000 tweets. The process presented classify social media messages by using ontology, word similarity, frequency of keyword, and evaluate results of natural language processing. We organize the messages into 15 categories and used as the classification algorithms with machine learning features of the count of each category word in the sentences. The result tweets were statistically compared with the keyword in each category to classify the content and collecting disaster information and using the result to build the analysis system.

Keywords: Disaster information · Word similarity · Twitter analysis · Tweet classification · Natural language processing · Neural disaster

1 Introduction

During the disaster, Japanese people utilize social media to exchange useful information in real-time. For example, during the 10 min from 8 o'clock immediately after the 2018 Osaka Northern Earthquake occurred, more than 270,000 tweets including the word "地震" (earthquake, in Japanese) were posted [1]. Even though many systems to use at the time of disaster have been created and used in disaster mitigation in Japan, most of them focused only on the Japanese people. Moreover, most information on social media during disasters does not help foreigners because the contents are written in Japanese. Therefore, we have been working on developing a system for foreigners in

Published by Springer Nature Switzerland AG 2020
Y. Murayama et al. (Eds.): ITDRR 2019, IFIP AICT 575, pp. 212–226, 2020.
https://doi.org/10.1007/978-3-030-48939-7_18

Japan, which is useful for obtaining necessary information in real-time during disasters. We use Twitter to gather information to be provided in our system because Twitter is the most utilized social media in Japan, with more than 45 million active users, and it is known that there are many tweets posted at the time of disasters [2, 3].

In this study, we propose a method to classify tweet data using WordNet as a step of developing a disaster information providing system. In the experiment, we used a dataset of more than 9 million tweets collected on June 18, 2018, the day when the Osaka North Earthquake occurred. We verify the accuracy of the proposed tweet classification method by calculating the confusion matrix.

2 Related Work

Lots of methods for the analysis of social media to create a disaster victims helping system. Several of them are explained in the following:

Disaster information tweeting system (DITS) and Disaster information mapping system (DIMS) is the application to share disaster information and help the user when disaster happens by use geolocation information and hashtag [4]. This system implemented as a web-based application. This application has unique features such that Tweets are posted as tweets from the user's own Twitter account, the user can send rescue information with the user's current geolocation information (the longitude and latitude coordinates) and share information between the users with texts and images. This application was launched in 2015 and the number of users of it is gradually increasing.

DETSApp is the applied research for disaster events by summarization of images on Twitter [5]. The proposed method in [5] has the following features: (1) image clustering process with a near-duplicate image detection algorithm, and (2) image summarization using textual information associated with each image. That possesses the ability to portray the real-time scenario of an ongoing disaster event accurately.

Sumalatha et al. proposed an emergency distress relief system using social networking platform, called GDSS (Geo Distributed Social Service System) to provide immediate assistance [6]. People can upload the picture and/or image taken at the time of incident once they come across disaster, using the mobile in social media to the system. The system informs the nearest relief center and people at the nearest place to provide service and to take measures for recovery.

DISAANA and D-SUMM are the systems that are using Twitter as an information source to analyze AI and be used to create a help system in a disaster event [7]. DISAANA provides a list of answers to questions as to location and information. D-SUMM summarizes the disaster reports from a specified area in a compact format and enables rescue workers to grasp the disaster situations quickly. In the 2016 Kumamoto Earthquake, DISAANA used by the Japanese government and provided a wide range of useful information. It shows the overall information of the earthquake by choosing from keywords and related words as a layer of information to find the answers that are most closely related to the question.

However, in the research to create a helping system for disaster, there are still many things that need to be considered and developed. Especially in Japan, there is an overwhelming lack of research and development on systems that provide disaster information for foreigners.

3 Methodology

Many types of study for sentiment classification use machine learning [8]. Based on these studies, we propose a method to extract disaster information from social media data. The first step of the classification process consists of conducting a few necessary pre-processing steps, i.e., tokenization and removal of stop words [9]. Next, we select ten keywords to create a category that relates to the requirement for surviving during a disaster based on the recommendation of well- known Japanese information. After that, we compute the ontology and the WordNet similarity between each word in the tweet sentence and category keywords to find the meaning of vocabulary. Then, we classify the tweet sentence by using the frequency of keyword matching with the category.

3.1 Word Similarity on WordNet

WordNet is a broad coverage lexical network of the English words, is organized into taxonomic hierarchies. Nouns, verbs, adjectives, and adverbs are divided into different groups named [10]. The process of computing the ontology and the WordNet similarity uses a library Java API for WordNet Similarity [11]. This process supports the semantic similarity between keyword and present similarity score with a percentage [12]. The lexical relations of WordNet include: the upper and lower position, synonyms, contains the property, causes [13, 14]. WordNet similarity equation compares words by finding the root word of both words with function HyperTrees(). For example, the root word of cat: HyperTrees(Keyword:cat) = ROOT*#n#1 < entity#n#1 < physical_entity#n#1 < object#n#1 < whole#n#2 < living_thing#n#1 < organism#n#1 < Keyword:animal < chordate#n#1 < vertebrate#n#1 < mammal#n#1 < placental#n#1 < carnivore#n#1 < canine#n#2 < Keyword:cat. The results of both words were kept in the parameters T1 and T2. Then, it calculates the depth of the similarity by equation Eq. (1).

$$DepthLCS = Depth(Keyword)$$
$$Depth1 = \min(depth(\{tree \text{ in } T1\} | tree \text{ contains } LCS)) \qquad (1)$$
$$Depth2 = \min(depth(\{tree \text{ in } T2\} | tree \text{ contains } LCS))$$

After that, we have a depth tree and results of T1 and T2, and we can calculate the similarity score by a use equation Eq. (2).

$$2 \times \frac{DepthLCS}{(Depth1 + Depth2)} \qquad (2)$$

From the calculating process with the WordNet similarity equation, we will get a similar score for each word when comparing. The result will be 0–1, where 1 means 100% related similar between two words and 0 will mean they are not similar at all.

3.2 Confusion Matrix

A confusion matrix is often used to measure the accuracy rate of the classifier. It uses new data that is not used in the training process of the machine learning model [15, 16]. The confusion Matrix has the following four values:

True Positive (TP): Both the prediction result and the actual class is true.
True Negative (TN): Both the prediction result and the actual class is not true.
False Positive (FP): The prediction result is true but the actual class is not true.
False Negative (FN): The prediction result is true but the actual class is true.

The measurement will measure all three things: accuracy, precision, and recall. Accuracy: The value that presents the accurate ratio of the prediction,

$$\frac{TP + TN}{TP + TN + FP + FN} \tag{3}$$

Precision: The value that indicates the correct answer rate when the prediction is true.

$$\frac{TP}{TP + FP} \tag{4}$$

Recall (True Positive Rate): The value that indicates how much of the true class can be predicted correctly.

$$\frac{TP}{TP + FN} \tag{5}$$

In this research, we use the confusion matrix to measure the accuracy of the prediction.

4 Data Collection and Analysis

4.1 Dataset Gathering

In this study, firstly, we derive a dataset from the previous process. It was tokenizing [17] from the Japanese sentences of the Osaka North Earthquake on June 18, 2018, such as; noun, verb, adverb, adjective, emoji, hashtag, link, and @Addfriend [18].

These APIs can also be used to access Twitter data [19] and the data from API is JSON String file [20]. Then, all of the keywords have been translated into English to know the meaning and understanding of each keyword by google translate API [21]. In the second process, the result has been selected for analysis only 149,938 unique noun keywords and classify sentences (The results are shown in Table 1).

Table 1. The top 20 most word noun.

No	Word	Count	No	Word	Count
1	地震 (earthquake)	12,116,336	11	水 (water)	667,229
2	大阪 (Osaka)	3,045,645	12	県 (Prefecture)	637,582
3	震度 (Seismic intensity)	2,409,063	13	熊本 (Kumamoto)	592,687
4	時 (Time)	1,841,154	14	余震 (aftershock)	588,481
5	北部 (North)	1,399,607	15	関西 (Kansai)	547,898
6	府 (Prefecture)	1,216,496	16	南部 (South)	536,719
7	情報 (information)	836,798	17	京都 (Kyoto)	494,031
8	発生 (Occurrence)	811,308	18	電車 (Electric train)	491,368
9	速報 (Breaking news)	693,661	19	緊急 (emergency)	478,020
10	震源 (Epicenter)	688,903	20	注意 (Caution)	466,612

4.2   Word Similarity and Frequency Process

To analyze the data, we selected ten words from the word groups that have emerged from this study. They are necessary to know when a disaster happens. The category focuses on events- before the disaster happens, during the disaster happens and after a disaster occurs. During the process of comparing word similarities, we have analyzed keyword categories in more than ten categories. However, after the translation process and word similarity process, the result found that some categories have the same meaning and similar keyword content. Then, we decided to summarize tweet data into ten categories (see Fig. 1); transportation (as a group of travel information, vehicles, roads), animal (as a group of living, human, animal, and pets), alert (as a group of information during and after the disaster happens), warning (a group of caution and self-defense before a disaster), place (a group of building or locations), damage (a group of effects and violence by disasters), emotion (a group of feeling information and ideas), action (a group of activities during the disaster), energy (a group of energy information), service (a group of helping information and sharing service).

Then, Japanese nouns have been translated into English and filter the words that have the same meaning to reduce the number of keywords. The results of the English word compare the similarities and calculate the score of word similarity between words using WordNet and counting the frequency of those words in each sentence (9,428,334 tweets) to classify the type of sentence.

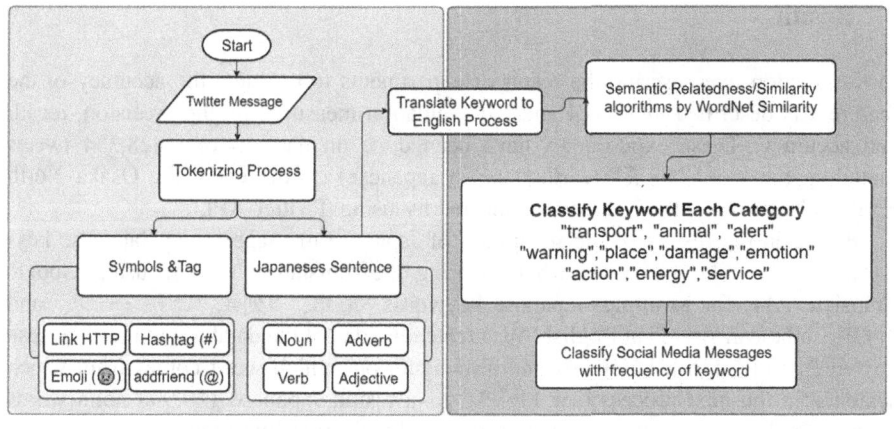

Fig. 1. The overall process of tokenizing, computing word similarities and counting word frequencies

4.3 Analysis of Words Frequency in Message

From the Japanese message on Twitter, such as "駅が地震で壊れたため、大阪の電車は停車しました" (The Meaning is "The train in Osaka stopped because the station has broken by the earthquake") to separate into each word. Then, all of the noun word grouping into ten categories of words based on their meaning. After that, the sentence will be counted frequency of the word in each category to rank the score (percent). The result of the score will present the main topic, the meaning of the sentence, and the rating of frequency used to classify messages to each category (see Fig. 2). However, several messages can be more than one category. It depends on the frequency score of the messages.

When the frequency score of each sentence has reached, we have verified and evaluated all the results by confusion matrix (measuring with Accuracy/Precision/Recall). The results of the process will compare to the real meaning of the actual content.

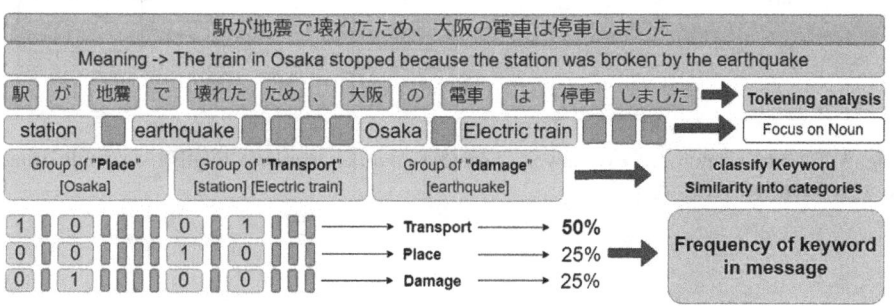

Fig. 2. The process of deriving word frequencies of each Twitter message.

5   Result

In this section, we describe the result of experiments to evaluate the accuracy of the feature sets described in Sect. 4 and the evaluation measured by the precision, recall, and accuracy. These experiments have been done on datasets of 9,428,334 tweets including the word "地震" (earthquake in Japanese) on the event the Osaka North Earthquake on June 18, 2018, that collected by using Twitter API.

Based on the results of the separation of Japanese message, many Japanese keywords have similar meanings when entering the translating process using Google Translate API; for example, Japanese keywords "電車," "列車," "トレーン," and "汽車," all mean "train" in English. We create relations of the database to link Japanese keywords and English keywords and also figure out which word comes from which sentence in the next process (see Fig. 3). As a result, Japanese 149,938 noun words become 59,236 English words. That used to find the similarity of the words in the next process.

When the result derived from the translation process and reduce the number of repeated meanings, the result keyword has to store in the database with the table linked to the original word table because all result should be able to connect to the tweet sentence. In the next step, we will compare the similarities and ontology of the 59,236 unique words. The number of results from all comparisons is $59,236 \times 10 = 592,360$ records. All calculation results from the word similarity process have stored in the database. In this regard, no matter how high or low the score is, we have to analyze results that can be used for the next research.

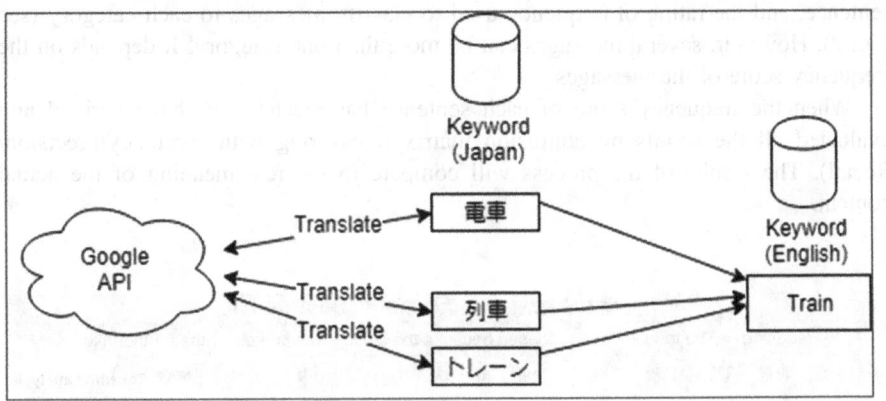

Fig. 3. The translation process between Japanese noun keywords to English keywords using Google Translate API.

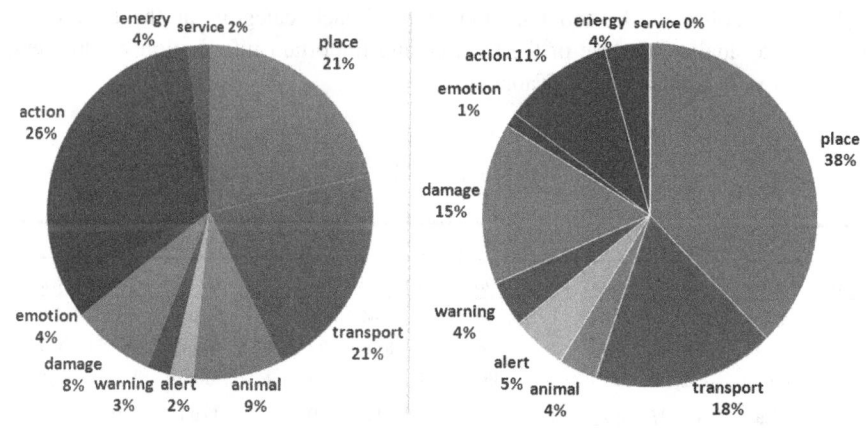

Fig. 4. Percentage of unique words per group (Left) and percentage of using times in message per group (Right).

Word similarity between all keyword with each category was calculated by using WordNet. For all noun keywords, we calculate the similarity score to ten categories. The total of keyword similarity in ten groups is more than 5,500 unique words and have been divided into the group of place 1,103 unique words (used 6,335,988 times in message), the group of transport 1,097 unique words (used 2,958,987 times in message), the group of animal 458 unique words (used 615,510 times in message), the group of alert 119 unique words (used 896,842 times in message), the group of warning 121 unique words (used 728,237 times in message), the group of damage 431 unique words (used 2,562,554 times in message), the group of emotion 176 unique words (used 226,251 times in message), the group of action 1,361 unique words (used 1,776,493 times in message), the group of energy 188 unique words (used 718,467 times in message) and the group of service and help 125 unique words (used 862,523 times in message). The number of keywords from the result in each category is derived from the comparison between keywords and ten categories to find the closest similarity rate, synonyms, and homonyms. The average result rate of each category depends on the ability to take advantage of the next process to find information. The scores of similarity rate are between 0.85–1.00 (see Fig. 4).

The word's similarity scores immediate difference in each category keyword due to the program find the result of the similarity based on the relationship and ontology of words. We have to analyze and select the most appropriate score in each category because a low similarity score that means, the word is not related and cannot filter the keyword of the sentence as we want. However, if we set too high a similarity score, the result will also lose that useful word. Therefore, the result has to determine the appropriate average rating from the keywords that can be analyzed and used in the content with the configuration as follows; the group of place: 0.80, the group of transport: 0.80, the group of animal: 0.70, the group of alert: 0.70, the group of warning: 0.75, the group of damage 0.75, the group of emotion: 0.75, the group of action: 0.75, the group of energy: 0.75, and the group of service and help: 0.75.

We have collected the top ten keywords of each category at the time of the earthquake to analyze the use of the term to find important information by differentiating the closest similarity rate (Table 2).

Table 2. The result top 10 most word noun in each category by similarity score.

Transport					Place					Animal		
No	Word	Count	Ratio	No	Word	Count	Ratio	No	Word	Count	Ratio
1	train	1,072,648	0.94	1	prefecture	1,216,496	0.94	1	cat	393,510	0.70
2	line	374,747	0.90	2	home	462,851	1.0	2	man	36,754	0.75
3	traffic	132,538	0.87	3	line	374,747	0.85	3	dog	17,661	0.75
4	release	46,207	0.82	4	work	226,212	0.80	4	head	9,085	0.70
5	delivery	35,071	0.80	5	station	218,792	1.0	5	horse	8,062	0.81
6	turn	31,748	0.89	6	target	216,486	1.0	6	bird	5,109	0.81
7	return	31,041	0.80	7	place	178,781	1.0	7	insect	3,504	0.80
8	transfer	29,027	1.0	8	area	127,034	0.94	8	creature	1,686	1.0
9	car	26,668	0.87	9	city	105,725	1.0	9	chicken	1,080	0.73
10	transport	25,572	1.0	10	center	100,094	0.80	10	beast	779	1.0

Damage					Emotion					Energy		
No	Word	Count	Ratio	No	Word	Count	Ratio	No	Word	Count	Ratio
1	intensity	2,409,063	0.93	1	feeling	74898	0.90	1	life	238,769	0.97
2	death	50,181	0.87	2	fear	37299	0.92	2	work	226212	0.94
3	loss	27,632	0.96	3	love	34264	0.93	3	light	101960	0.95
4	change	26,627	0.81	4	hate	13314	0.93	4	power	91402	0.90
5	injury	25,192	1.0	5	care	8930	0.90	5	force	67929	0.92
6	damage	24,584	1.0	6	panic	4796	0.93	6	weather	48568	0.75
7	cost	16,292	0.75	7	spirit	2894	0.90	7	sun	8141	0.82
8	price	16,292	0.94	8	emotion	839	0.90	8	heat	3247	0.82
9	break	15,918	0.89	9	joy	614	0.90	9	energy	2803	1.0
10	harm	6,283	1.0	10	concern	585	0.93	10	electricity	1206	0.76

Alert					Warning		
No	Word	Count	Ratio	No	Word	Count	Ratio
1	caution	466612	0.78	1	caution	466612	0.90
2	preparation	209549	0.92	2	rumor	215501	0.85
3	alarm	93425	1.0	3	advice	30863	0.92
4	signal	24030	0.70	4	report	11804	0.90
5	notification	22277	0.85	5	account	3097	0.90
6	wake	2222	0.80	6	lesson	1728	0.93
7	horn	885	1.0	7	recommendation	1425	0.88
8	sign	692	0.70	8	threat	1225	0.91
9	indication	342	0.87	9	comment	176	0.87
10	threat	225	0.90	10	example	159	0.93

(Continued)

Table 2. (*Continued*)

	Action				Service		
No	*Word*	*Count*	*Ratio*	*No*	*Word*	*Count*	*Ratio*
1	operation	320172	0.88	1	work	226212	0.91
2	stop	126677	0.94	2	use	98831	0.78
3	fire	125801	0.93	3	force	67929	0.91
4	cause	110637	0.90	4	company	64728	0.90
5	end	73924	0.93	5	staff	26410	0.75
6	case	61262	0.90	6	service	25210	1.0
7	release	46207	0.90	7	support	13313	0.78
8	change	26627	0.90	8	law	11120	0.80
9	effect	23658	0.93	9	aid	5128	0.83
10	war	17868	0.90	10	help	3699	1.0

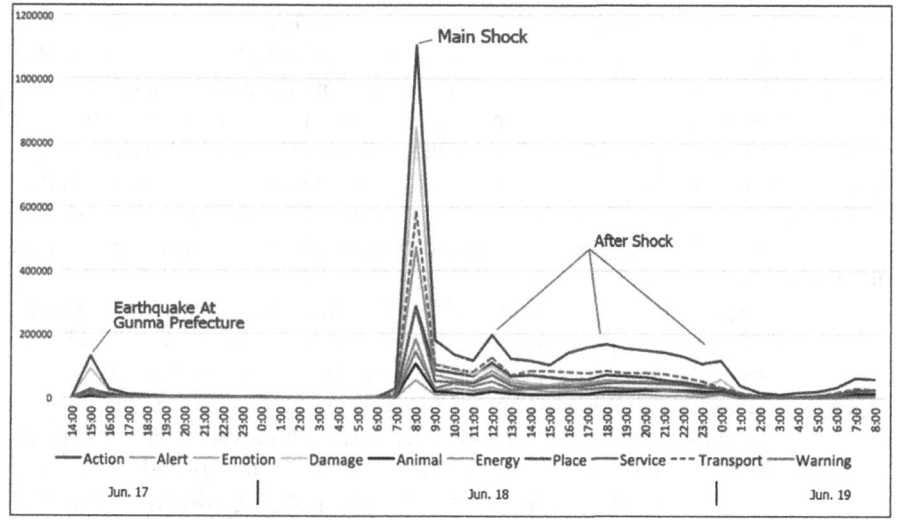

Fig. 5. The number of tweets per hour before and after the occurrence of the Osaka Northern Earthquake.

All calculations result presented on the graph is showing the amount of usage data of each category during the Osaka North Earthquake on June 17–19, 2018. From this graph, the line of data in each category is following the same direction as the earthquake situation. However, the amount of content in each category is different (see Fig. 5).

As shown in the graph, the most tweet message on the graph is in the place category. Most of the content in place category refers to the location of the earthquake, such as " 【地震情報】18日07時58分頃、大阪府北部で震度6弱の地震がありました。　　　　　　　　　震源地は

大阪府北部で、震源の深さは約10km、　　　　地震の規模はM5.9と推定されます。この地震に　　　　よる津波の心配はありません。　　　　　この地震について、緊急地震速報を発表しています。震度6弱:大阪北区、高槻市、枚方市など" (In English: [Earthquake Information] An earthquake of less than 6 intensity occurred in northern Osaka Prefecture around 7:58 a.m. on the 18th. The epicenter is in northern Osaka Prefecture, the depth of the epicenter is estimated to be about 10 km and the scale of the earthquake is estimated to be M5.9. There is no concern about a tsunami caused by this earthquake. An earthquake early warning for this earthquake was announced. The seismic intensity of 6-lower: Kita Ward of Osaka, Takatsuki City, Hirakata City, etc.).Also, the second rank of the graph is damage categories because of the "intensity" keyword that has a volume of 2,409,063 tweets. The Tweet message contents about the strength of the earthquake and the shaking, for example, "07 時58分頃、地震がありました。[震度6弱] 大阪北部 [震度5　　　　強] 京都南部 [震度5弱] 兵庫南東部、奈良 [震度4] 嶺南地方、滋賀北部、　滋賀南部、大阪南部、淡路島 [震度3] 三重北部、三重中部、京都北部、兵庫北部、兵庫南西部、和歌山北部" (In English: An earthquake occurred around 07:58. [seismic intensity of 6-lower] northern Osaka [seismic intensity of 5-upper] southern Kyoto [seismic intensity of 5- lower] southeastern Hyogo, Nara [seismic intensity of 4] Reinan region, northern Shiga, southern Shiga, southern Osaka, Awaji Island [seismic intensity of 3] northern Mie, central part of Mie, Northern Kyoto, Northern Hyogo, Southwestern Hyogo, northern Wakayama.). Then the third of the overall graph will be the "transport" category related to travel. The most tweet content is about traveling by trains as they are the main transportation of Japanese people. The content is mainly about the train information and the train stopped disrupted information. It is helpful information. Also, the other two important information is data before and after an earthquake happens. We expand both graphs to see data fragmentation information (see Figs. 6 and 7).

When we expand the graph, we can find the distribution of information. We found and the trend of the line graph in the group of transport categories that occurred before the Great Earthquake happens. There was a fewer tweet, but after the earthquake happens, it became the second most tweet. Another important graph is in the category Warning is the third highest in the pre-disaster period; however, after the disaster, the amount of tweets has decreased. The most content in that period of Warning category　　　is　　"地震発生後余震への備え　　①断水に備えお風呂に水を貯める②停電に備え懐中電　　　　　　　　灯の用意 ③食器棚の扉にはガムテープで食器が落ちない工夫を…" (In English: Preparations for aftershocks: (1) Keep water in a bath to prepare for a water outage, (2) prepare flashlights for A power outage, (3) prevent falling objects, such as stopping the door of the cupboard with gum tape. …). Also, the graph of Action and Service category that rises after the earthquake happens. In this section can be analyzed to find guidelines for helping when an earthquake happens.

However, the summary of the graph result is the amount of information for each category that cannot present the meaning in each message. There will be more than one keyword noun. Therefore, the next step is to count the frequency of the categories in each sentence. This step will help us know the meaning of the contents.

The sentence of the Twitter message is very short words (only 140–280 characters) and the keywords in each message use word's similarity scores as a comparison. Therefore, some words can be grouped in more than one category but have different scores. We have created calculation rules of counting as follows.

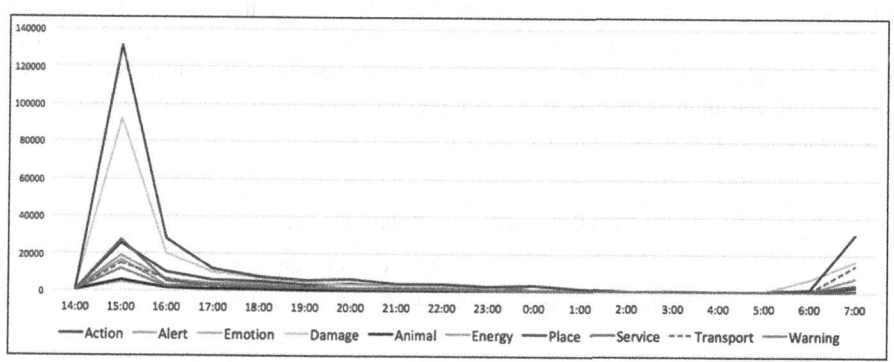

Fig. 6. The number of tweets per hour before the occurrence of the Osaka Northern Earthquake.

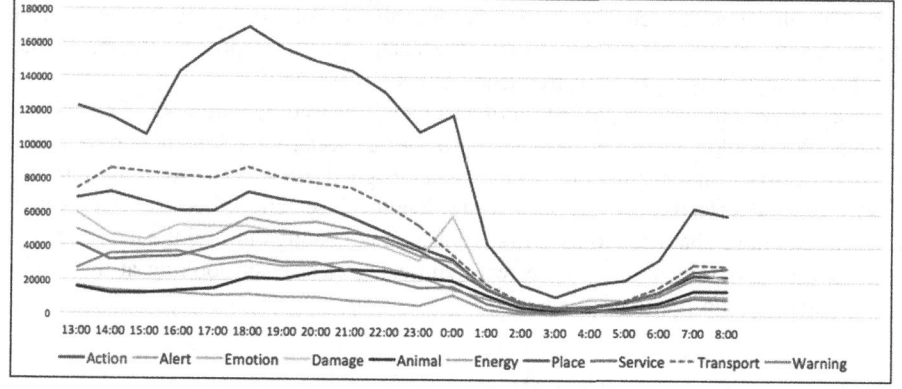

Fig. 7. The number of tweets per hour after the occurrence of the Osaka Northern Earthquake.

- In the case that two categories with the same keyword, compare the similarity score of each category to find which category is more accurate.
- In the case that the keyword has more than one category, the second category that has top of similarity score will be used to find the frequency as well.

For example, in the case of the content of the Twitter that separates the nouns is [caution] [intensity] [prefecture] [preparation]. The keyword caution is a word in both categories Alert and Warning, but the score is different. The system retrieves both categories to counting frequency. Therefore, this content is in the group [Alert | Warning] [Damage] [Place] [Alert] and summarizes the results of the word frequency count as follows: Alert $2 = 2/5 \times 100 = 40\%$, Warning $1 = 1/5 \times 100 = 20\%$,

Damage $1 = 1/5 \times 100 = 20\%$, Place $1 = 1/5 \times 100 = 20\%$. From the results of calculations, summary the content of this Tweet message as a primary category "Alert" within that message, there has the content of category damage and category places inside.

We tested the accuracy of calculation frequency in content counting using the confusion matrix. We random 10,000 tweets from all tweets in the database to calculate the results of the accuracy. By comparing the result of prediction from the calculation program (from counting the frequency of words and classified into ten categories) and the actuality meaning of tweets when reading and translating typically by a human. (The results are shown in Table 3.)

Table 3. Accuracy of classification.

	Accuracy	Precision	Recall
Confusion matrix score	0.874	0.97	0.861

From the results, it presents the accuracy score of the use of classifying messages in social media. The accuracy is as much as 87% because classified by use group of the category to reduce the variety of keyword in social media. Moreover, the use of word similarity effects with accuracy score is because the use of word similarity will select the words to analyze and group it into the category. These process decreases the number of keywords to find the frequency in each message.

We analyzed that the imperfection of accuracy is caused by a number of categories defined. We should increase the number of categories because the sentences have many kinds of words than categories that have been designed, such as question groups, etc. Also, other imperfection of accuracy is the length of sentences because the Twitter message can have characters only 140–280. It was not enough to find the max score of one category. As sentences must be two main categories, when looking at the actual content, then group into one category.

6 Conclusion and Future Work

We proposed the method to classify tweets posted at the time of disaster. The verification experiment using Osaka North Earthquake tweet dataset showed that the accuracy of the proposed method is over 80%. In future research, it would be useful to compare the results obtained with other datasets of disasters and use different machine learning, such as SVM to compare the results to find out the midpoint of the score using for developing the best helping system for foreigners in the natural disaster situation in Japan.

We found that the accuracy of the classified content depends on the number of categories defined. Therefore, it should increase the number of categories that affect the content of disaster to increase the accuracy of the result, especially the category that can separate contents between the question sentences and knowledge sentences. Moreover, the system should have an information filter that correctly classifies fake information and truth knowledge information as well. However, we found some keywords that cannot be translated into English ultimately, such as the keyword "Neko" which means "cat" in an English word. The problem has come from that the Twitter user does not type correctly or type Japanese words in English, so this information was missing some keyword. The database should have a table for translation Japanese important proper nouns (including famous locations name and brands name) into English.

Acknowledgment. This study was supported by JSPS KAKENHI (Grant Number 18K11553) and the Tokai University General Research Organization.

References

1. Kemavuthanon, K., Uchida, O.: Social media messages during disasters in Japan: an empirical study of 2018 Osaka North Earthquake in Japan. In: Proceedings of 2019 IEEE 2nd International Conference on Information and Computer Technologies, pp. 199–203 (2019)
2. Yamada, S., Utsu, K., Uchida, O.: An analysis of Tweets during the 2018 Osaka North Earthquake in Japan -a brief report. In: Proceedings of 5th International Conference on Information and Communication Technologies for Disaster Management (2018)
3. Uchida, O., et al.: Classification and mapping of disaster relevant tweets for providing useful information for victims during disasters. IIEEJ Trans. Image Electron. Vis. Comput. **3**(2), 224–232 (2015)
4. Uchida, O., et al.: A real-time information sharing system to support self-, mutual-, and public-help in the aftermath of a disaster utilizing Twitter. IEICE Trans. Fundam. **E99-A**(8), 1551–1554 (2016)
5. Layek, A.K., Pal, A., Saha, R., Mandal, S.: DETSApp: an app for disaster event tweets summarization using images posted on Twitter. In: Proceedings of 2018 5th International Conference on Emerging Applications of Information Technology (2018)
6. Sumalatha, M.R., Basta, P., Sinha, A., Shrinath, P.: Social media for disaster relief—geo distributed social service system. In: Proceedings 2015 7th International Conference on Advanced Computing (2015)
7. Mizuno, J., et al.: WISDOM X, DISAANA and D-SUMM: large-scale NLP systems for analyzing textual Big Data. In: Proceedings of 26th International Conference on Computational Linguistics: System Demonstrations, pp. 263–267 (2016)
8. Naradhipa, A.R., Purwarianti, A.: Sentiment classification for indonesian message in social media. In: Proceedings of 2012 International Conference on Cloud Computing and Social Networking (2012)
9. Cavalin, P.R., Moyano, L.G., Miranda, P.P.: A multiple classifier system for classifying life events on social media. In: Proceedings of 2015 IEEE 15th International Conference on Data Mining Workshops, pp. 1332–1335 (2015)
10. Li, H., Tian, Y., Ye, B., Cai, Q.: Comparison of current semantic similarity methods in WordNet. In: Proceedings of 2010 International Conference on Computer Application and System Modeling, pp. V4-408–V4-411 (2010)
11. Nguyen, L.T., Huynh, K.M.: Using WordNet similarity and translations to create Synsets for ontology-based Vietnamese WordNet. In: Proceedings of 2016 5th IIAI International Congress on Advanced Applied Informatics, pp. 651–656 (2016)

12. Hasi, N.-U.: The automatic construction method of mongolian lexical semantic network based on WordNet. In: Proceedings of 2012 Fifth International Conference on Intelligent Networks and Intelligent Systems, pp. 220–223 (2012)

13. Pedersen, T., Patwardhan, S., Michelizzi, J.: WordNet: similarity - measuring the relatedness of concepts. In: Proceedings of Nineteenth National Conference on Artificial Intelligence (2004)

14. Zhang, Y.-L., Hasi: A constructing method of Mongolia-Chinese-English multilingual semantic net based on WordNet. In: Proceedings of 2015 International Conference on Computer Science and Applications, pp. 195–198 (2015)

15. Kale, S., Padmadas, V.: Sentiment analysis of tweets using semantic analysis. In: 2017 International Conference on Computing, Communication, Control and Automation (2017)

16. Indra, S.T., Wikarsa, L., Turang, R.: Using logistic regression method to classify tweets into the selected topics. In: Proceedings of 2016 International Conference on Advanced Computer Science and Information Systems, pp. 385–390 (2016)

17. Janssens, O., Slembrouck, M., Verstockt, S., Van Hoecke, S., Van de Walle, R.: Real-time emotion classification of tweets. In: Proceedings of 2013 IEEE/ACM International Conference on Advances in Social Networks Analysis and Mining, pp. 1430–1431 (2013)

18. Twiter. https://twitter.com/

19. Riyadh, A.Z., Alvi, N., Talukder, K.H.: Exploring human emotion via Twitter. In: Proceedings of 2017 20th International Conference of Computer and Information Technology, pp. 22–24 (2017)

20. Matsumura, N., Miura, A., Komori, M., Hiraishi, K.: Media and sentiments in the Great East Japan Earthquake related tweets – social media as "Meta Media". In: Proceedings of 2016 IEEE Tenth International Conference on Semantic Computing, pp. 465–470 (2016)

21. Google API. https://cloud.google.com/translate/

Workshop Program on Disaster Prevention and Mitigation for Young Generation Utilizing Disaster Information Tweeting and Mapping System

Osamu Uchida[1]($\boxtimes$), Sachi Tajima[2], Yoshitaka Kajita[3], Keisuke Utsu[4], Yuji Murakami[5], and Sanetoshi Yamada[6]

[1] Department of Human and Information Science, Tokai University, Hiratsuka, Kanagawa, Japan
o-uchida@tokai.ac.jp
[2] Center for Liberal Arts, Tokai University, Hiratsuka, Kanagawa, Japan
stajima@tokai-u.jp
[3] Department of Civil Engineering, Tokai University, Hiratsuka, Kanagawa, Japan
yokaji@tokai-u.jp
[4] Department of Communication and Network Engineering, Tokai University, Minato, Tokyo, Japan
utsu@utsuken.net
[5] Department of Electrical Engineering and Computer Science, Tokai University, Kumamoto, Japan
my072539@tsc.u-tokai.ac.jp
[6] Research and Information Center, Tokai University, Hiratsuka, Kanagawa, Japan
S.Yamada@star.tokai-u.jp

Abstract. Various large-scale natural disasters occur every year in Japan. Then, various disaster education is conducted at schools and in local communities for alleviating the damage caused by such natural disasters. However, according to various surveys, disaster prevention awareness among young people is known to be lower than in other age groups in Japan. Therefore, we worked with Kanagawa Prefecture, Japan, on establishing a program of workshops on disaster prevention and mitigation utilizing ICT equipment such as smartphones or tablet PCs to raise awareness of disaster prevention and mitigation among young people. The program is based on town watching and group discussion using DITS and DIMS (disaster information tweeting and mapping system) proposed in the previous studies. In this paper, we introduce the contents of the developed workshop program using DITS/DIMS. Moreover, we report on the results of the workshops for disaster prevention and mitigation using this program at several junior high and high schools. The results of the post-questionnaire show that many participants of the workshops had a positive impression on the disaster prevention and mitigation workshops using DITS/DIMS.

Keywords: Disaster prevention and mitigation · Disaster information · Town watching · Social Media · Twitter

Y. Murayama et al. (Eds.): ITDRR 2019, IFIP AICT 575, pp. 227–236, 2020.
https://doi.org/10.1007/978-3-030-48939-7_19

1   Introduction

Various large-scale natural disasters occur every year in Japan [1]. For example, more than 6,000 people died in the Great Hanshin-Awaji Earthquake of 1995 [2], and more than 15,000 people died in the Great East Japan Earthquake occurred in 2011 [3, 4]. Damages caused by typhoons, heavy rains, and heavy snows are also frequent. Then, various education on disaster prevention and mitigation has been conducted at schools and local communities for alleviating the damage caused by such natural disasters [5, 6]. In the Great East Japan Earthquake, there was a school where students could take appropriate evacuation behaviors due to the results of daily disaster education [7, 8]. Therefore, the effect of disaster prevention education attracts a great deal of attention recently. However, according to various surveys, disaster prevention awareness among young people is known to be lower than in other age groups in Japan. Therefore, we have worked with Kanagawa Prefecture, Japan, (http://www.pref.kanagawa.jp/english/) on establishing a program of workshops on disaster prevention and mitigation utilizing ICT equipment such as smartphones or tablet PCs to raise awareness of disaster prevention among young people, especially junior high and high school students. The reason why we tried to utilize ICT equipment for disaster prevention education is mainly due to the following two reasons.

- It is becoming common to utilize social media in the event of a disaster [9–11].
- The generality of junior high school and high school students have a smartphone and use it actively in Japan.

The established program is based on town watching and discussion using DITS and DIMS (disaster information tweeting and mapping system) proposed by us in the previous studies [12, 13]. In this paper, we introduce the contents of the established program of workshops on disaster prevention and mitigation. Moreover, we report on the results of the workshops for disaster prevention and mitigation using this program at several junior high and high schools.

2   Utilization of Twitter at the Time of Disaster

To minimize damage in case of large-scale disasters, it is important to collect and distribute information quickly and accurately. Therefore, the potential for the use of social media, especially Twitter, during disasters has attracted worldwide attention [9–11]. In recent large-scale natural disasters, Twitter has actively been used as a communication tool during the Great East Japan Earthquake on March 11, 2011, for example, many people used Twitter to find information about the tsunami, shelters, the state of public transportation services, and so on [14–16]. When Hurricane Sandy hit the U.S. East Coast in 2012, many people used Twitter to share disaster-related information more than 20 million tweets that included the words "sandy," "hurricane," "#sandy," and "#hurricane" were posted between October 27 and November 1, 2012 (https://twitter.com/Twitter/status/264408082958934016). Over a quarter million tweets were posted in the first 72 h after Typhoon Haiyan destroyed large areas of the Philippines [17], and a crisis map was made using crowdsourcing [11]. During the

10 min from 8 o'clock immediately after the 2018 Osaka Northern Earthquake occurred, more than 275,000 tweets including the word "地震" (earthquake, in Japanese) were posted [18]. Nishikawa et al. [19] showed that many tweets including the hashtag #救助 (救助 means rescue) were posted fore rescue request in 2018 Japan Floods.

The following text is an actual tweet posted after the 2016 Kumamoto Earthquake occurred: "There is no food or drink at Ubuyama Junior High School. The people there are really in trouble. Please send them food. Please help them. They need disposable diapers because there are many seniors" (original tweet is written in Japanese). Such tweets may be useful not only for disaster victims but also for governmental agencies to gain a better understanding of current conditions and thus help them make more informed decisions. For the reasons noted above, many Japanese national and local governmental agencies began to use Twitter to collect and distribute information during disasters. For example, the city government of Wako, Saitama Prefecture, Japan, decided that the hashtag "#和光市災害" (和光市 and 災害 mean Wako City and disaster, respectively, in Japanese) would be used as the official hashtag for posting disaster-related tweets. The use of hashtags with the form "#(municipality name) disaster" has been spreading to other municipalities in Japan in recent years.

3 DITS/DIMS: Disaster Information Tweeting and Mapping System

We give an overview of the disaster information tweeting and mapping system developed by Uchida et al. [12, 13].

3.1 DITS: Disaster Information Tweeting System

DITS (Fig. 1) has the following features.

- The user's current geolocation information is acquired by using location specification functions, such as the Global Positioning System (GPS). Based on the acquired location information, the street address of the user's current location, the hashtag of the form "#(municipality name) disaster," and the Military Grid Reference System (MGRS) code [20] are automatically attached to the tweet.
- In cases when the user needs rescue, the hashtag #救助 (救助 means rescue) is also attached to the tweet.
- An image can be attached.
- When a tweet is posted, the following information is stored in a database: (i) username, (ii) screen name, (iii) tweet ID, (iv) tweet text, (v) date and time of tweet post, (vi) latitude, (vii) longitude, (ix) MGRS code, (x) address, (xi) presence of the rescue hashtag ("\#rescue"), and (xii) URL of the attached image (if any).
- Tweets are posted from the user's own Twitter account (Twitter authentication is conducted at the start of system use).

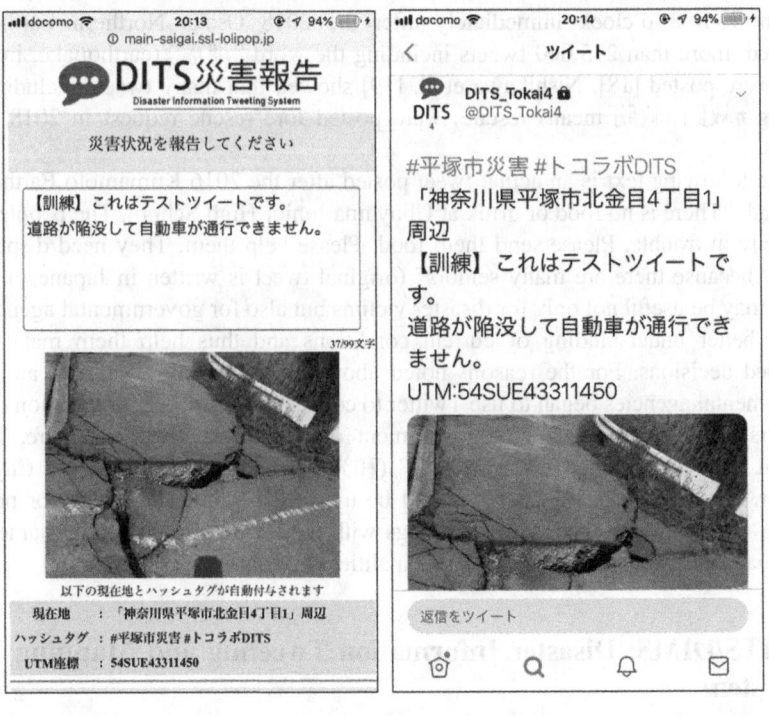

Fig. 1. Tweet posting page of DITS (left) and an example of a tweet posted by DITS (right)

Because the information posted using DITS is also posted on Twitter as tweets from the user's Twitter account, it can be used not only by users of this system but also by other disaster victims and organizations.

3.2 DIMS: Disaster Information Mapping System

DIMS has the following features.

- A Twitter account is not required to use this system.
- It displays a map with the most recent 30 tweets posted via DITS within 20 km of the user's location.
- The map is centered on the user's current position.
- The shape and color of the icon used to indicate the position of the tweet change, depending on whether the rescue hashtag (#救助) and an image are attached or not.
- The places of shelters within 2 km from the user's current location are displayed on the map. If user click (tap) a shelter icon, the shortest route from the current location of the user to the shelter is displayed.

Since the DIMS map displays centered on the user's current position, it is possible to obtain only nearby information efficiently.

4 Workshops on Disaster Prevention and Mitigation Utilizing DITS and DIMS

4.1 The Established Program

The established program of workshops on disaster prevention and mitigation is based on "town watching" using DITS and "group discussion" using DIMS. The main objectives of this disaster education program are as follows.

- to arouse awareness of disaster prevention through town watching,
- to learn the advantages and disadvantages of using Social Media at the time of disaster.

The schedule of this workshop program is as follows (in case that the total workshop time is 100 min).

1. Introduction: 15 min.
2. Town watching (using DITS): 45 min.
3. Group discussion (using DIMS): 20 min.
4. Report on group discussion: 10 min.
5. Summary: 5 min.
6. Questionnaire: 5 min.

In town watching, the participants post a tweet with a photo by DITS. DITS is originally a system to post disaster-related information such as damage situation and needs of victims in the event of a disaster. However, in this workshop program, DITS is used as a tool for getting the awareness of places and things in terms of disaster and disaster prevention. When the participants find an important site or thing from the viewpoint of disaster prevention and mitigation, for example, a dangerous site such as steep slope and a useful thing such as a fire extinguisher, in the town watching, they post a photo of such a place and a thing with a comment using DITS.

After the town watching, group discussion is conducted. In the discussion, the participants utilize DIMS to look back to the town watching. By using DIMS, the participants can browse the tweets posted by DITS in the town watching. The following subjects are given to the participants;

- Look back the tweets you posted. Explain what points you took notice of while showing the tweets you posted in the town watching. Moreover, describe your idea what kind of attention is needed in the event of a disaster.
- What kind of tweets do you think is useful at the time of disasters? What should we pay attention to when posting a tweet on disaster information? What should we pay attention to when receiving disaster information from Twitter?

After the group discussion, the representative of each group reports the conclusions obtained from the group discussion.

4.2   Implementation of Workshops at Junior High and High Schools

We conducted workshops based on the established program at six schools (three junior high schools and three high schools) in Kanagawa Prefecture, Japan (Table 1). In town watching, we lent one tablet PC (HUAWEI MediaPad T3 LTE model) to each group (5 or 6 people/group) and asked the students to post a tweet by DITS (Fig. 2). Figure 3 shows examples of the tweet posted by DITS in the town watching. The left figure of Fig. 3 is a tweet on a storage warehouse for disaster prevention and mitigation. The right figure of Fig. 3 is a tweet on a sign indicating 4.7 m above sea level. Every student posted tweets at least twice. Figure 4 shows the group discussion using DIMS. Figure 5 shows an example of a tweet displaying on DIMS.

Table 1. Outline of workshops conducted at six schools

School City	Date and time	# of participants
Hadano High School Hadano City	July 9, 2018, 14:30–16:30	34
Minamigaoka Junior High School Hadano City	July 13, 2018, 8:45–12:35	109
Nishiikuta Junior High School Kawasaki City	July 17, 2018, 14:00–16:00	62
Hiratsuka Commercial High School Hiratsuka City	Sept. 10, 2018, 10:50–12:50	35
Kanazawa-Sogo High School Yokohama City	Oct. 29, 2018, 13:35–15:25	35
Fujino Junior High School Sagamihara City	Oct. 31, 2018, 13:40–15:30	51

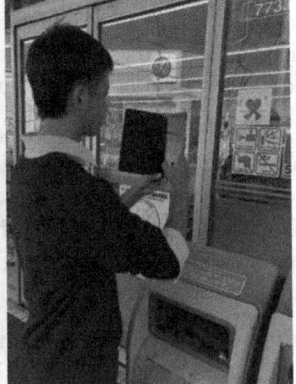

Fig. 2. Tweet posting using DITS in town watching

Fig. 3. Examples of the tweet posted by DITS in the town watching

Fig. 4. Group discussion using DIMS

4.3 Summary of Post-questionnaire of Workshops

A post-questionnaire was carried out in each workshop (16 items). The results on several major questions are shown below (we ask students to evaluate each question item on a scale of one to four; 1: I do not think so at all. 2: I do not think so. 3: I slightly think so. 4: I strongly think so.).

- Q.3: Did you discover new things in the town watching from the viewpoint of disaster prevention?
- Q.4: Did you discover new things in the group discussion after the town watching from the viewpoint of disaster prevention?
- Q.5: Have you raised awareness of disaster prevention by receiving today's class?

Fig. 5. An example of tweet displaying on DIMS

- Q.6: Was today's class more interesting than previous disaster prevention drills and disaster prevention?
- Q.8: Do you want to participate in the disaster prevention workshop using ICT equipment again?
- Q.10: Do you think DITS/DIMS is easy to use?
- Q.11: Do you want to use DITS/DIMS yourself in the future?
- Q.12: Do you think DITS/DIMS will be useful in the event of a disaster?

Figure 6 shows the results of each question (reply rates for each scale). As shown in the figure, many participants of the workshops had a positive impression on the disaster

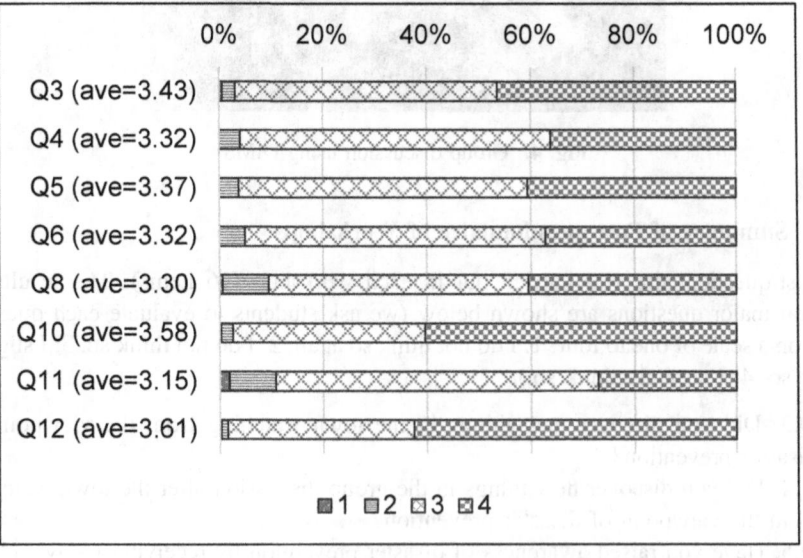

Fig. 6. The results of the questionnaire

prevention and mitigation workshops using DITS/DIMS. Below are some of the comments:

- This workshop was an opportunity to think about what I can do in the event of a disaster.
- I think it is very important to act while assuming the occurrence of a disaster from usual.
- I think this workshop should be done in other places.
- When posting information at the time of a disaster, I want to check the contents to post carefully.
- I want to use Social Media positively to protect the area where I live.

5 Conclusion

In this paper, we introduced the contents of the program of workshops on disaster prevention and mitigation established with Kanagawa Prefecture, Japan. Moreover, we reported on the results of the workshops for disaster prevention and mitigation using this program at several junior high and high schools. The results of the post-questionnaire show that many participants of the workshops had a positive impression on the disaster prevention and mitigation workshops using DITS/DIMS.

In the future, we will examine which of the conventional workshops on disaster prevention and mitigation, that is, the one without using ICT equipment, and the proposed workshop program is better.

References

1. Cabinet Office: Government of Japan: Disaster Management in Japan (2015)
2. Nakamura, H.: Overview of the Hanshin-Awaji Earthquake disaster. Acta Paediatr. Jpn. **37**, 713–716 (1995)
3. Mimura, N., Yasuhara, K., Kawagoe, S., Yokoki, H., Kazuma, S.: Damage from the Great East Japan Earthquake and Tsunami - a quick report. Mitig. Adapt. Strat. Glob. Change **16** (7), 803–818 (2011)
4. Okada, N., Ye, T., Kajitani, Y., Shi, P., Tatano, H.: The 2011 eastern Japan great Earthquake disaster: overview and comments. Int. J. Disaster Risk Sci. **2**(1), 34–42 (2011)
5. Komura, T., Hirano, A.: On disaster imagination game. In: Proceedings of Annual Conference of the Institute of Social Safety Science, vol. 7, p. 139 (1997). (in Japanese)
6. Yamori, K.: Disaster risk sense in Japan and gaming approach to risk communication. Int. J. Mass Emerg. Disasters **25**(2), 101–131 (2007)
7. Suppasri, A., Shuto, N., Imamura, F., Koshimura, S., Mas, E., Yalciner, A.C.: Lessons learned from the 2011 Great East Japan Tsunami: performance of Tsunami countermeasures, coastal buildings, and Tsunami evacuation in Japan. Pure. appl. Geophys. **170**, 993–1018 (2013). https://doi.org/10.1007/s00024-012-0511-7
8. Kodama, S.: Tsunami-tendenko and morality in disasters. J. Med. Ethics **41**(5), 361–363 (2013)

9. Imran, M., Castillo, C., Diaz, F., Vieweg, S.: Processing social media messages in mass emergency: a survey. ACM Comput. Surv. **47**(4), Article 67 (2015)
10. Simon, T., Goldberg, A., Adini, B.: Socializing in emergencies - a review of the use of social media in emergency situations. Int. J. Inf. Manag. **35**(5), 609–619 (2015)
11. Meier, P.: Digital Humanitarians: How Big Data is Changing the Face of Humanitarian Response. CRC Press (2015)
12. Uchida, O., et al.: A real-time information sharing system to support self-, mutual-, and public-help in the aftermath of a disaster utilizing Twitter. IEICE Trans. Fundam. **E99-A**(8), 1551–1554 (2016)
13. Kosugi, M., et al.: Improvement of Twitter-based disaster-related information sharing system. In: Proceedings of 4th International Conference on Information and Communication Technologies for Disaster Management (2017)
14. Peary, B.D.M., Shaw, R., Takeuchi, Y.: Utilization of social media in the east Japan Earthquake and Tsunami and its effectiveness. J. Nat. Disaster Sci. **34**(1), 3–18 (2012)
15. Toriumi, F., Sakaki, T., Shinoda, K., Kazama, K., Kurihara, S., Noda, I.: Information sharing on Twitter during the 2011 catastrophic Earthquake. In: Proceedings of 22nd International Conference on World Wide Web Companion, pp. 1025–1028 (2013)
16. Wilensky, H.: Twitter as a navigator for stranded commuters during the Great East Japan Earthquake. In: Proceedings of the 11th International Conference on Information Systems for Crisis Response and Management, pp. 697–706 (2014)
17. Takahashi, B., Tandoc Jr., E.C., Carmichael, C.: Communicating on Twitter during a disaster: an analysis of tweets during Typhoon Haiyan in the Philippines. Comput. Hum. Behav. **50**, 392–398 (2015)
18. Yamada, S., Utsu, K., Uchida, O.: An analysis of tweets during the 2018 Osaka North Earthquake in Japan - a brief report. In: Proceedings of 5th International Conference on Information and Communication Technologies for Disaster Management (2018)
19. Nishikawa, S., Uchida, O., Utsu, K.: Analysis of rescue request tweets in 2018 Japan Floods. In: Proceedings of 2019 International Conference on Information Technology and Computer Communications (2019)
20. Military Map Reading 201. http://earth-info.nga.mil/GandG/coordsys/mmr201.pdf. Accessed 09 June 2019

Author Index

Printed in the United States
by Baker & Taylor Publisher Services